Recent Titles in
Contributions in Political Science

INTERNATIONAL
THEORY

J
R
Ca
Tra

INTERNATIONAL THEORY

To the Brink and Beyond

ANDREW P. DUNNE

Foreword by Morton A. Kaplan

Contributions in Political Science, Number 378

GREENWOOD PRESS
Westport, Connecticut • London

Library of Congress Cataloging-in-Publication Data

Dunne, Andrew P., 1956–
    International theory : to the brink and beyond / Andrew P. Dunne ;
foreword by Morton A. Kaplan.
        p.   cm.—(Contributions in political science, ISSN 0147–1066
; no. 378)
    Includes bibliographical references and index.
    ISBN 0–313–30078–X (alk. paper)
    1. International relations—Philosophy.   2. International
relations—Methodology.   3. International relations—Historiography.
4. Political science.   I. Title.   II. Series
JX1395.D796   1996
327—dc20   96–18227

British Library Cataloguing in Publication Data is available.

Library of Congress Catalog Card Number: 96–18227
ISBN: 0–313–30078–X
ISSN: 0147–1066

First published in 1996

Greenwood Press, 88 Post Road West, Westport, CT 06881
An imprint of Greenwood Publishing Group, Inc.

Printed in the United States of America

The paper used in this book complies with the
Permanent Paper Standard issued by the National
Information Standards Organization (Z39.48–1984).

10 9 8 7 6 5 4 3 2 1

To Giordano Bruno,

and other burning minds

Contents

Foreword

International Theory: To the Brink and Beyond by Andrew Dunne is the most important book on the theory of international politics in more than thirty years. Dunne is one of a new generation of political scientists who are much better versed in the philosophy of science than were previous generations.

Using this background, Dunne demonstrates the minimal requirements for a theory of international politics and shows how properly constructed theory can be developed and subjected to empirical analysis. He is then able to explain from a consistent framework the flaws in past attempts in theory—from Lasswell and Carr to Waltz and his critics—that goes to the heart of their methods as well as the particulars of their failures. The same methodology is employed to show that successful, or at least partly successful, theory meets these requirements.

This incisive book provides the profession with a much needed teaching manual, as well as a major contribution to international theory. Although bipolar theory is treated only briefly in this book, Dunne offers a new theory of the bipolar system in a companion volume, already in draft, on the postwar loose bipolar system.

Dunne's work has integrity. Unlike some attempts at criticism, this segment of his book is, as far as I can determine, faithful in rendering the positions under review, sympathetic to the efforts involved, and yet often devastating when exposing fundamental mistakes.

It is difficult to understand why theorists of international politics have been so slow in recognizing at least some of the requirements of theory. The major point that Dunne makes about theoretical concepts has been recognized by at least some writers for more than a hundred years. For instance, the nineteenth century anthropologist, Lewis Morgan, in his *Systems of Consanguinity*—the book in which his contributions to linguistic analysis are prominent—noted that in one Indian tribe "mother" referred to any female in a specified age group with respect to any child in a correlative age group. "Mother" was thus a theoretical term, the meaning of which depended in part on the theory in which it was employed, much as "mass" has meanings that are not identical in Newtonian and Einsteinian theory.

One cannot correlate across types of systems, whether family or international, and use terms such as mother or state as if they were identical across types. And even with comparable systems, care is required with respect to boundary conditions. Yet generations of theorists of international politics have continued to use terms such as "nation" or "state" in undifferentiated ways, as if this made no difference to the legitimacy of the analysis.

Because writers did not understand the analytical requirements of theory, they could not properly distinguish between different types of systems. Despite the prominence of the concept of bipolarity from the late 1940s, bipolarity was viewed merely as a special case of balance of power systems. This persisted until the mid-1950s, when two writers for the first time recognized the postwar system as a different type of system, one that differed from "balance of power" systems, even those in which the balance revolved around two specially powerful actors.

The great Australian political scientist, Arthur Lee Burns, was justifiably regarded by many knowledgeable professionals as the preeminent theorist of international politics, in part because he made a theoretical distinction between the two systems but also because of the power and novelty of his analyses. Unfortunately, by the late 1960s this advance with respect to differences of types of international systems had been lost amidst a welter of confusion on the part of critics.

There are two general reasons why—with the possible exception of economics, in which fungible units are available—fully deductive and general theories are not available in the social sciences. Independent measures and covering laws do not exist in the social sciences, which introduces the possibility that different theories will be needed for different but comparable systems. In this respect theory differs in the social sciences from what is possible in physics, where except for the divide between relativity and quantum theory—some physicists believe a grand unifying theory will be found and others doubt this—the theories apply universally to the subject matter and independent measures usually permit fully deductive methods.

Complexity also may forbid fully deductive methodologies. Because social systems are inherently complex, fully deductive formal theories are not possible in the social sciences. It is interesting that the logic of the "balance of power" theory could be explored with a type of computerization that parallels later developments in physics with respect to problems that are too complex for fully deductive analysis. This "realization model" then could be compared with the partly deductive verbal model.

Dunne does note some confusions in my formulations and finds one of my major formulations "ugly." Perhaps I could argue that the formulation he rejects is ugly only from a mathematical point of view and that when using words my formulation is preferable, as long as shifts in the focus of examination are clearly indicated. But this is of small moment in the search for adequate method.

Although Dunne's treatment of the bipolar system will be presented fully only in a subsequent book, I note something of interest. His other two readers, Duncan Snidal and Charles Lipson—perhaps doubting the charge I get from professional controversy—urged me not to underestimate the positive contribution he has made to the theory of the bipolar system. Although I do not agree with all of Andrew's formulations concerning bipolarity, I agree that he has made a major advance in understanding the bipolar system. Indeed, unlike Andy, who regards his theory of bipolarity as an application of my theory, I see it as a major new formulation in its own right. Particularly because I have never been fully satisfied with my own account of bipolarity, I view Andy's contribution with special appreciation.

Morton A. Kaplan

Preface

This book is a treatise on macrotheoretical social science, particulary in the discipline of international politics. It states the fundamentals for macrotheory and shows how they can be empirically applied. This objective is accomplished largely through a critical appraisal of landmark works in international relations. Although most contemporary literature is intentionally eschewed, the meaning and methods of most contemporary debates—with the possible exception of game-theoretic and rational choice approaches—are nonetheless directly covered. The reason this is possible is relatively simple. Most of the great debates in the field of international relations, both originally and today, are operating with a world view generated in Descartes' division of reality into a mind-body dualism. In international relations this dichotomy is manifest in many forms, such as theory versus reality, or idealism versus realism. This dependence on dated conceptions is often explicitly, if not self-consciously, recognized. I recently heard a senior professor in international relations suggest to a younger colleague that his paper implied "we need to get to Locke." And no student of the field can get through a course without some reference to Hobbes. Thus, at its most general level, much of the current literature is three to four hundred years behind the great theoretical developments that have taken place in the twentieth century. I realize that this is a very serious claim, but it might be more difficult to accept if I directly criticize current practitioners. Since the reason we have come to this point is based on the transmission of ideas from our predecessors, it is sufficient to analyze their works.

In the twentieth century the importance of language and logical structure becomes dominant in theoretical science. In this world view, false absolutes derived from modern political philosophy—such as cooperation versus conflict—are integrated into coherent systems in which each proposition has its reciprocal and the objective of theory evolves into the analysis of transformations and permutations. To divide one's intellectual structure into the false absolutes of cooperation or conflict is, as Edward Shils once said, like trying to walk with one foot. The terms are polar correlatives, like night and day, that are unintelligible without their reciprocal.

Hopefully, it will become clear that this book is not a wrecking operation. Macrosystems analysis has been largely misunderstood for almost forty years, and the reason lies not so much in the clarity of exposition by which these ideas have been transmitted—though that is somewhat a problem—as in the fundamentally paradigmatic shift that their formulation engenders in the way international politics is framed and practiced. The approach is "structural," "operational," or "constructive," as those terms are used in the sciences. Readers familiar with Jean Piaget's *Structuralism* will find similarity in our meanings of these terms, though I would raise questions about a number of his specific formulations. Nonetheless, only by understanding this paradigmatic shift, represented by the transition between the book's two parts, can we prehend the truly constructive criticism that can improve our professional standards.

The constructivism that I employ aspires to the ideals of logical and objective analysis as those terms are used in the analytical pragmatic tradition of C.S. Peirce, M.R. Cohen, and W.V.O. Quine. Thus, it is post-modern in the sense of rejecting false absolutes in favor of the analysis of meaning, but it is not a trendy post-modernism that collapses meaning into an idiosyncratic solipsism. Well-trained scientists form a community that communicates through an analytically and empirically objective language. This book presents a version of such scientific standards for communication in the social sciences, particularly in international politics. And it presents the theory of international politics that we have been formulating on these grounds.

The title of the book indicates its basic argument. There is a brink that separates an explanatory macrotheory of international politics from approaches that fall outside the confines of such a theory. I refer to theory beyond the brink as *international theory*. That brink is defined by seven basic standards, which I argue are presuppositions for the construction of international theory. They delimit the basic subject matter of such a theory, frame the meaning and limits of explanation, provide guidelines that relate models to empirical evidence, and demand that time factors be explicitly incorporated into analysis. In this book I show that most of the landmark paradigms used in the field of international relations fail to meet these basic standards. As a result, there has been considerable crowding at the brink of international theory. Few have moved beyond it.

The book in general and the basic standards in particular are formulated on the basis of a pragmaticist—or pragmatic—philosophy of science. Its most general arguments cross the boundaries of the social sciences, not to mention the standard subdisciplinary boundaries of international relations. Although the substantive theories in this book tend to be about systems usually referred to as power-politics, the basic approach and categories could, for example, be used to analyze systems of international political economy, international organization, or comparative politics. If used skillfully it is possible that the approach might contribute to the formulation of more powerful theories in these disciplines.

My approach to criticism is similar to the systems approach—not systems theory—that I use to construct international theory. I start with a model, and then engineer it to particular cases. In this book the basic standards are the model; and individual landmark authors are the cases. Other parameters outside my model are employed to explain each author. But the basic standards are the main instruments of appraisal. The landmark authors are well known to those familiar with the history of international relations research. They include Edward Hallett Carr, Hans J. Morgenthau, Stanley Hoffmann, Richard N. Rosecrance, Kenneth N. Waltz, J. David Singer, Harold D. Lasswell, Quincy Wright, and Morton A. Kaplan. My appraisals demonstrate that the standards are necessary in order to move knowledge beyond the brink that separates the field of international relations from a theory of international politics.

Criticism in the field of international relations is often theoretically underdeveloped. Criticism tends to be a transparently partisan argument between competing perspectives. This problem is understandable in the social sciences, disciplines in which students invariably enter the field with partisan beliefs of some kind. The use of the basic standards does not cross swords on these grounds. As a result, the book is not an easy read, because it analyzes the meaning and relationships of many concepts that are often taken for granted.

The issues in this book are largely questions of whether the landmark authors can—at least in principle—explain the ways that international systems function on the basis of their own assumptions, if we follow the implications of their conceptions to their logical and empirical conclusions. Rather than attacking the realist or liberal position, the basic standards focus on the statements and arguments that the landmark authors make. As a result, some readers may find the text somewhat unrelenting, but I believe that at this point in the discipline's evolution, sustained, blunt critical analysis is preferable to elegant, subtle, and persuasive discourse. My bluntness should not be interpreted as irreverence. Whatever limited contribution this book makes to international theory, it would not have developed as it did without the contributions—and even errors—that the landmark authors make. As a pragmatist, I start with problems, and in theoretical work those problems are shaped by our forethinkers. On the other hand, the landmark authors are not deities, and science is not a modern myth based on the authority of priests and priestesses. Science advances only in self-conscious recognition of error. If my style in presenting those errors is indelicate, I plead *nolo contendere*. I am willing to trade indelicacy for truthfulness.

The introductory chapter has two main objectives. It first sets the groundwork for the study by analyzing the fatal problems of historiographical, national-interest approaches to international relations. Historiographical approaches have been unbounded by any meaningful international typologies and have resulted in unanswerable and interminable debates about conflict versus cooperation. These debates have been theoretically unproductive, and without at least the basic standards, they will remain interminable. Second, this chapter contrasts these traditional approaches to international relations—competing historiographical conceptions of national interest—with the seven basic standards. The basic standards form a logically interdependent system; drop even one presupposition and international theory will be seriously flawed if not fundamentally destroyed.

Because there are seven standards, each of which is fairly technical and interrelated, the basic standards form a complex structure. Such structures are not thematic, and as a result many readers not trained in scientific reasoning will find the argument somewhat difficult to absorb. But this is not unlike the situation that occurs whenever one tries to learn something that is operationally practicable. Readers should think back to the first time they tried to learn a new word processing program. I would be happy if I could make the book simpler and less demanding of my readers. But as with any new operational activity, I can only recommend that if you find the ideas are not being absorbed, try again later.

A theory of international politics presupposes the following basic standards:

1. The *focal* presupposition sets the analytical scope of international politics. A theory of international politics means that we are focused on how and why different types of international relationships among international actors imply optimal action patterns, and how departures from those optimal patterns modify the structure of those relationships;

2. The *explanatory* presupposition sets the ideal standard for scientific knowledge but tempers this ideal to take account of the complex phenomena that social scientists face. A theorist's ideal aspiration is to formulate deductive arguments that rigorously establish specific hypotheses about the international system, though in practice we often have to settle for partly deductive and plausible reasoning rather than strict logical system;

3. The *conditional* presupposition specifies sets of concrete variables for international theory. Thus this presupposition governs the subject matter that makes the first two presuppositions concrete. The three sets of variables are international structure, optimal international action patterns, and the regime characteristics of the actors;

4. The *coding* presupposition mandates that the scope of theoretical categories be explicitly limited by "signs" that link the theoretical categories to their empirical referents. It is particularly important to provide coding criteria for the model's initial conditions;

5. The *motivational* presupposition is a standard for confirmation in macro-political analysis. In small *n* systems in particular, actor motivation is a necessary part of the confirmation process. Social and political theories are confirmed when actors act in conformity with the reasons proposed in a theory.

In order to distinguish intended (theoretical) from unintended (accidental) consequences in international theory, the actors must be motivated by the values in the international system rather than alternative values;

6. The *valuational* presupposition is the correlative of the focal presupposition. It mandates consideration of the alternative value systems (domestic, bureaucratic, psychological, etc.) that might motivate actors;

7. The *durational* presupposition mandates that analysts specify their procedures for isolating the duration of a system and its varying processes over time. This presupposition is necessary to avoid the selection of evidence that affirms what we want to demonstrate.

The remainder of the book is divided into two parts. Part I covers authors who, at most, moved theoretical discourse "to the brink" of international theory. Chapters 2, 3, and 4 illuminate the most common theoretical errors in analyzing international systems. Chapter 5 shows the unfortunate consequences of these theoretical failures, particularly the failure to distinguish systems by type. Part II examines arguments that go "beyond the brink," meaning that the particular formulations adequately integrate the seven basic standards, even though further development is required. Chapter 6 introduces the theory of international politics. Chapter 7 presents applied macrotheoretical research results. And chapter 8 analyzes the logical characteristics of international macrotheory. Because they show the relationship between theoretical hypotheses and empirical fit, chapters 5 and 7 are the heart of the book.

Chapter 2 examines the approaches of E. H. Carr and Hans Morgenthau. I argue that Carr's approach merely provided two historiographical orienting principles: utopianism and realism. Orienting principles in effect provide only thematic guidance for the writing of history. Carr's thematic approach was manifest in his examples, which merely characterized thinkers according to their liberal-utilitarian or their realistic attitudes. But a classification of attitudes about international relations is not international theory. I also argue against his inductive conception of science. My overall appraisal is that Carr's approach completely misses five of the basic standards. He demonstrates some affinity only for the motivational and valuational standards.

Next, Morgenthau's orienting principles are analyzed in terms of the universal function that power played in his writings. I compare his interests-as-power principle with the covering law model of scientific explanation. This comparison is relevant because the covering law model is a scientifically rigorous approach to universal propositions. Morgenthau's universals are shown to be incompatible with the requirements of the covering law model both in practice and in principle. I also show that his balance of power concept is incapable of distinguishing the intended from the unintended consequences of a statesman's actions. In particular, Morgenthau employed both a hidden-hand and a self-conscious conception of balancing. The former does not require motivational analysis; the latter most certainly does. But Morgenthau denies the relevance of motives, and these must be necessary if balancing is not actually universal. My overall appraisal of Morgenthau is mixed. Except for the explanatory and durational standards, Morgenthau showed some appreciation for each of the other basic standards. But his usage was vague and often contradictory. As a result he failed to meet the focal, conditional, coding, and motivational standards.

Chapter 3 analyzes the approaches of Stanley Hoffmann and Richard Rosecrance. In contrast to universalized principles, their approaches used an investigatory framework. Both authors failed to meet the focal, explanatory, and—even within their framework—coding standards. Their employment of the other standards is seriously weakened by these general failures. Trained in the tradition of historical sociology, Stanley Hoffmann dismissed deductive scientific procedures in order to use a framework of core questions to uncover empirical causes. This failed to meet the explanatory standard and did not incorporate coding criteria. These failures resulted in part from a failure to employ the focal presupposition. I specifically argue that Hoffmann's fondness for ideal types is consistent with scientific procedure, but that he failed to develop an appropriate typology. His particular typology—revolutionary and stable systems—generally employed criteria that characterize the "external" behavior of states (units), rather than specifying the "internal" political relations that order the units into international systems. The international system was instead treated as an outcome of state policies, a sort of accidental rather than an analytical system.

Richard Rosecrance applied a similar research program that characterized systems as stable and unstable, but he also avoided a typology of the political relations among the international actors. Rosecrance did step right to the brink of a developed vision of international politics as a distinct disciplinary enterprise. He recognized that there were different regulatory features in different international systems, but he failed to distinguish adequately among these regulatory features or develop them into a typology. He also included so many elements from outside the boundaries of the international system that he was unable to integrate them in one theory. The complexity and number of subcomponents that he included from the domestic systems of the international actors distracted his attention from international analysis, and led him to seek the causes of stability and instability in the foreign policies of the units rather than in the political relationships in the international system.

Chapter 4 analyzes Kenneth Waltz's neo-principled approach to international relations. Unlike previous traditionalists, Waltz set his position in a scientific context, an approach that warrants separate treatment. After arguing that Waltz's conception of "reductionism" is used as a polemical device unrelated to that term's technical usage among scholars of the sciences, the analysis focuses on his particular view of international relations. I show that Waltz's argument is essentially unsustained at every juncture. His claim to distinguish international politics from other international domains avoids his own objective, choosing instead to distinguish international and domestic politics. That position violates the focal standard. Then because international politics lacks what domestic politics has—government—Waltz called it a system of structural anarchy, and claimed that only the distribution of capabilities applies to both international and domestic politics. However, the concept of anarchy is merely a definition of Waltzian structure, and it is difficult to comprehend why Waltz called it a theory after earlier embracing the explanatory function of scientific theory. Stipulated definitions do not meet explanatory standards. Waltz's further claim, that balance of power theory is a development of structural anarchy, moves from structural anarchy to balance unsupported by the motivational standard. Regardless of a state's motives, balance just occurs (also a violation of the valuational standard). Although Waltz presents analogies with economic theory, he displays a poor understanding of economic theory. He specifically confuses the relationships between free and oligopolistic markets, doesn't comprehend the role that rationality plays in economic theory, and confuses the relationship between numbers of actors, interdependence, and stability. Thus, his economic analogy departs further from the explanatory standards. He does have some codings, some notion of duration, and a truncated conditional standard. Each of these standards are employed as part of his bipolar-multipolar dichotomy, which is scrutinized in chapter 5.

Chapter 5 examines the empirical applicability of the multipolar-bipolar dichotomy. In both Waltz and Singer this dichotomy cannot explain—even in postdictive application—relatively simple macroproblems. I argue that this inapplicability results largely from underspecified models. Waltz hypothesizes that only changes in organizing principle or consequential changes in the number of actors transform international systems, that bipolar systems balance by internal means, and that uncertainty diminishes in a bipolar system. I show that these hypotheses are not empirically corroborated. This inapplicability largely results from failures to meet the focal, conditional, coding, and motivational standards. I then analyze J. David Singer's correlates of war approach to international relations, showing that his correlational approach—as well as the now common formulation of the levels-of-analysis problem—partly originated in order to avoid decision-making approaches. These correlations completely fail the motivational standard. The approach also fails to meet the focal and conditional standards by attempting to identify system-types (bipolarity and multipolarity) by aggregating the properties of units. As a result of these latter failures, Singer's correlations have been marked by inconsistencies. Moreover, the effort to treat system-types as ranged along a continuous scale does not meet coding requirements for continuity. The bipolar-multipolar dichotomy presupposes that different types of international systems are instances of a single axiom set, and there is neither argument nor evidence in the international politics literature that will sustain this position. Next I examine the objectivity of decision-making analysis, a major problem that the bipolar-multipolar conception fails to address. By removing decision-makers from the international system level, these kinds of correlational approaches have substituted a pseudo-objectivity of facts for what should be the objectivity of the social scientist, and sundered real causality from the system. After examining some derivative applications of nonactor models, I conclude that

the exclusion of decision-makers from the international system level has not and
cannot produce the causal patterns that were originally used to justify the effort.
Decision-makers and action are the central features of social science, despite the
fact that this makes research projects laborious.

Chapter 6 opens Part II. It analyzes four essential presuppositions that
distinguish a theory of international politics from the field of international
relations. Morton Kaplan's approach figures prominently throughout the
remainder of the book. Kaplan's incorporation of all seven standards places his
approach "beyond the brink." The chapter first describes the psychological
orientation of Quincy Wright and Harold Lasswell. This background is
necessary to understand Kaplan's usage of levels of analysis. Kaplan's
formulation must be distinguished from other approaches in the field in that
Kaplan's levels·are not locational, and the decision-maker is not conceived in
atomic terms. All the levels of analysis are analytical distinctions in the
decision-making mind, and thus the international system level includes the
decision-maker. Second, international actors are conceived as embedded in
international systems that manifest characteristically different types of relationships. Third, he holds that a theory has to state the explicit actions that are
optimal in maintaining the system in which the actors are embedded. Finally,
the verification of such a theory in historical cases depends on whether the
specific actions of real actors conform to the statements of optimal behavior, and,
moreover, that their conformity was motivated by the strategic rationale of the
international system rather than by domestic or psychological values. These
distinctions are illustrated by a simple example of a teenager whose strategic
situation varies depending on which of three types of systems he is embedded
in. The three types are used to illustrate his adoption of three different action
patterns in order to optimize his interests. This kind of explanation is then
contrasted with those that, lacking a role for motives, are merely historiographical and with those that are not based on international relationships, and are
thus atomistic.

Chapter 7 primarily analyzes the applicability of the "balance of power" and
loose bipolar types of systems. I first distinguish Kaplan's conception of
"balance of power" from other conceptions and then analyze how that conception
has been used in comparative case studies. Compared to the original publications, my presentation of the case studies is more accessible to students at the
introductory level. I analyze the entire life of the Italian city-state and Chinese
warlord systems and the final years of the European state system. I then analyze
the loose bipolar model and discuss some of the difficulties that arise in its
application. A comprehensive presentation and application of my extended
theory of bipolarity, which remodels Kaplan's basic theory, will be published
separately. Finally, I analyze the unit-veto system—a system in which widespread nuclear proliferation has occurred—to show the onerous requirements for
its stability.

Chapter 8 presents the most technical arguments of the book. It specifies
central logical relationships among central theoretical foci in international theory.

It also uncovers problems in some of Kaplan's analytical formulations. These problems are resolved in a set of formal protocols that give more precise meaning to the concepts of equilibrium, stability, and transformation in terms of the relations among the various sets of initial conditions in the international system models. Also included is an analysis of the Reinken-Kaplan computer model of the "balance of power" system. As with the comparative case studies, my presentation of the computer project is geared to non-specialists.

The final entries in the text are two appendices that would have interrupted the argument in chapter 8. Appendix A analyzes the use of Lanchester equations in the Reinken-Kaplan computer project in light of later criticism. Appendix B is an analysis of the meaning of "conditions"—both necessary and sufficient—in scientific analysis.

My acknowledgements start with the able staff at Greenwood Press. In particular Mim Vasan, Jim Dunton, Norine Mudrick, and Joanne Freeman, a freelance copyeditor, made this book more real, more readable, and more handsomely styled than it otherwise would have been.

Except for chapter 7, most of the early research and writing of the book occurred at the Center for International Studies at the University of Missouri-St. Louis (UMSL). As the Center's Theodore Lentz Postdoctoral Fellow in Global Issues, International Conflict, and Peace Research, I was provided with a spacious office, gracious staff assistance, and generous use of Center resources. In particular, I wish to thank the director of the Center, Joel Glassman, as well as Robert Baumann, Kathy Cochrane, Marty Rochester, and Kenny Thomas. Gene Meehan provided critical encouragement. Pat Mulligan, Mary Hines, and Sylvia Muléstagno provided invaluable staff assistance. The Lentz Peace Research Association provided primary support, for which I am most grateful. It is both unique and commendable that the Association encouraged research on fundamental aspects of reasoning in the international and social sciences. If we are ever to consolidate the peaceful potential in the emerging democratic epoch, it will be because we have pushed back the boundaries of ideological and dichotomous thought. UMSL's Department of Political Science also provided support, and a collegial spirit of encouragement. The able staff, Jan Frantzen and Lana Vierdag, made each day a little bit brighter.

I benefited from the input of numerous individuals. At UMSL Edwin Fedder was a source of encouragement, practical advice, and good judgment (and very entertaining political poetry). Dave Robertson read all of Part I. His comments led to extensive revisions and clarifications. While I was in Montreal, Marcus Kreuzer of Columbia University, and Janine Clark of the University of New Hampshire, commented on chapter 1. And Sara Zaborovski, my research assistant, performed her duties professionally and cheerfully and helped create the index. The highest hurdles had to be surmounted at The University of Chicago, both as a graduate student and later. The book is an outgrowth of a dissertation chapter, suggested independently by David Laitin and John Mearsheimer, both of whom thought I should clarify how my approach compared with main currents in the field. My disposition in this regard was amplified as individuals confused my arguments with the opinions of others. Reminded of Peirce's dilemma with William James' use of the term "pragmatism," I even thought of renaming the approach "systemicism." But I feared that even a word as ugly as that might not be safe from kidnappers, so I have stuck to the original meaning of systems analysis and tried to drive home how the approach is to be used to develop theory beyond the brink. The earliest arguments that have become Part I were systematically challenged by Duncan Snidal and Charles Lipson. Lipson in particular focused me on ambiguities and ambivalences in my formulations until I could take better aim. My arguments against continuous bipolar-multipolar conceptions are noteworthy in this regard. Snidal pushed me to systematize my scattered critical comments of the landmark authors. The basic standards, initially presented in the dissertation and specified in chapter 1 of this book, are the result of his suggestion.

As an undergraduate at The City College of New York, Willard Hutcheon guided me through the history of philosophy. He taught me how to read carefully and precisely analyze arguments. That provided me with basic ideals and problems—or is that redundant—in the philosophy of science and political theory that has enlightened many a dark and dreary day. I learned the most about logic and science from another teacher at City whom I never met. Morris Cohen's writings inspired much careful reflection about the relationship between theory and empirical application. Often without appropriate acknowledgement in the text, I use his works for general reference to problems in logic and mathematics, in both reason and nature.

Morton Kaplan read and commented on the manuscript almost as many times as I wrote it. Throughout this process, as well as our other interactions, he has been a consistent opponent of faulty reasoning. He could have set lower standards, ones which encouraged me at my own expense to adopt a partisan position of some sort. Instead he took the harder, longer, and riskier road of challenging me, and encouraging me to challenge him. The language was usually direct and literal, the conversations were generally spirited and provocative, and the process was always judged on the basis of fairness and justice to the subject matter under scrutiny. What specific differences exist in our formulations should not obscure our common ground. For without qualification, I always think of Professor Kaplan as a scientist.

1

Basic Standards in International Theory

The study of international relations as an academic enterprise began after World War I. The recent death of the bipolar system, the lack of consensus about the current system's identity—not to mention the policies to maintain it—and the continuing, repetitious debates between the traditional camps in the field have produced a widespread sense of doubt about the professionalism of macrolevel research. In this context, academic theories about international relations warrant appraisal.

Any appraisal requires a close look at the ideas of those thinkers who formulated the dominant paradigms in international relations. They include Edward Hallett Carr, Hans J. Morgenthau, Stanley Hoffmann, Richard Rosecrance, Kenneth N. Waltz, J. David Singer, Harold D. Lasswell, Quincy Wright, and Morton A. Kaplan. Although others will be mentioned occasionally, no effort has been made to include all twentieth century contributors to the field. The writers analyzed here are representative of the presuppositions held by the international relations community in general, although writers employing rational choice approaches are given little or no attention. The appraisal of the selected writers provides a basis upon which we can build more specific and useful international theory.

There are two main objectives in this chapter. It sets the groundwork for the study by analyzing the fatal problems of historiographical, national interest approaches to a theory of international politics. It also states the analytical plan of the book, including specification of seven basic standards necessary for a theory of international politics.

In particular, I first make some preliminary analytical distinctions about the scope of the discipline, followed by illustrations of the fatal problems of traditional historiographical approaches in international relations. Next I present standard conceptions of the national interest focus in international relations and show the limits of this focus. This is followed by the general analytical plan of the book. Then, the central planks of this chapter are presented: basic standards for international macrotheory. Finally, I mention the interdependence of the basic standards and how this approach differs from traditional ones. Part I then shows that failures stem from incomplete employment of these basics standards, while Part II shows how to use the basics to build and apply international theory.

PRELIMINARY DISTINCTIONS

A few preliminary analytical distinctions about the scope of the discipline are necessary to avoid confusion. The term "theory" does not mean the same thing to all writers analyzed in this book. Sometimes it means principles of practical politics, sometimes a framework, and sometimes an explanatory model. Those differences will be elucidated later in this chapter. Also, it is important to note that they do not all apply their theory to the same subject matter. Subject matter is a question of scope; that is, range of category. Debates in the field often occur without sufficient regard to this analytical problem.

I find it useful to distinguish international politics from the field of international relations. Since Quincy Wright, the field of international relations has covered all the special sciences and disciplines that impinge upon international action: international law, international politics, foreign policy, international political economy, strategic studies, development, international organization, anthropology, international economics, geography, diplomatic history, sociology, and so forth. Based on our current understanding of the philosophy of science, a theory of international relations is as inconceivable as a theory of science or social science. There are theories of mechanics and biochemistry, for example, but no unified theory of science.

On the other hand, Wright defines international politics as an art of influencing, manipulating, or controlling major groups in the world.[1] This definition is inadequate to define what a theory—as opposed to an art—of that subject matter would include. So I offer an alternative conception.

As a specialized discipline and subject matter, a theory of international politics must explain how and why different types of political relations among international actors (types of structures) imply different optimal action patterns, and how and why departures from those optimal action processes modify the structure of those relations. In the real world, all subject matters that comprise international relations cross-cut one another. The real world is a world of causal contingency. But a theory attempts to generalize about a particular type of order. Thus, it is bounded. It formulates the necessary relationships that connect the elements of a system. The ideal theory is not *a priori*, but it does attempt to

---

1. Quincy Wright, *The Study of International Relations* (New York: Appleton-Century-Crofts, 1955), 130.

explain the general characteristics of concrete systems by abstractive rather than descriptive procedures.

Thus, in a theory of international politics a brink must be established that delineates what is international politics and what is not, so that that subject matter can be treated as an analytical system. This book examines the meaning and scope of this frontier between the field of international relations and a theory of international politics. Models that explain actor behavior as a function of international political relationships—particularly alignment, alliance, institutional, and organizational relationships—are beyond the brink. That is, these models embed the actors within explicit international boundaries, and explain those aspects of their behavior that are rationally motivated by strategic calculations within those boundaries.

However, explanation requires more than a mere move beyond this threshold. It requires basic standards once you get there. Such standards are provided later in this chapter. Based on my understanding of scientific reasoning, these standards are necessary to make a theory well specified. I refer to such a well-specified theory of international politics as international theory. International theory, like all sciences, requires specialized discipline.

HISTORIOGRAPHY IN INTERNATIONAL RELATIONS

One way to analyze landmark approaches to international relations is through historical synthesis of the literature. Two synoptic perspectives are the most general guides for organizing such a history. Events can be presented in either a linear or a cyclical pattern. Linear patterns represent events as progression toward (or regression from) some event, whereas cyclical patterns represent events as endless repetition. Christian, Marxist, and Comtean historians tend to adopt a linear pattern—the second coming, the classless society, scientific progress—whereas Classical, Renaissance, and Enlightenment historians tend to adopt a cyclical pattern—recurring conflict, for example.[2]

In international relations the obvious starting point for such a history is to consider the representatives of realism and idealism. The former tend to adopt a cyclical perspective of recurring international conflict, and the latter a linear perspective of evolving peace and harmony. Hans Morgenthau, for example, stated that a system of checks and balances "was a universal principle for all pluralist societies." On the other hand, Francis Fukuyama's linear perspective, which recently achieved notoriety, argues that liberal democracy has reached "the end of history."

If a history of ideas approach is adopted with respect to the field of international relations, then a decision must be made as to whether to treat the

---

2. A most useful overview of these issues is Willard Hutcheon, "Reason in History and Its Rationale," in Martin Tamny and K. D. Irani, eds., *Rationality in Thought and Action* (New York: Greenwood Press, 1986), 137-163.

development of the academic enterprise as: a. progression towards the viewpoint of one group of representatives (for example, neoliberal institutionalists), or b. a cycle in which preeminence waxes and wanes depending, perhaps, on the intensity of international conflict (with realism dominant in the 1950s and early 1980s and idealism preeminent in the late 1970s and, perhaps, the early 1990s).

A notion of science often plays a role in such a history. The idea of science has been intimately tied up with international relations because of two intellectual currents that streamed through Europe at the same time. The rise of the modern state system, and the rise of a physics based on individuated bodies in motion, occurred as part and parcel of the same historical age. All the memorable political theorists from Hobbes to Kant were engaged in these earlier debates, and their views represented, to varying degrees, an attempt to grapple with the new science of individuated bodies in motion. Thus, Thomas Hobbes can state—in a political tract!—that: "The cause of sense is the external body . . . which presseth the organ proper to each sense . . . by the mediation of the nerves . . . continued inwards to the brain and heart, causeth there a resistance, or counter-pressure. . . . for motion produceth nothing but motion."[3]

From the standpoint of the contemporary philosophy of science, this is obviously bad science. Nonetheless, this individuated conception of science has continued to influence twentieth century international relations. In traditional historical thinking, to the extent that science has been advocated, it has been pressed into service to support the view that individuals are, or can be, rational. Edward Hallett Carr believed this to be the objective of utopians such as Bentham, who "provided a plausible confirmation of the 'scientific' assumption of the eighteenth-century rationalists that man would infallibly conform to the moral law of nature once its content had been rationally determined."[4] If this is true, then the development of science and rationality can be used to change history!

Note, however, that the interpretation that science demonstrates historical progression does not actually address the meaning and methods of science or social science. Such interpretations are about the effects of science on some aspect of human culture, and are thus only using science to vindicate their presupposed historically progressive perspective. However, the traditional opponents of science have a legitimate counterattack.

There is absolutely no evidence that the increasing numbers of rational individuals have led to any moral advance. The twentieth century produced the most advanced scientific reasoning in recorded human history, and the most horrific barbarism imaginable. And the same developed cultures produced both

3. Thomas Hobbes, *Leviathan: or the Matter, Form, and Power of a Commonwealth, Ecclesiastical and Civil* (Oxford: Blackwell, 1955), chap. I; also, cross-reference chap. V, "Of Reason and Science," where Hobbes states an instrumentalist and nominalist view of science.

4. Edward Hallett Carr, *The Twenty Years' Crisis, 1919-1939: An Introduction to the Study of International Relations*, 2nd ed. (London: Macmillan and Co., 1946), 23.

kinds of individuals. Thus, science and reason demonstrate nothing about history, where individuals still seek their own interests.

The very appearance of fascism not only in Germany and Italy but in our own midst ought to have convinced us that the age of reason, of progress, and of peace, as we understood it from the eighteenth and nineteenth centuries, had become reminiscences of the past. Fascism is not . . . a mere temporary retrogression into irrationality. . . . It is mastery of the technological attainments and potentialities of the age, it is truly progressive—were not the propaganda machine of Goebbels and the gas chambers of Himmler models of technical rationality?[5]

A debate of this character could easily be carried on throughout a book of this length. But there is already a vast—and vapid—literature that adopts one variant or another of a history-of-ideas approach to the field of international relations. And many of the empirical studies that are undertaken are designed to vindicate one perspective or the other. Because the only way to vindicate a perspective is to select the evidence that is consistent with it, historiographical theses always tend toward ambivalence: "Thus, Gilpin's assertion that 'the role of the nation-state in economic as well as political life is increasing' in no way contradicts our assertion that transnational relations are becoming more important."[6] As this quote illustrates, it is impossible to resolve the realism-idealism dispute by these methods. If one could measure the degree of consensus at the final determination of history—the end of international relations—this could perhaps vindicate one theory of historical determination. However, even this notion is dubious: after all, nothing can contradict an assertion.

THE NATIONAL INTEREST FOCUS

The historiographical approach led to the national interest focus. Beginning during the inter-world war period, a debate raged in the United States about what constitutes the proper theory for international politics. As would be expected of a debate that began so early in the century, the discussion is rooted in nineteenth century conceptions of international politics, and relies almost exclusively on differing conceptions of national interest as the focus for analysis. Despite the increasing use of sophistic arguments and methods, as well as a variety of new labels, these conceptions still constitute the bulk of theoretical discourse among students of international politics, including those sympathetic to science. The result of these efforts has been to reroute analysis away from systematic explanatory paths.

---

5. Hans J. Morgenthau, *Scientific Man vs. Power Politics* (Chicago: University of Chicago Press, 1946), 6.

6. Robert O. Keohane and Joseph S. Nye, Jr., eds., *Transnational Relations and World Politics* (Cambridge: Cambridge University Press, 1972), 375.

The so-called theoretical choice posed by students has largely been between two alternative conceptions of national interest, one of which is based on case-by-case analysis and the other which seeks either first or universal principles of politics.[7]

Universal Principles

The most traditional approach to the national interest views nations as real individuals with interests that are permanent, coherent, and independent of the sentiments and passions of its citizenry. The advancement of these interests is often treated as a self-evident universal principle of politics. The use of the term "objective" to describe the national interest is usually associated with those advocating these universal (or first) principles of politics. It is meant to evoke in the listener a conception that there is a singular or prime tendency inherent in the nature of things, a sort of *principium politica* analogous to Newton's principle of inertia.

This conception obviously has its origins in a Newtonian age, one in which a ruler could say, "I am the state" and mean it in a virtually literal sense. This process can, of course, become ritualized: de Gaulle apparently thought this way. In such a mind other nations are each likewise organic beings engaged in a struggle for life, and thus the national interest is everywhere the same—to seek power. This camp tends to identify the nation with the state and the state with its rulers or government. But because real nations presented the analyst with glaring differences in style and substantive policy, the initial formulation required constant adjustment and re-interpretation.

Two general classes of adjustment have been used. First, power-seeking could be defined in an all-inclusive conception on the grounds that radical egoists arbitrarily define all human actions as self-interest, because otherwise the self performing the action would not have undertaken it. Second, whenever this claim of power motives was challenged by evidence to the contrary it could still be argued that power, though a first or real principle, was nonetheless not the only principle—thus it could be deflected or moderated by intermediate variables.

Intermediate variables were conceived variously, but almost always in terms of human or national diversity. Governments are known to have different operational codes and individuals are known to have different psychological propensities. To deal with this problem an effort was made to avoid it. In what has become a bit of a dogma in the field, the level-of-analysis problem was contrived in order to eliminate the effects of "causes" arising from subsystemic levels-of-analysis.[8] This clever research strategy justified the elimination of

---

7. This section relies heavily upon Thomas I. Cook and Malcolm Moos, "The American Idea of International Interest," in *American Political Science Review* 47 (1953): 28-44.

8. A meaningful approach to the levels of motivation problem is presented below in the valuational standard, and in chapter 6.

decision-makers and choice from the systems level. It is hoped that by the end of the book this popular dogma will be seen for what it has become, a ritual that avoids the difficulties of empirically meaningful investigation.

Case-by-Case Approaches

Case-by-case approaches originate in eighteenth century Enlightenment thought. In this conception, the national interest should remain flexible, for prudence suggests that its interpretation should depend upon the specific characteristics of the situation which the decision-maker confronts. Moreover, the nation is in some sense tethered conceptually to the loyalties and interests of the citizenry, a formulation which amplifies the variability of each situation. The term "subjective" to describe the national interest is usually associated with those advocating these case-by-case approaches. It is meant to evoke the conception that elemental, psychologically independent interests (e.g., utility-maximizers) are being aggregated into an ever-changing democratic impulse. After all, the interests of a living citizenry develop over time. In this view the focus tends to be on the "real" interests of the population, who really desire peace and economic development. The great statesman is usually conceived as the objective assessor of these ever-changing interests. Although the state is merely an instrument in the achievement of these ever changing interests, it is so only nominally. For even contemporary practitioners, the state has remained the locus and expression of the national interest, whereby the great leader—a Churchill or de Gaulle—represents the will of the people.

The American Variant

In essence, though, these conceptions are of European origin, where the state has been a centerpiece of political life. Although there has been an alternative American conception, one which is a variant of the case-by-case approach, this conception is also based on a theory of national interest rather than a theory of international politics. The American version is certainly a substantially different doctrine. It is historically based not on a political conception of the nation's interest but an emotive attachment to local values of freedom, family, and community. In the United States, mention of the national interest—the need for military bases, for example—tends to elicit the question, "Whose national interest?"

The American variant of the case-by-case approach is explained partly by the Puritan and revolutionary history of the original colonies. The anti-statist sentiments of the American conception are still present in contemporary America, as evidenced by various critical remarks about the "imperial presidency" or frequent congressional attempts to restrict the latitude of the president in foreign affairs. The War Powers Resolution or the Boland Amendment are good examples of these sentiments. The fact that the United States is not a parliamentary democracy is significant, because the forging of the national interest in practice is based on consensus rather than a single party's or coalition's dominance. That consensus must overcome the perennial organizational rivalry between the executive and legislative branches, a rivalry that is present regardless of the party affiliations of the various office holders. In many ways the postwar period has obscured much of this tradition, perhaps owing in part to the centralization of the national security state, as well as the more central role which the United States has come to play in the international system. However, these conceptions have tended to re-emerge following the fall of the Berlin Wall.

Despite the different conceptions of national interest, in all cases there are serious drawbacks. By presupposing the individuated nation as the focus of analysis, the systemic and organizational features of international action are treated merely as an unintended consequence—an outcome—of differing interests and conditions, rather than as variable situations in which actors are embedded and in which problems and prospects for choice are not reducible to individual or aggregate interests. Although there were many efforts during the postwar period to examine "systemic" factors, most of these efforts have remained stuck on a conception of national interest that is either largely irrelevant for explaining action patterns in international systems, or have proposed models which were severely underspecified for such an explanation. Most dangerous has been the tendency to overlook the international role functions of the human actors who comprise the international system, instead opting to treat them largely as residual entities whose behavior is "caused" by forces either domestically or international- ly external to the human decision.

The Limits of a National Interest Focus

These various approaches to the national interest certainly seem to imply different theories of what the national interest is or should be. However, there is no statement of conditions that determine what the national interest will be, along the lines that a biologist might employ in determining the interest of an animal or animal group in protecting its territory. Whereas the biologist would almost certainly state the type of animal, its form of social organization, the type of competitors, and the type of environment in which that animal is found, and from that system of relations develop hypotheses to explain the behavior of the animal, theorists of national interest tend simply to define the interest they deem appropriate, based on the needs of the nation which they consider legitimate.

From all definitions of the national interest, analysts usually commit the fallacy of selectivity—selecting the evidence from history that supports the chosen definition. The use of such selected materials is extremely problematic. Often the evidence offered in support of theoretical propositions is the mere testimoni- als of individuals who agree with the perspective of the writer. Such debates are not representative of a developed conception of macrotheoretical social science.

Careful reading of the debates about the national interest, about the relationship between domestic and international levels-of-analysis, about whether the national interest is based on the state or other values, and about whether realist and liberal theories of international politics are old or new reveals an historiographical approach to theory. Such an approach may or may not be a correct characterization of the history of ideas. It may or may not be a correct description of the social and political development of the value identifications that a community shares. But compared to theoretical approaches of other sciences, it is not science. It explains nothing about the action patterns of different types of actor-systems operating in different environmental situations, but instead substitutes either a constant principle of politics, a relativistic subjectivism, or a secular eschatology. The general attitude prevailing among those who focus on the definition of the national interest—realist or liberal—has constituted an attempt to convince the scholarly and policy-oriented international community that their characterization of the world, or their characterization of the direction of historical forces is true. Thus, concepts in international relations often suffer from theoretical dualism, in that one camp attempts to prove conflict based on its own arbitrary assumptions about either human nature or the national interest while the other camp attempts to redefine our conception of either the national interest or national security in order to prove the possibility of cooperation.

THE ANALYTICAL PLAN

The succeeding chapters analyze the leading approaches to the study of international relations in the twentieth century as measured against the basic standards stated below. These standards are based on the author's understanding of theoretical science and the empirical material of human action out of which any social scientific theory must be fashioned. Science primarily implies the search for truth by logical methods. Readers are cautioned not to necessarily read their own conceptions of science into this book. No presumption of rational social progress resulting from the development of science is entertained in this book. I am not a positivist, and am skeptical of many quantitative approaches to international theory. If a label must be used, the approach adopted might be characterized as logical pragmaticism.[9]

---

9. My philosophy of science has been strongly influenced by a wide array of writings. See, for examples, Charles Sanders Peirce, *Philosophical Writings of Peirce*, edited with an Introduction by Justus Buchler (New York: Dover Publications, 1955); W. V. O. Quine, *From A Logical Point of View* (Cambridge: Harvard University Press, 1953), especially chap. II; Morton A. Kaplan, *Science, Language, and the Human Condition* (New York: Paragon House, 1984); Morris R. Cohen, *Reason and Nature: An Essay on the Meaning of Scientific Method* (New York: Harcourt, Brace and Co., 1931); Morris R. Cohen and Ernest Nagel, *An Introduction to Logic and Scientific Method* (New York: Harcourt, Brace and Co., 1934); Carl G. Hempel, *Aspects of Scientific Explanation and Other Essays in the Philosophy of Science* (New York: Free Press of Glencoe, 1965); Ernest Nagel, *The Structure of Science: Problems in the Logic of Scientific Explanation* (Indianapolis: Hackett Publishing Co., 1979).

The origins of international relations thinking as an academic endeavor goes back to the period following World War I, and my analysis includes some of this earlier work. With respect to all selected writers, the book attempts to bring major problems of international theory within a common framework of scientific discourse.

One cannot assume that the history of ideas progresses. Along with World War I the importance of mass society and strategic propaganda techniques rose to prominence in the history of ideas. This phenomenon had never before occurred, and it seems to have forestalled the development of analytical clarity among students of international relations. As a result, much "theory" in the field represents little more than a partisan agenda. I hope to avoid this trap. In order to appraise others fairly, standards of appraisal must be stated. The basic standards are a benchmark of appraisal that may be applied to individual theoretical formulations. Doing so will show that, on occasion, writers have gone to the very brink of a scientific vision of the international system, but like a modern Moses, most have failed to enter the promised land of cultivated scientific discourse.

Although this analysis focuses primarily on established works in the field, younger scholars should not feel that they have somehow risen above the myriad intellectual problems that reroute analysis away from systematic explanatory paths. Students of international relations owe most of their conceptual debts to the thinkers analyzed in the following pages, though these thinkers differ substantially while often committing similar errors. However, because these differences are usually hidden within a naive nominalism—which defines abstract universal concepts such as "system" by stipulated definitions—the real differences among theorists is obscured and trivial characteristics are grossly magnified. It is therefore essential to distinguish among their research projects by more rigorous standards.

Three fundamental perspectives—practical politics (usually characterized as realism), historical sociology (currently labeled neoliberal institutionalism), and social science—have directed research in international relations during the twentieth century, and controlled isolation of these perspectives is a prerequisite for comparison. Theory and its associated methods do not mean the same thing to all these theorists, and their research projects are not of equal analytical status. Although any conceptual process can be called a theory, careful analysis indicates that within each perspective researchers have differed as to whether to erect principles, frameworks, or explanatory models in order to approach the international world.

When it is argued that most writers have not moved beyond the brink separating the field of international relations from international theory, it is to state that their systems of thought are incapable of explaining action as a function of particular types of international political relations. A major reason for this situation seems to be that most thinkers in the field have conflated historiographical and social scientific theory. Almost all of them are attempting to vindicate a particular perspective about the national interest. But, as stated above, only the end of history can fulfill this objective.

BASIC STANDARDS

The standards proposed here are by no means sufficient to conduct empirical analysis. Any specific theory will have to make further, more specific presuppositions and assumptions than are here indicated, but none of the basic standards can be eliminated without sacrificing important explanatory information. These standards provide a checklist for the critical commentary that comprises much of the book. To varying degrees, it is on these grounds that most of the landmark authors failed to construct successful explanatory models of international politics, and this partly includes the social scientific approach with which the author identifies.

The following basic standards seem unavoidable if a social scientific theory is to be well formed. These standards are not a general theory, only requisites—really prerequisites—for theory. Whereas a basic international theory would explain the functioning of a particular type of system, the basic standards specify those analytical components that make possible an explanation of international politics. There are seven such standards.

1. International Political Relations

The first basic standard for a theory of international politics specifies its subject matter. It may be thought of as the *focal* presupposition. A basic macrotheory of international politics focuses on two sides of one analytical coin. First, it must explain why different types of relations among international actors reasonably motivate optimal international action patterns. Second, it must explain how departures from optimum modify the structure of those relations.

An explanation requires specification, in concrete cases, of variables that are relevant to the subject matter. There are three sets of variables that seem relevant: international structure, the regime characteristics of the international actors, and the optimal action patterns. The concrete specification of the variables in these sets constitutes the initial conditions of a macromodel. These are discussed further in basic standard number three.

This focal presupposition should not be interpreted as a metaphysical truth about the real causes of human activity. It is simply a judgment about how to mark off the subdiscipline of international politics from both other aspects of international relations and other subdisciplines of political science.[10]

---

10. The focal presupposition entails merely a choice of subject matter. One could substitute any other system—national, subnational, or supranational—and perform the same two-sided analysis concerning the relationships among the actors and the action patterns of the actors. This standard is necessary to facilitate discourse among students of international politics and international relations by establishing a more central focus.

It should be obvious that actors may be motivated to act internationally for any variety of noninternational reasons (bureaucratic, personality, public opinion, the national), and it is unlikely that any actor has ever acted purely from international motives. International motives nonetheless exist. What is needed is knowledge about how internationally motivated actors *would* act in different systems of international politics. Propositions about these relations are distinctly within the scope of the concept of international theory whereas other foci properly belong to the field of international relations conceived broadly.

Thus, international theory was peripheral to Truman's decision in early 1950 not to increase the defense budget. Truman's decision supported his budget director, and was based on a theory of fiscal conservatism. In effect, Truman made a decision that was based on domestic rather than international considerations. Neither theory has authoritative status.

In fact, the broader conception was captured by William T. R. Fox when he titled the journal *World Politics*. Fox did not wish to limit the journal exclusively to the subject of international politics. His conception clearly implies that international politics does not exhaust the analysis of international relations. But it does not imply that all relevant subjects are identical with international politics.[11]

At a very general level this focal presupposition reaffirms the answer to the long asked—either implicitly or explicitly—question in international theory: What is the distinct subject matter of the discipline? Within this answer there may be macroanalyses which focus on the political relations among numerous collective actors or microanalyses which focus attention at the level of individuated actors who exhibit motives and preferences about those relations. The international system may be used in analyses as a cross-sectional or a dynamic entity. But the point is that if one claims to do international theory, then one must presuppose those political relations. Only then can relevant variables be selected.

The specific meaning and content of variables chosen for analysis must be fitted to the particular structure of relations among a particular configuration of international actors. Capabilities may be taken as the simplest example. The meaning of a variable such as capabilities will change from theoretical system to theoretical system, being within the scope of blocs in bipolar systems, nations for "balance of power" systems, and perhaps restricted to military command in

---

Practitioners of any discipline must be able to agree on subject matter if they aspire to be characterized as professionals.

11. The distinction between world politics and international politics is presented in Quincy Wright, *The Study of International Relations*, 130ff. To some extent, the journal *World Politics* is closer conceptually to the meaning of international relations. World politics is the study of territorially independent groups in contact. International politics is a subset of this in which the specific groups are primarily national actors. See, for example, chap. 7 in which the Italian city-state and Chinese warlord systems are discussed. Both of these systems fit Wright's definition of world politics.

unit-veto systems.[12] In a system of nondirective, economically interdependent actors, international capabilities might, for example, be treated as within the scope of central banks.

If one were talking about family capabilities, this would be obvious. A traditional nuclear family might have a single home and savings plan. More contemporary families, headed by two professionals who have careers in different cities, might have two comparatively separate plans. Still different might be the meaning of capabilities for a cohesive immigrant group that provided loans to new members of the community.

2. Explanatory Theory

The second standard is the *explanatory* presupposition. A subject-matter does not make a theory scientific. A theory is an explanation that is deductive, and its operations are performed within the constraint of specifically stated initial conditions. In deductive accounts, there exists a set of premises which include general statements about the entity under investigation (all nonhierarchical bloc actors have collective action problems during détente) and a set of initial conditions (NATO is a nonhierarchical bloc actor) from which a conclusion necessarily follows (NATO has collective action problems during détente).[13] The general statements thus offer the *reasons* a particular statement is true.

Generalizations and initial conditions are usually called antecedents, and the conclusion is called the consequent—though in the philosophy of science the terms explanans and explanandum are the respective terminological substitutes; the former do the explaining and the latter is that which requires explanation. In the philosophy of the exact sciences the generalizations in the explanans are usually called either laws or theories; it is generally held that laws explain empirical events whereas theories explain laws. However, because theories in this sense are often simply another set of laws from which the explanandum law is deduced, this distinction is somewhat context dependent. In the social sciences, where we do not have covering laws or truly general theories, the distinction need not be adopted in an unqualified sense. Theories may be conceived broadly as the set of implicit and explicit hypotheses about the possible transformations of a system, within explicit boundaries. The ideal of scientific system denotes consistency and connectedness of the part-systems

---

12. These different theoretical systems are discussed in Morton A. Kaplan, *System and Process in International Politics* (New York: John Wiley, 1957), chap. 2.

13. The particular statements employed in the example are elliptical. In the actual presentation of a theory, it is necessary to specifically explain why a nonhierarchical bloc would have collective action problems during periods of détente, and terms such as "détente" require coding criteria. Moreover, social science statements do not apply to the real world in the strictly deductive fashion implied by the examples. In the application of a theoretical formulation, other factors will modify the theoretical pattern. On this last point, see chap. 7.

which comprise it. In this sense, Euclid's geometry was the first scientific system.

What constitutes a scientific community's choice between theories is partly the extent to which a theory implies novel conclusions—that is, new consistent connections which are potentially verifiable, in addition to those it was originally intended to explain. These conclusions must, however, have some systematic relationship to the theory. Thus "greater female economic dependency" is systematically consistent with a theory of the nuclear family in which a homemaker role exists for the female and a breadwinner role for the male. However, a conclusion about "greater psychological dependence" of one gender upon the other would be ad hoc, and not necessarily related to a theory of the nuclear family (which does not mean the empirical hypothesis is false).

In using explicit definitions, undefined terms, postulates, and theorems, deductive arguments are the most specific and rigorous model of reality possible, though it is also reasonable to characterize any sign system—images, metaphors, analogies, graphs, templates, paradigms—as a model if it is used to represent reality. In the following pages it is argued that theoretical knowledge is formed only in models which are at least partly deductive, because only deductive arguments allow for necessarily true conclusions. However, no claim to *a priori* reasoning is necessarily entailed in this position, though it should be obvious that only animals with a capacity for higher logical functions can produce a deductive argument.

The qualifier "partly" is used because it is important to distinguish applied theory, which is science, from pure theory, which is logical-mathematical. At the apex of scientific thought stands physics, where the applied and the pure overlap most closely, though not completely. In international relations there is much less integration between these two aspects of reason. This weakness is unlikely to change, because the nature of social subject matter is recalcitrant. Social phenomena cannot be coded as precisely as physical phenomena. The variables in actual social systems are highly interdependent, mutually sensitive, and open to external influences. There is no central logical system to which all human decision-making or social systems conform. And—at most—there are very few cases for comparison.

In applied international theory the standards of logical completeness and rigor will require some relaxation and at the empirical level evidence will tend to be less direct, accurate, and precise. Theory, therefore, may be sketchy in that the reasoning process may be partly deductive and partly plausible; but the ideal of theoretical explanation should not be abandoned in favor of distinctly non- or atheoretical approaches. Thus, throughout the book, except when referring to another author's meaning, the terms "theory" and "model" are used in the sense of explicit, at least semi-deductive, argument forms.

The meaning of deductive theory is distinct from two other approaches prevalent in the field—namely, investigatory frameworks and orienting principles. Investigatory frameworks are usually designed to place the field of international relations on the infinite road to theory. Although the process of gathering information, organizing it into categories, and reaching for conclusions may provide scaffolding for greater insight, it is not theory. There is no such thing as inductive logic. Investigatory frameworks in the service of inductive reasoning may be regulated by criteria—systematic indexing, statistics, historical detail, extensive data collection—and with some luck and creativity may hit upon a theory. Until this occurs, one has merely a notebook approach to understanding the world, a sort of journalism. And increasing the number of categories provides only more breadth and no systematic knowledge.

Although this enterprise is valuable in its own right, and even necessary in the process of discovery, it does not constitute an explanation. The danger of identifying too closely with the inductive enterprise lies in conflating this psychological process of discovery with the logical structure of the knowledge thus discovered. No theory of the actual world can be built without experience, and from that experience one reaches up for the unifying system of relations that explain the particulars. But what goes up must come down if it is to be designated a theory. Rolling around in mud is not an inductive approach to physics, unless empirical generalizations are uncovered in the process.

Another conception of theory current in the literature is that theories are images, orienting principles, or metaphors which merely describe the general character of the world. This conception is most prevalent in the so-called realist literature but is not confined to it. Hidden-hand conceptions of balance, for example, are not deductive. And those who aspire to substitute liberal "theories" of interdependence have often offered merely an alternative description of world politics without providing any greater analytical sophistication. When international politics is practiced in this fashion, both realist and internationalist conceptions are traditional rather than scientific in character.

Like notebook approaches, the use of images cannot be eliminated from the reasoning process. Great scientific theorists generally have in their minds and employ in their presentations metaphors and images or both. Einstein reportedly "felt" the universe in his arms, and his illustrations of special relativity theory employ simple everyday concepts such as railroad cars moving along an embankment. Such devices permit wider dissemination of theories but are not substitutes for the detailed explanations which deductive arguments imply. Images, feelings, or metaphors are mytho-poetic devices to which most humans are susceptible, but they are not verifiable as such, and they are not capable of tests for logical consistency.

3. Initial Conditions

The third standard specifies the *conditional* presupposition. Initial conditions are the material premises in a scientific argument. In pure theory—logic and mathematics—the material truth of axioms is irrelevant. A logician employs a system of axioms to deduce theorems, and if the chains of reasoning are consistent the logician is satisfied. He does not, for example, decide whether Euclidean or Riemannian geometry is materially true. The physicist, however, is granted no such freedom. He cannot rest on the fact that a materially true event follows from certain axioms but must also show—sometimes indirectly—the material truth of the axioms.[14]   In international politics the same argument applies, or the axioms become merely ethereal instruments to hide behind.

Three sets of initial conditions are necessary parts of international theory: the particular type of international structure in which the actors are embedded; the regime characteristics (intra-actor structure) of the international actors; and the patterns of international action which are consistent with the regimes and international structure of the system. In a basic theory, each of these conditions is assumed—each is a counterfactual conditional proposition—and conclusions inferred, however loosely.   In assessing real world action, evidence for each initial condition must be adduced, or there is no way to determine if conclusions are explained or merely epiphenomenal.

Not all configurations are equilibrial. A major purpose of well formed theory is the specification of those types of systems that are equilibrial, and the conditions for their stability. The analysis of system-types is treated in detail in chapters 5 and 7. This section examines the components that comprise such systems. The analytical interrelationships among these components are discussed in detail in chapter 8, where they are used to make the concepts of equilibrium, stability, and transformation more precise.

International Structure. There are four variables that are most relevant to the meaning of international structure: the number of actors, their international capabilities, their role functions, and the informational transparency of the system. The structure of the international system cannot be collapsed into a mere bipolar-multipolar distinction. Efforts to do so have been feeble reformulations of the distinctions introduced by Kaplan and Burns[15] in the mid-1950s. And current debates about institutions or the democratic peace also tend to be structurally feeble.

---

14. cf. Albert Einstein, *Relativity: The Special and the General Theory*, trans. Robert W. Lawson, 15th ed. (New York: Crown Publishers, 1952), 1-4, 21-23. It is instructive that Anatol Rapoport, trained as a mathematician, gets this wrong, opting instead to treat axioms about pendulums, for example, as false. See his "Various Meanings of Theory," *American Political Science Review* 52 (1958): 972-988. On the meaning of conditions, see appx. B.

15. Kaplan, *System and Process*, chap. 2; Arthur Lee Burns, "From Balance to Deterrence," *World Politics* 9 (July 1957): 494-529. The reformulations include Karl W. Deutsch and J. David Singer, "Multipolar Power Systems and International Stability," *World Politics* 16 (April 1964): 390-406; Richard N. Rosecrance, "Bipolarity, Multipolarity, and the Future," *Journal of Conflict Resolution* 10 (September 1966): 314-327; and Kenneth N. Waltz, "The Stability of a Bipolar World," *Daedalus* 93 (Summer 1964): 881-909; idem., *Theory of International Politics*, (Reading, MA: Addison-Wesley Publishing Co., 1979), chap. 8.   These concepts have not been successfully applied to the international system. See chapter 5 of this book.

Actors play different roles in different systems. In a system of national actors such as nineteenth century Europe, each actor's strategies are formulated largely in national terms. In a bloc system, the actors' strategies are substantially formulated in bloc terms. There will be differentiation, however, between regular bloc members and bloc leaders. It is not necessary to derive role function from something else, such as power. One cannot derive the role of "balancer," for example, from arbitrary indices of power alone. Geography will obviously influence the ability of an actor to play that role. But these factors will vary from case to case. Instead, role function is presupposed as an irreducible category of analysis. In some systems there may be little differentiation. In others there may be tremendous differentiation. The United States and Luxembourg did not play the same role in the post-1945 international system. The United States did not play the same role in the international system when it acted through NATO as it did when it acted in the Middle East or Asia. None of the countries who were members of NATO and the Warsaw Pact acted as they would have if the alliance were not in place.

Actors may be classified as having essential and nonessential role functions, and as being national or supranational. Supranational actors may be further subdivided into blocs and universal actors. Further distinctions in the class of supranational actors would almost certainly be useful, but are beyond the scope of this book.

In systems as small as international systems, the number of actors and their relative international capabilities clearly influence all the relations in the system. Capabilities refer primarily to the physical instruments actors have available to achieve international objectives. In past international systems, examples of capabilities include military forces in being, the technological quality of weaponry, and logistical capabilities. It is possible that in an empirical case, the availability of foreign assistance funds and international economic instruments would also be treated as capabilities (Israel, for example).

Informational variables are related to capabilities but entail other factors. Transnational actors, for example, are not direct international actors. However, they can at times be analyzed as part of the informational transparency, as well as content, of the system. The same is true of the presence of a permanent diplomatic corps and regularized international conferences. Satellites and intelligence structures also illustrate informational characteristics of a system.

These four variables are necessary to analyze an international structure in a meaningful way. It would be impossible to analyze meaningfully even a simple family structure by numbers alone. Consider a "family" of twelve, all related by blood ties. The normal patterns of action are certain to be radically different depending on whether the twelve comprise a single nuclear family; two nuclear families in which the fathers are brothers; four nuclear families one of which is headed by the parents of the other three; a similar system headed by grandparents with the other units headed by children and grandchildren; or four nuclear units that operate as an extended family. The child-rearing practices are likely to be very different across types, the economic organization will vary across types, the economic role of biologically fertile women is likely to vary across types, and the solidarity of the group is likely to vary across types.

Even a system with only two primary communities requires an analysis of their relations. The action patterns will be radically different depending on whether the two groups are the Hatfields and the McCoys or the interdependent coastal and inland village system in Melanesia that Bronislaw Malinowski analyzed. It follows that researchers must start with what is relevant to the specific type of relations under investigation. For example, the recently deceased bipolar system had bloc relations; it was not merely dyadic. In social and political systems more than numbers and capabilities of the actors are relevant. Actors play different roles in different systems. In Melanesia the coastal inhabitants supplied fish and the inland inhabitants supplied vegetables.[16] In the bipolar system the bloc leaders played distinctively different roles than the bloc members. These relations cannot be assumed away without undermining meaningful explanatory material.

Regime Characteristics. In a narrowly international theoretical formulation, exogenous factors such as the domestic or intra-institutional political characteristics of the actor-systems would have no effect on international action. This is equivalent to the assumption that psychological factors have no effect on the economic system, or that a corporation's chief economic officer is not an alcoholic whose problem effects oligopolistic price coordination. Thus all actors must first be treated as internationally rational.[17] This assumption renders analysis and deduction manageable and the results intelligible. But it should be obvious that this assumption cannot necessarily be maintained in empirical analysis. To believe that democracies and dictatorships, for example, will operate according to the same operational code is not necessarily false, depending on a host of factors including the state of the international system. But such factors are likely to have significant disturbance effects that demand analysis. In no case is empirical analysis advanced by sweeping away the problem under some presumption of rationality or unitary action.

Because so many factors are involved in a regime's characteristic operational style, it is necessary to treat this factor in terms of intra-actor structural typologies. In nontechnical terminology, regime characteristics for national actors would include whether they are democratic, authoritarian, or totalitarian. Bloc actors are divisible into hierarchical, mixed-hierarchical, and nonhierarchical

---

16. Bronislaw Malinowski, *Crime and Custom in Savage Society*, (London: Routledge and Kegan Paul, 1926).

17. The presupposition of rationality need not take the form of von Neumann and Morgenstern's "all embracing and complete" preferences. See John von Neumann and Oskar Morgenstern, *Theory of Games and Economic Behavior*, 3rd ed., (Princeton: Princeton University Press, 1953), 17-20. Instead, the looser—and more realistic—form of the term, "bounded rationality," is appropriate, whereby actors are presupposed to be rational with respect to the system within which the theory is bounded—a particular state of the international system, for example.

actors. Other supranational actors such as the United Nations or the European Union may be analyzed in similar terms.[18] International rationality is likely to be facilitated to the extent that these actors possess long-lasting administrative machinery and legitimacy in the conduct of international policy.

International Action. The function which action serves in a theory, especially at the macrolevel, is usually under- or misspecified. It has often been common in the social sciences to treat behavior merely as an outcome. This conception, left over from the rise of modern physics, views human or social systems as behaving as a function of forces that are external or internal to the actors. Such a conception makes all humans victims of their conditions and renders the analysis of responsible action impossible. Action, however, is a necessary feature of dynamic analysis. Action connects the equilibria and transformations of material conditions across time. The equilibrium between Malinowski's coastal and inland villages is in part maintained and transformed by the exchange relations of fish and vegetables. The Soviet-American strategic equilibrium was in part maintained and transformed by the production and control of armaments. One cannot explain how an international system is maintained and transformed without reference to the patterns of action which occur, because actions can modify a system's structure. Thus, all social systems have implicit or explicit rules that are necessary for system stability.

The existence of rules does not necessarily entail a formally sanctioned enforcement mechanism. Enforcement mechanisms will obviously influence what kinds of rules are stable. (The direct taxation of citizens in the NATO countries by NATO would obviously not be stable). Although all social systems require an entire set of rules, singular examples are at present sufficient to illustrate the point. Coordinated prices are a rule of oligopolistic economic systems. A balanced diet is a rule of good health, as is exercise, and abstinence from smoking. "Marry and multiply" is a rule of agricultural societies. Limit family size is a rule of post-industrial societies. "Do not burn any bridges" is a rule of the U.S. Senate and the nineteenth century "balance of power" international system. Do not weaken alliance solidarity is a rule of bipolar international systems. At least in principle, the function that rules play in social action is really not a very difficult concept to master.

4. Coding

The fourth standard is the *coding* presupposition. A general discussion of coding requires an analysis of language far beyond our scope. It would minimally include a discussion of concepts, meaning, signs, logic and reality. Some relationships between logic and reality already have been adumbrated under the headings of international political relations, explanatory theory, and

---

18. For technical terminology see Morton A. Kaplan, *System and Process*, chap. 3.

initial conditions. One cannot, however, draw meaningful conclusions between models and reality without some middling device, and signs are this device.

Variables and parameters are the primary analytical entities that must be coded. As previously stated, the relationships among the necessary sets of initial conditions will be discussed in chapter 8, where the reasons that each set can be either a variable or a parameter will be stated. But regardless of how these sets function in an argument, they must be coded. Take the example of a family as an analogue. Family structure could, for example, be coded as "nuclear" or "extended." The former coding could refer to the presence of a husband and wife in a domicile, who constitute the basic units of authority and legitimacy for all decisions regarding child-rearing, family norms, and economic management. An extended family structure could refer to the presence of a clan, where the elders constitute the basic units of authority and legitimacy for child-rearing, marriage, and economic distribution within the clan.

In the social sciences there is occasionally a tendency to associate coding with quantification, but quantitative analysis—in the numerical sense—is not the only form of definite and rigorous thought. It is primarily useful in situations where a one-to-one correspondence exists between a sign and a real world referent, the latter being measured by independent instruments, such as measuring rods. Such coding permits the rules of mathematics to be employed if operator terms, such as "plus," can also be defined operationally. These conditions do not generally exist in the social sciences, and attempts to force the issue do violence to the concepts employed. Qualitative signs may also be arranged to represent the order of things and may be employed in propositional form to reach necessarily true conclusions.

Not everything in a theoretical system can be coded—that is, employ specific symbols associated with real world referents. There are undefined terms in any theory (such as points in Euclidean geometry, which are defined only implicitly through the other terms in the theory). However, the initial conditions of a theory must be coded in terms of referents; otherwise the selection of evidence is unregulated. And if unregulated, then there is no reason why the length of Cleopatra's nose, to echo Pascal, should not be treated as a variable in the analysis.

Especially in a qualitative study these codings must not be too rigid, because meaning is so context dependent. In a bipolar system, for instance, the number of bloc members and the capabilities of the blocs are central variables. One cannot, however, provide a bright-line boundary between attempts to increase bloc membership and attempts to increase capabilities. A new member generally increases a bloc's capabilities and an increase in capabilities may be a consciously chosen means to persuade or coerce a new member. In the early postwar period, for example, when does one affirm Western efforts in West Germany as membership expansion and when as an increase in capabilities?

These questions are highly context-dependent. However, the range of a category cannot be set so widely or loosely that everything is within its scope or is subject exclusively to subjective interpretation. In the case of West Germany, for example, restricting membership to variations in diplomatic relationships and capabilities to variations in military relationships provides a tool for sorting out these kinds of questions. A useful coding scheme provides observation criteria for propositions in a theory. Without such schemata a theory has no objective observational possibilities, and instead collapses into an idiosyncratic private language. The fact that a particular community appears to share the same meanings is no guide that the language is objective.[19] Consider merely the widespread usage in democratic societies of the symbol "freedom" and the divergent—often antithetical—meanings, such as autonomy, license, selfishness, or self-transcendence.

5. Motives and Confirmation

The fifth standard is the *motivational* presupposition. In international politics, humans should be brought back into analysis. Most of the authors considered in the book treat international actors as residual entities whose behavior is the product of some recondite causes, either international or domestic. That conception is a little outdated at this point in history. It is better to conceive the actor as the nexus at which relationships are integrated, roles are embodied, and motives are activated.

The section entitled "initial conditions" implied the theoretical function of international action: actors either act consistently or not with respect to some system of values. In a theoretical formulation, system-rational action must be hypothesized. It is the action that rational actors would take if they valued the theoretical situation under scrutiny, and nothing else. System-rational action does not mean "acting for the good of the system," nor does it presume that every real actor acts rationally. Every individual does not act as a price-rational economic actor. But the reader may consider a reasonable economic presupposition: If prices are all that actors take into account, they will always buy at the lowest price.

Personality systems, however, do not necessarily behave in theoretically determined ways. In the real world actions may be accidentally consistent with a system's equilibrium. Consider a consumer who buys the best quality shoes in a store that always has the lowest advertised prices. Clearly this could occur for non-price reasons. An interview might indicate that this person frequents the shoe store because of fondness for the clerk, and, moreover, their fondness is based on the fact that the clerk is a descendent of powerful beings from another planet!

---

19. By "objective" I mean that a concept is coded by signs such that the concept applies to specific empirical referents. Thus a drinking glass exists objectively when the signs "cylindrical," "fluid reservoir," "open-topped," and "hand holdable" are applicable to an object of reference, though the context of the situation will always require assessment. In the context of a marital spat a "glass" may in fact be a "weapon" or a "projectile."

The truth of any scientific theory rests partly on whether the subject-entity behaves in accordance with the reasons proposed in that theory. When the subject-entities are international actors, researchers must adduce evidence for the conformity of motives with the assumptions postulated in their theory. When practicable, the assessment of motives should include stated motives as well as corroboration with behavior. A person who claims to be a serious scholar, for example, should on occasion read a book. Likewise, an international decision-maker who claims that they want to settle a dispute peacefully should not return to the party faithful and state that the original statement is a ruse to deceive the enemy. These are illustrative examples of corroboration. In general an analyst can place higher confidence in an explanation to the extent that there is great congruence between stated motives and behavior. In systems with very large numbers of actors, such as the international coffee market, direct confirmation may be difficult and often unnecessary. In an international system that focuses primarily on a comparatively small number of essential actors, confirmation requires much greater corroboration of motives and actions.

According to the focal presupposition, the actors must be motivated by international political relations. Otherwise an international theory does not necessarily apply. For instance, an increase in international capabilities that is consistent with a theoretical hypothesis must be motivated by something arising in the international system rather than domestic or personality factors. With respect to the actors' mind-sets, therefore, it is necessary to make a basic conceptual distinction between motives and preferences, the latter conceived as an analytical subroutine of the former. Policy preference "x" may occur as a result of, say, two motives—international or bureaucratic. Although the policy implications may be largely similar, the explanation of the action requires different theories. Otherwise, any preference which led to an international outcome could be considered international theory. Although such preferences may explain particular international actions, those actions would not be explained by the particular system of international political relations in which the actors are embedded, and thus would not constitute international theory.

Assessments must be used in determining an actor's motives for action. In the next section Truman's motives about the defense budget are used to illustrate that the president was motivated by domestic rather than international considerations. In that case the evidence is fairly unambiguous: the decision was hotly debated, the budget director and the Joint Chiefs of Staff presented their respective cases in domestic versus international terms, and the determination is consistent with the wider context as it is known. Other cases are often much more difficult. At the end of any particular analysis some motives will undoubtedly remain unknown. The ethical and professional social scientist will state so, or at least not attempt to cover up or obfuscate the matter.

The key point here is that theories are not primarily designed to predict or to describe characteristics of a system—though a good theory will incorporate these functions in part. The objective is to explain; social analysis that is sundered from motivation is nothing more than mythology.

6. Values (Levels of Motivation Problem)

The sixth basic standard is the *valuational* presupposition. Any theory in the social sciences must have value components if it seeks to be explanatory. Human actors tend to seek objectives which they believe are valuable. Any specified theoretical system will have some values which are consistent with its structure and others which are not. The term "values" is an abstract universal concept, and particular values vary according to the system under scrutiny. It must be emphasized, however, that anything deemed valuable is so only within the boundaries of a particular type of system. This proposition is meaningful both for abstract and concrete systems.

The Euclidean geometrical system has the Pythagorean theorem as one of its values. This is to say that it follows from the structure of the axioms. The purely free market economic system values profit and private property and dismisses governmental ownership. And these values are consistent with premises of instrumentally autonomous individuals. The Leninist system of democratic centralism values decisions of the Vanguard and diminishes those of the masses. This follows from some collectively conceived premises. And in a bipolar system each bloc values itself and diminishes its opponent. Even claims of universal or absolute values presuppose that human beings are in some sense identical systems, perhaps morally or biologically.

In any particular system an actor may or may not view a particular system of international political relations as valuable. More specifically, an actor may view that system or its components as more or less valuable when compared to alternative systems, including systems at alternative levels. Alternative levels include both the domestic system and subsystems of which the actors are members, as well as the actors' personality systems. Only through such a matrix of values is it possible to assess the motives for actions, and thus the truth of a theory.

Consider a simple example of different systems of value as they impact upon decision-making. In early 1950, for instance, Truman decided that the defense budget would be approximately $14 billion. The Joint Chiefs of Staff argued that they needed about $17 billion if they were to maintain a foothold in Europe in the event of a Soviet invasion. Truman discounted such a threat. Truman's decision supported the position of his budget director, and the grounds of the decision were based on the need for fiscal conservatism. Whether that fiscal conservatism was motivated by inflation, a personal bond between Truman and his budget director, or the election environment is of no relevance, per se, to international theory. The United States government made that decision in order to promote domestic values.

The point here is not to criticize Truman's decision. The purpose is to classify it in terms of the level of motivation which Truman valued most in that decision. There was a trade-off in this case between domestic and international value judgments, and Truman's decision judged the maintenance and expansion of domestic values to be more important in that case.

Keeping wider values in context clarifies that international structural questions do not have absolute priority. Whether actors choose to increase or decrease their military capabilities, for example, may be motivated by the relative value which they place on international security, but may also be motivated by some intersection of values of all the systems of which the actor is member. And it is certainly possible that international security may not be the motive whatsoever.

7. Time

The seventh basic standard is the *durational* presupposition. Although not considered intensively in this book, the issue of time is central to a well formed theory. It is necessary to isolate both the duration of a particular type of system (its life and death), and its varying processes (phases) over time. Isolating different types of international systems is partly a question of coding and partly of identifying initial conditions for international structure, whereas a system's phase variations are a question of intrasystemic timekeeping.[20]

Phase demarcation is the more challenging intellectual problem. In highly interactive systems which exhibit sensitive dependence on initial conditions—such as the weather system—patterns do not exhibit explicit temporal divisions. Even the seasons shade into each other, and it requires astronomical theory about the relation of the sun and earth to mark precisely when seasonal change is instantiated. Imagine the uselessness that would result in the comparison of seasonal temperature averages if meteorologists did not share theoretically meaningful temporal boundaries.

The less complex a system, the less this is a problem. Some international systems are less sensitive and complex than others. In "balance of power" international systems, phases are easily identified by the war frame. The initial conditions for all the variables and parameters may be determined in the pre-war period. In domestic political systems, phases are usually set by elections. Macroeconomic systems have the boom and bust phases of the business cycle. In the twentieth century bipolar system, no comparable natural "clock" is obvious, a problem that has led researchers to select time frames arbitrarily. Selecting a year—1953, 1956, 1969, 1973, and 1989—as marking a significant change in the characteristics of the bipolar system has been used by various researchers. But such selections are seldom tethered to explicit theoretical criteria that would explain why that year was chosen. Instead, dramatic selection criteria—change of ruler, wars, treaties, and so forth—are the custom. This problem—the fallacy of selectivity—cannot be eliminated, but theoretical controls related to the focal presupposition, or to variations in the initial conditions of a model, can temper this danger.[21]

---

20. See chap. 7 (footnote 44).

21. Andrew P. Dunne, *The Life and Death of Bipolar Systems* (manuscript). In the postwar system the changing phases of bipolarity indicate a recurrent pattern of action

INTERDEPENDENCE OF BASIC STANDARDS

Although no author can claim absolute status for any particular proposition or part-system of knowledge, a very strict threshold must be crossed before these basic standards can be parsed. The basic standards form a logically interdependent system, because each part prehends and is prehended in other parts. Together the standards form the formal subject matter of theoretical discourse at the macrolevel of international politics (and of social science if the appropriate substitutions are made for the concrete subject matter in the focal presupposition and initial conditions), though only as a minimal system that mandates further prehension and refinement.

These standards are analytical distinctions and are thus distinct from traditional historiographical standards in the field of international relations. Realism, idealism, and neoism are theorism, not theory. Quite literally, only the end of history can vindicate one perspective or the other. As has been remarked, the traditional schools are best characterized by two perspectives: a school of practical politics, and a school of historical sociology. The former have sought to erect principles of politics, whereas the latter have attempted to expand analysis to include a framework. The first part of the book is about these kinds of approaches, which have moved to the brink that separates the field of international relations from a theory of international politics. These approaches lack explanatory capacity and are caught in the web of nineteenth- and early twentieth-century debates about the proper conception of the national interest. There is, however, no control in any of these conceptions. A practitioner usually selects the kind of problem or the kind of evidence deemed appropriate to support the presupposed conception. In the process, they create a hornets' nest of confusion. The frailty of these methods will become obvious as these approaches are subjected to strict analysis in the first part of this book. In each case, major failures to employ one or more of the basic standards are shown to entail serious consequences for sustained argument. The issue of whether the world is becoming rational and peaceful, or is stuck in a futile and fruitless cyclical impulse is of no direct concern in this book. What is of importance is whether or not the individual social scientist is to be rational, and to exhibit some basic cognitive consistency and clarity.

The basic standards attempt to provide these kinds of criteria: that the subject matter of international theory be explicitly bounded, that deductive or semi-deductive arguments be employed where possible, that specific initial conditions be stated, that the variables and parameters of analysis be coded, that actor motivations toward the international system be treated as evidence, that the other values which could be motivational factors be considered, and that time be

---

that tends to switch between phases of "détente" and "cold war." Phase-switching has been controlled reasonably well by tethering these switches to major changes in the bloc leaders' doctrines of world order. See also some of the discussion in chap. 7 about phase-switching in the Italian city-state system.

incorporated in the analysis. These elements are necessary presuppositions; drop even one, and the analysis is seriously damaged, if not fundamentally destroyed.

ORDER OF TREATMENT

Analysis now turns to authors whose theoretical efforts fail one or more of these standards, which precluded their development of international theory. The authors are presented in order of increasing complexity of argument form.

Chapter 2 opens with Edward Hallett Carr's standard historiographical dualism, a dualism that characterizes the field. Carr was fairly well balanced in his approach to realism and utopianism, though he did not believe he had formulated a theory. It is perhaps useful to bear this in mind from the outset.

PART I:

_____

To the Brink . . .

2

Orienting Principles

International politics was practiced by soldiers and statesman long before it became an academic enterprise. The mind-set of such individuals is usually one of practical politics. Words and ideas are used to express oneself in the ordinary language necessary to communicate practical problems and solutions. Naturally, our professional language evolved from this practical discourse. World War I was a great catalyst in making international relations and international politics permanent elements of academic life. As would be expected, the policy debates and analytical standards of soldiers and statesman became incorporated in the orientation of pioneer academic writers. In order to orient themselves, and orient the field, there was a tendency to tailor the emerging academic discourse to the practical political language that had preceded it.

To some extent this interpenetration is inevitable and fruitful. Otherwise international politics runs the danger of divorcing itself from the materials it studies. But many statements formulated in practical discourse are not capable of systematic investigation. As a result they generate debate rather than answers.

Although sophisticated approaches to international politics now exist, they often include a great deal of baggage. Much of that baggage is a result of the unconscious incorporation of the practical discourse that originally informed the field. In particular, the meaning of international theory is usually conflated with the meaning of practical political thought. Adoption of a theory in international politics often means adoption of a partisan platform: realism or liberalism, for example. The writings of Edward Hallett Carr and Hans Morgenthau are paradigmatic examples of this problem. This chapter presents their conceptions of the realism-idealism dispute in order to show that, at best, these conceptions are orienting principles that tell us how to write a history; at worst, they are shibboleths that infuse scholarship with a secular religious dispute.

EDWARD HALLETT CARR

To most, it will come as no surprise that a diplomatic historian such as Carr does not meet the basic standards stated in Chapter 1. My overall appraisal is that Carr completely misses five of the basic standards and demonstrates only meager affinity for the motivational and valuational standards. But Carr's distance from the basic standards puts into sharp relief many of the current debates about theory. The realism-liberalism debate undoubtedly served some academic function when it was formulated. Today, however, this debate has a function similar to that of the human appendix: while it is an element in the organon, it doesn't seem to change the performance of the system. An appendix should be left alone if it causes no problems. But if it is infected it should be removed from the system so that healthy functions can be maintained. Many contemporary debates are unproductive largely because they invest a great deal of time in research on an element that is no longer useful for our professional evolution.

Focus and Method

Since E. H. Carr, most heated debates among students of international relations have been about the relative weight of what Carr called "utopian" and "realist" attitudes.[1] Carr stated that the academic origins of the field resulted after World War I, when English-speaking populists opposed the secret treaties that they claimed were one of the war's causes. This history of the field's origin is generally accepted. Genesis, however, is not function: historiographical and policy debates do not constitute professional research standards. That the expression of research standards was not Carr's objective is no surprise. Carr's mind-set was that of an historian. The maturation of the social sciences was not a consideration for him. But the kind of reasoning that Carr employed, and that so permeates much subsequent discourse, is very much at odds with the basic standards presented in chapter 1. By applying those standards to Carr—and Morgenthau after him—we may be able to learn what baggage to leave behind in the effort to build a theory of international politics.

The first point to make is that Carr became a victim of an age that based both realism and idealism on the concept of national interest. That both Carr's realism and Carr's idealism are united in a common framework based on historiographical methods about the national interest is easily shown.

Utopia and Reality. In a chapter entitled "The Utopian Background," Carr attributes the origins of modern utopianism to Benthamite utilitarianism. Carr specifically mentions Bentham's reliance on individuated reason as the arbiter of morality, and refers to his ethical formula: "the greatest happiness for the greatest number." This formula helped to justify public opinion and majority rule as the

---

1. Edward Hallett Carr, *The Twenty Years' Crisis, 1919-1939: An Introduction to the Study of International Relations*, 2nd ed. (London: MacMillan and Co., Ltd., 1946).

arbiter, if not the literal manifestation, of the "greatest" happiness. Public opinion, acting in the light of reason, was by definition always right. It was bound to prevail in the democracies, at least in the long run. These conceptions led to the belief that international public opinion, once aggregated, was a force for good in the world. This article of faith was strongly internalized by Woodrow Wilson, for example, who expected that the League of Nations, disarmament agreements, and territorial compromises would be guaranteed by the court of public opinion.[2]

Carr also stated that utopian thinking was based on faith in the "harmony of interests," a faith that the highest interest of the individual and the highest interest of the community naturally coincide. Carr claimed that this doctrine resulted primarily from the efforts of the *laissez-faire* school of political economy, particularly from Adam Smith's argument that individual competitive action in the free market leads by an "invisible hand" to the promotion of the public interest. It was a small step to equate the nation with individuals and thereby promote free trade among countries as well. All states could then be said to have an economic harmony of interests. Carr states that this doctrine, though it avoided the question of which interests would have to be sacrificed in pursuit of the true interests of mankind, was promoted by the United States after World War I. As a political doctrine it stated that all nations desired peace; as an economic doctrine it stated that all nations desired the benefits of free trade.

On the other hand, Carr characterized realist thinking as an analysis of actual political practices. History, the "whole course of human evolution," was contrasted with ethics. Whereas utopians, according to Carr, believe that ethical notions apply to all individuals, the realist school believes that ethical notions are a product of historical conditioning, and that thoughts are in general wedded to purposes. It was through this notion that Carr virtually equated theory and policy principle as one in the same: "If theories are revealed as a reflexion of practice and principles of political needs, this discovery will apply to the fundamental theories and principles of the utopian creed, and not least to the doctrine of the harmony of interests which is its essential postulate."[3]

And from whence comes the notion of a community interest? Carr is plain: "Theories of social morality are always the product of a dominant group which identifies itself with the community as a whole, and which possesses facilities denied to subordinate groups or individuals for imposing its view of life on the community. Theories of international morality are, for the same reason and in virtue of the same process, the product of dominant nations or dominant groups."[4]

---

2. Ibid., 23-24; on Wilson, 31-36, but cf. Alexander L. George and Juliette L. George, *Woodrow Wilson and Colonel House: A Personality Study* (New York: Dover Publishing, [1956] 1964), 320-322.

3. Carr, *The Twenty Years' Crisis*, 75.

4. Ibid., 79.

The universal form in which Carr makes this statement is certainly overstated. Neither Marx nor the early Christian writers represented dominant groups when they wrote. And it inanely suggests that any differences among the moral characteristics of Nazi, Stalinist, American, or Colonial doctrine is unimportant or irrelevant. Even if Carr meant that social morality becomes important only if a dominant group expresses it, he still uses the word "theory" in a scientifically naive sense. In that form, the statement that every dominant group claims to be acting in the interest of the larger community is an historiographical premise (a methodological device) that describes the world and selects evidence according to a certain standard—namely, that of first selecting the dominant group. Whether this is a good historiographical standard is, however, not relevant to the issue at hand. It is essential to recognize the fundamentally nonscientific character of such an argument, and the common basis it shares with utopianism as an orienting principle.

Carr's concepts of utopianism and realism violate both the focal and explanatory presuppositions. His focus is not on the international political relationships that comprise a particular type of international system, and no explicit deductive reasoning is employed. It follows that both the conditional and durational presuppositions are violated as well. The latter two standards would be used only if deductive reasoning was at the center of analysis.

The Realm of Judgment. The purpose of Carr's book was to orient the attitudes of academic and popular thinkers; to counteract the tendency to neglect the factors of power in analyzing international affairs.[5] Carr mostly oriented himself towards realism and is today remembered by that label. However, Carr's personal thinking was a little more balanced than his realist reputation suggests:

But there is a stage where realism is the necessary corrective to the exuberance of utopianism, just as in other periods utopianism must be invoked to counteract the barrenness of realism. Immature thought is predominantly purposive and utopian. Thought which rejects purpose altogether is the thought of old age. Mature thought combines purpose with observation and analysis. Utopia and reality are thus the two facets of political science.[6]

The backdrop for Carr's study was the dissolution of the Versailles peace agreement. Carr did not universalize his realism. His argument was focused against world government and League of Nations advocates who implied that the mere institution of good ideas would guarantee the maintenance of good institutions. Nor did Carr view the state as a constant of international intercourse. He explicitly stated that territorial-unit bases of power were neither the only historical form nor the only possible future form of international authority.[7]

---

5. Ibid., vii.
6. Ibid., 10.
7. Ibid., 226-232.

Moreover, he did not think that the element of power was sufficient to analyze international stability.

If, however, it is utopian to ignore the element of power, it is an unreal kind of realism which ignores the element of morality in any world order. Just as within the state every government, though it needs power as a basis of its authority, also needs the moral basis of the consent of the governed, so an international order cannot be based on power alone for the simple reason that mankind will in the long run always revolt against naked power. Any international order presupposes a substantial measure of general consent.[8]

These ideas indicate Carr's weak affinity with the motivational and valuational presuppositions. His characterization of mature thought as inclusive of both realist and utopian orienting principles indicate a limited role for these standards. Two points are clear regardless of Carr's mixture of utopian-realist thinking. First, the naked pointing to "camps" among many students in the field has led Carr's somewhat balanced opinions to be obscured by his realist label. Carr thought that more benign forms of world order could be real. Second, and more important, Carr was not developing an explanatory theory.

Carr's Dualism

Carr's intellectual background contributed to his subsequent classification as a staunch realist, because he accepted historiographical principles that continually suggest a superficial choice as to how to interpret the political world. First and foremost, this problem resulted from Carr's coding scheme.

Coding. Carr does not explicitly employ coding criteria. But it is impossible to use language effectively without some kind of coding scheme. Carr's codings are consistent with the academic debates that resulted from the success of Newtonian science. The rise of modern physics following the sixteenth century fostered a mind-body dualism which was still prevalent during the nineteenth and early twentieth centuries. Carr fully operated within this mind-set. Virtually all of Carr's analytical categories are implicitly coded according to this dichotomy. Utopianism is associated with mind, theory, purpose, hope, harmony of interests, and morality. In contrast, realism is associated with bodies, practice and analysis, interests, empirical facts, relativity of thought, and power. Although this coding scheme can be employed—albeit arbitrarily—to characterize world history, it has nothing to do with international political relations, the focal standard stated in the introductory chapter. Instead, Carr's dualistic categories are merely orienting principles; an historiographical device by which to select information to describe international thought. These categories do not treat systems of international politics as exhibiting structural variability which would

---

8. Ibid., 235-236.

affect the action patterns of real actors embedded in the system. These categories are used merely to characterize the thought of other thinkers.

Carr himself became a victim of these characterizations. Because of the rigid, dualistic framework, his treatment of other writers tended toward caricature. For example, Carr categorized Hegel as a realist, a term that in Carr's coding is linked with empirical facts. Hegel was anything but an empiricist, as even a cursory understanding of his Absolute would have indicated.

Caricatures such as these raise doubts about the practical value of the realism-idealism dichotomy. The rigidity of the coding scheme permits only limited use of evidence. For example, most of the evidence Carr used to support the position that national interests were not harmonious were quotations from individuals who believed such interests were discordant. No consideration of alternative evidence is offered. Although Carr's evidence is consistent with the motivational standard, it cannot get at the questions that the contemporary political scientist needs to ask. The latter questions are bounded by the focal presupposition. And within those boundaries, national interests surely have a wider range of possibility than that indicated by a dummy variable for "harmony." To continually rehearse Carr's dichotomy produces merely endless and unproductive ideological wars.

Explanation or Description? The problem with this dichotomous coding scheme becomes particularly acute in any attempt to move beyond descriptive categorization. Carr was not doing explanatory theory: deductive accounts and the explicit coding of initial conditions are ignored. It is fairly clear that Carr did not understand modern science. Stuck as he was in Bacon's preoccupation with facts he never grasped the essentially hypothetical character of theoretical science. He believed science was an enterprise rooted in facts. Modern science, however, unambiguously presents itself as a triumph of human reason, as a formal system of relations which unite the objects of study within an intelligible order.

This misconception of science precluded Carr's adoption of theoretical objectives. In fact he called neither his study nor realism a theory. He spoke of realism and utopianism as political thinking. His few examples of the word "theory" (sometimes meaning purpose, sometimes a moral policy) indicate that Carr did not believe the term had explanatory meaning. And by science Carr clearly means the suppression of wishful, purposive aspirations in favor of a study of the real causes and consequences of facts. Theory is characterized as rationalized and purposive thought—something distinct from facts, not something to unite the facts in a coherent explanatory system.[9]

---

9. Ibid., 2-5, 12-13, 67-71. It can hardly be claimed that Newton's laws of motion are based on facts. First, these laws establish *invariant* relationships among variables in a system. Newton could not have perceived invariance in the real world. In this sense, realists are correct that the facts are changeable. As a fact, the fall of feathers and billiards balls are quite different, but in the system of Newtonian equations both phenomena are products of the same relations among the variables of force, mass, and

After World War II, students of international relations, especially in the United States, often pursued goals of theory building. Many kept Carr's orienting principles at the forefront of their efforts, others not. These orientations, however, are not relevant to theory building. Hedley Bull seemed to understand the difference and to agree with Carr when he stated that the traditional approach was based on judgment, and, that the confines of theory-building in the scientific sense would allow us to say very little about international politics.[10] But if theory-building is our objective, then Bull and Carr are not the baggage that will get us there.

The approach of Carr sets us on the wrong path in the development of international theory. The orienting principles that are proposed are not capable of refutation; they ask the wrong questions, and they select the wrong facts. The focus on individual attitudes ignores the requirements to focus on types of international political systems, to make deductively valid arguments, to specify initial conditions and a coding scheme about the variables and parameters that define the international system. At best, we can make judgments about motives and values. But we can only determine the relevant actor motivations and valuations when these other standards are well specified. Without them we wind up with approaches such as Carr's, with a focus on political thought in general.

HANS J. MORGENTHAU

Hans J. Morgenthau also employed orienting principles, but always with a hint of something more developed. Except for the explanatory and durational standards, Morgenthau vaguely incorporates each of the other standards. However, the ambiguities and unbounded scope of his central terms undermine the efficacy of those standards. A fair appraisal must conclude that Morgenthau's approach failed to adequately meet any of the basic standards.

Morgenthau's relevance to the history of explanatory theory in international politics is best examined in his conceptions of universal principles and balance of power. These concepts have a ring to them, and seem to sound like what it is that a scientific theory should sound like. Moreover, among practitioners in the field, his opinions had long-term implications on the sociology of knowledge.

---

acceleration. Newton could not have been following Bacon's method. On Newton's thought see John Hermann Randall, *The Career of Philosophy* (New York: Columbia University Press, 1962), vol. I: 563-594; and Alfred North Whitehead, *Science and the Modern World: Lowell Lectures, 1925* (New York: The Macmillan Co., 1925), 45-58.

10. Hedley Bull, "International Theory: The Case for a Classical Approach," in *Contending Approaches to International Politics*, Klauss Knorr and James Rosenau, eds., (Princeton: Princeton University Press, 1969), 20-38.

The Function of Power

Morgenthau's tone differed explicitly from Carr's. He called his realism a theory and stated that his purpose was "to discover the forces underlying social phenomena and how they operate," because that was the "natural aim of all scientific undertakings." However, he did not believe international relations required any specialized form of political analysis. He instead viewed a system of checks and balances as "a universal principle for all pluralist societies."[11] Such universal applicability is in conflict with the first basic standard: that of specifying a distinct focus for the subdiscipline of international politics, a focus based on different types of international political relationships. However, perhaps theories more general than those entailed by focal presuppositions are possible. If so, Morgenthau's principle might serve as an example of such a methodology, and could perhaps be accomplished by his successors. The question is reasonable, but I will show why it is wrong. First consider Morgenthau's claims.

Morgenthau claimed that, unlike utopians, his science was basically empiricist in form. He did not consider his universal principle of checks and balances to be abstract, by which he generally meant *a priori*. Instead, one would study the historical record, develop principles related to "reality," determine if the concepts were somehow consistent, and then point to the facts as they "actually are" to support the theory.

The test by which such a theory must be judged is not *a priori* and abstract but empirical. . . . The theory . . . must be judged not by some preconceived abstract principle . . . but by its purpose; to bring order and meaning to a mass of phenomena. . . . It must meet a dual test . . . [Do] the facts as they actually are lend themselves to the interpretation the theory has put upon them, and do the conclusions at which the theory arrives follow with logical necessity from its premises. In short, is the theory consistent with the facts and within itself.[12]

In very general terms these are adequate criteria for the assessment of a theory. In Morgenthau's case the theory was a set of principles, the first of which asserted that objective laws rooted in human nature govern all of politics and society. Morgenthau believed that these laws operated regardless of human preferences. This position was consistent with his monistic view that there is a primary reality underlying political phenomena in general. But it was a consistency achieved through one principle, which was the main junction in his approach. The "main signpost . . . of interest defined as power" was the link between reason and facts, between theory and reality, between principles and the

---

11. Hans J. Morgenthau, *Politics Among Nations: The Struggle for Power and Peace*, 3rd ed. (New York: Alfred A. Knopf, 1963), 3-4, 16; cf., 172.
    12. Ibid., 3.

historical record. Thus the function of power was to orient, but like a statue it always pointed in one direction.

Universal propositions—that is, covering laws—have been demonstrated in the exact sciences. In the following section I show how a universal proposition can be used in a deductive argument. Then I discuss the covering-law model of scientific explanation. The covering-law model provides the most rigorous approach to universals in human thought. That discussion provides a basis for assessing why Morgenthau's power-seeking principle cannot be universalized. Morgenthau's approach—or any other—cannot meet the rigorous coding and conditional requirements necessary to establish universal propositions. Next I state why the failure to establish universal propositions mandates the analysis of motivation, which Morgenthau rules out of court. I then argue that the function of power in Morgenthau's approach was designed for the writing of history, not the construction of international theory.

Universal Principles. Morgenthau often referred to "iron laws" or, to "general laws of international politics, applicable to all nations at all times." By these laws he meant that the national interest in power-seeking was the supreme value by which statesmen operated. He claimed that: "The question which Richelieu, Hamilton, . . . or Disraeli would ask . . . was: Does this decision increase or decrease the power of this and other nations?"[13]

Statements like these are replete throughout Morgenthau's writings, and constitute substantial evidence that we are dealing first and foremost with a theory of national interest rather than one of international politics. However, is it possible to develop a theory of international politics from a theory of national interest? The answer to that question depends in part on how the power-seeking principle could conceivably function within an explanatory model.

Despite the fact that Morgenthau's position doesn't develop a specialized standard for the study of international politics, perhaps a theory more general than that implied by the focal presupposition is possible, in which case Morgenthau's objective laws—his various concepts of power—could function within a deductive framework in one of two ways.

1. As a Consequence to be Explained: if a universal interest in power exists, then it must be a consequence deducible from other generalizations about human psychology;

2. As a Premise to Explain Behavior: such a principle could itself be taken as antecedent generalization from which behavioral consequences about

---

13. Morgenthau, *Scientific Man vs. Power Politics* (Chicago: The University of Chicago Press, 1946), 101. On "iron" or general laws, see idem, *In Defense of the National Interest: A Critical Examination of American Foreign Policy* (New York: Alfred A. Knopf, 1951), 144, 147, 154.

international relations could be derived. In this latter case behavioral events would be explained by the principle.

Morgenthau is somewhat closer to this second approach. However, he gives little indication—other than the statement that a theory must be consistent within itself—that he recognizes the import of deductive theory. In fact, because he states that rational theory is supposed to "reflect" the objective laws, it is highly unlikely that he comprehended the manner in which deductive procedures are used in the sciences.

Morgenthau never worked out the meaning of "reflect," but seems to be groping toward a concept of truth based on correspondence, whereby the principle of power-seeking is shown to be associated with a statesman's behavior. He assumed, and claimed that the evidence confirmed, that statesmen actually behaved congruently with the power principle.[14] If we adopt the standpoint of scientific procedure, there are two reasons this claim does not survive scrutiny. These reasons are covered below in the sections on coding and initial conditions. First, however, it is necessary to discuss the covering law model of scientific explanation.

Covering Laws. As stated above, the logical nature of scientific theory is deductive. In the developed sciences the ideal of theoretical explanation is represented by the deductive-nomological (D-N) version of the covering law model. D-N models are designed to answer "why questions," such as, "Why do satellites travel in elliptical orbits?" In D-N models the premises, called explanans, are of two kinds: empirical conditions (facts) and general laws (principles).[15]

It is the conjunction of these premises that constitutes the explanation of an event. General laws are statements of universal applicability for a specified class of systems (subject entities). Such statements specify an invariant relation between a subject and its properties. The proposition "all satellites travel in elliptical orbits" relates satellites and orbital characteristics. If supplemented by a minor premise such as "x is a satellite," then the conclusion, called the explanandum, that "x travels in an elliptical orbit" can be proven to be a logically valid consequent of the premises (explanans).

If "the space shuttle Discovery" is substituted for "x," two more statements can be made. First, it can be stated that if the space shuttle Discovery happens to be

---

14. Idem, *Politics Among Nations*, 18; and idem, "Another Great 'Debate': The National Interest of the United States," *American Political Science Review* 46 (1952): 965-966.

15. The covering law model has been used as a label to describe both the deductive-nomological (D-N) as well as statistical models of scientific explanation. The treatment of it which follows is based exclusively on the D-N model. For a comprehensive treatment of these models in scientific explanation, see Carl G. Hempel, *Aspects of Scientific Explanation and Other Essays in the Philosophy of Science* (New York: Free Press of Glencoe, 1965), 331-496.

in an orbit, then the shape of that orbit will be elliptical. Second, if the question is asked: "Why is the space shuttle in an elliptical orbit?," then the explanation is complete by stating that Discovery is a satellite and all satellites travel in elliptical orbits.[16]

To repeat, Morgenthau's principle of interest defined as power could function in a deductive argument in one of two ways: as an explanandum (consequence to be explained) or as an explanan (premise to explain behavior).

As an explanandum event the principle would be treated as a consequent, to be explained by some logically prior principles, say of human psychology. In this case a question such as "Why do all nations seek power" could be answered by the conjunction of favorable conditions (e.g., political, financial, personal) and universal laws (drives) of human psychology. In this kind of explanation favorable social conditions would serve as releasing mechanisms for the primitive psychological drives. The drives might be ego gratification or rerouted biological needs. Morgenthau sometimes made statements along psychological lines, such as when he stated that objective laws are rooted in human nature and that general laws of international politics are applicable to all nations at all times.

Were it true that all nations seek power at all times—if it were a constant akin to Einstein's speed of light—then an explanation of this "general law" could be based exclusively on a psychological theory of human nature, perhaps including phylogenetic adaptations of human neurophysiological structure. Although Morgenthau often stated that the national interest in power-seeking was a universal law, under criticism he backed off from this position, stating that it was a principle of social conduct that permitted violations, and thus was unlike a law of nature.[17] Therefore, the less than universal explanation would have to include the conditional releasing mechanisms as minor premises in the argument.

The less universal explanation would require specification of the conditions—social and psychological—that must be present for the manifestation of power-seeking behavior. It would also require that power-seeking be defined in a nontautological way. Morgenthau did neither, and thereby fell short of both the conditional and coding standards. Therefore, he did not offer a theory to explain power-seeking.

The second way power-seeking could function as part of an explanatory theory is as a premise. Morgenthau, in training and emphasis, was focused on history and the lessons which could be drawn for foreign policy. In technical terms, he

---

16. It must be noted that the statement "all satellites travel in elliptical orbit" is a shorthand statement for Newton's universal law of gravitation. This law explains the path of any particular satellite and its particular orbital characteristics once values are provided for each of the variables in the system.

17. See Robert Tucker, "Professor Morgenthau's Theory of Political Realism," *American Political Science Review* 46 (1952): 214-224; which also contains Morgenthau's response, "Another 'Great Debate'," 962n.

was not primarily seeking to explain power—to make it an explanandum—but using power-seeking as an explanan to explain behavioral patterns.[18]

In this function the power-seeking principle could be treated as an anteced-ent—covering law—used to explain a statesman's actions. Thus, the question "Why did Bismarck seek power in Alsace-Lorraine?" could be answered by the conjunction of favorable conditions—favorable public sentiment, political and financial capabilities, weak opponents—and a theoretical law that all humans or all statesmen have a dominant drive towards power. And when all these conditions are present, then statesmen seek territory.[19]

As stated previously, Morgenthau's position is closer to this second explanato-ry objective. It must be remarked, however, that there are strong conditions that attach to the use of a theory as a covering law in an explanation. With respect to the question of power-seeking, it is not necessary to specify all of these conditions. Instead, two will be mentioned that undermine the theoretical extension of Morgenthau's claim that statesmen universally seek power. First, the covering law must state the specific operational observations of theoretical terms. That is, terms like "statesman" and "seek power" must be coded in terms of empirical referents such as "Secretary of State James Byrnes" and "seek greater military capabilities." Second, the initial conditions under which the law is supposed to operate must be stated, such as whether the statesman has control of the defense budget or is constrained by public opinion.

Coding. However, in none of Morgenthau's writings is a statesman's behavior well specified with respect to the term "power." It is certainly possible that a national leader will start a war, make peace, increase the defense budget, decrease the defense budget, form an alliance, or break an alliance in order to increase power. Any of these actions could be an example of power-seeking, a mechanism by which man attempts to dominate man. There is virtually nothing in Morgenthau's writings that explicitly precludes such an expansive interpreta-tion of power-seeking. This problem constitutes a failure to incorporate the fourth basic standard, that of providing coding criteria for the theoretical terms in the analysis.

This unlimited scope is essentially the problem analysts confronted when power-seeking was offered as the means by which a statesman was supposed to behave. The category of power had no fixed meaning and could include anything which could be used by man to dominate man—military preparedness,

---

18. To be fair, Morgenthau was doing neither, but if one wanted to establish a sound scientific basis for his position, then to satisfy the standard of deducibility, "power" would probably serve in one of the two functions that have been specified.

19. However, the evidence is strong that animals, including humans, do not have a dominant drive governing any particular action, with the possible exception of the escape drive during times of extreme danger. Instead, there is a great "parliament" of instincts. See Konrad Lorenz, *On Aggression*, trans. Marjorie Kerr Wilson (New York: Harcourt, Brace and World, 1966), and Irenaus Eibl-Eibesfeldt, *The Biology of Peace and War: Men, Animals, and Aggression* (New York: Viking, 1979).

geography, natural resources, national morale, to name merely a few. This sign system is problematic, because power is not coded with respect to international politics but drawn in an unbounded fashion across the entire field of international relations. Morgenthau thus would have little trouble making the theory bring order to "the facts as they actually are," especially since he viewed the "facts" as ambiguous and changeable. Because the concepts and facts have such wide scope, the analysis of behavior, supposedly based on power, reduces to a truism. In Morgenthau's position there exist no objective criteria to determine either the precise problem or the initial conditions of the empirical world.[20]

Hempel makes it quite clear that an explanandum event—power-seeking—must be stated in terms of specific observational regularities. The subject-entity (statesmen) must exhibit behavior characterized by a series of "that-clauses." Examples would be: that the statesman went to war, that he engaged in an arms buildup, that troops mobilized, and so forth. Unless these actions are specified as part of the problem, the problem to be explained lacks the characteristics of a scientific problem. It is quite possible, at least in principle, to specify a situation with respect to such behavioral observation criteria.[21]

Initial Conditions. A second essential requirement of using a single principle—a covering law—as the theoretical explanation of such a precisely stated explanandum event is that the law must be universal and must in principle permit no exceptions.[22] Morgenthau did not believe this was true of his principle, despite his careless usage of terminology like "iron laws." However, if the principle is not universal, then it is incumbent upon the analyst who seeks to explain a statesman's behavior to tell us why the statesman would seek power. What is it in the features of a situation which would trigger aggressive, power-seeking behavior? Morgenthau, of course, never specified initial conditions. His power-seeking principle was a generality, not a conditional generalization.

Motivation. Once it is admitted that the power-seeking principle is not a universal determinant of human behavior or statecraft, then it is implicitly admitted that either there exist different motives or different drives in the action frame. This constitutes the principle reason that we cannot determine if power is the main signpost of politics: even if an actor behaves in arguable conformity with a principle, the non-universalized principle itself cannot tell us whether the actor's behavior is consistent with the principle. An actor's behavior which looks like it conforms to a principle may simply be a coincidence, an irrelevant

---

20. Morgenthau, *Politics Among Nations*, 18-21.

21. This delimitation is usually easier to accomplish at levels-of-motivation that are restricted in the scope of behavioral outcome rather than the vastness of concepts implied by international relations theory. See, for example, John J. Mearsheimer, *Conventional Deterrence* (Ithaca: Cornell University Press, 1983), 15-17, where the specification of what it is that is to be explained is stated with reasonable precision. It is unfortunate that most writers at the level of the international system have not adopted similar standards.

22. Such generalizations are, even in principle, extremely difficult to formulate. See Hempel, *Aspects of Scientific Explanation*, 338-342.

correlation.   After all, all killings are not murders and it is ambiguous that America's rise to superpower status resulted from an interest in power. Morgenthau specifically avoided this problem by stating that motives and ideological preferences were analytically irrelevant. This is a clear violation of the motivational standard. But it seems that only the rigid dualism of utopian-realist thinking precludes the theoretical necessity of motives in explanations of international action, because there is absolutely nothing in the evidentiary record to support such bald assertions about power-seeking.

Although in practice motives are extremely difficult to discern with precision, without some motivational evidence for behavior there is no means of determining whether a theoretical proposition has been confirmed or merely rationalized according to the interpretation the author wishes to support. In Morgenthau's position we are left merely with an obscure metaphysical doctrine in which the actors are residuum whose behavior is determined by a something we know not what.

Science or Historiography? In the first excerpt cited above, Morgenthau states that a theory must be judged according to whether it brings order and meaning to a mass of phenomena. A good argument can be made that the attempt to bring order and meaning to a mass of phenomena is the purpose behind all cultural and intellectual endeavors.[23]   There are many forms of thought—mythical, historical, and scientific—with differing epistemological criteria and goals that contribute differently to the growth of knowledge. Although research projects in the social sciences often combine manifold forms, one is usually central and the others auxiliary. Morgenthau's truism allows an unregulated interpretation of order and meaning, and because there are no criteria (codings) for truth, we cannot possibly falsify Morgenthau's proposition that a statesman was acting in accordance with his principle.

This failure to adopt explicit standards for assessment is, of course, one of the major problems with the approach of diplomatic historians. And despite his use of the term "science," there is slight similarity between Morgenthau's approach[24] and that of any well-trained modern scientist in any field. What is abundantly clear throughout his writings, is that Morgenthau is completely preoccupied with the organizing principles by which the historian should write about international politics and foreign policy.

---

23. Ernst Cassirer, *An Essay on Man: An Introduction to a Philosophy of Human Culture* (New Haven: Yale University Press, 1944).

24. There is substantial evidence that Morgenthau did not identify his own approach as science. What else could be the meaning of the following sentence: "In order to refute a theory which *pretends* to be scientific, it is first necessary to understand what a scientific theory is" [emphasis added]. It seems from the context of the article that Morgenthau is referring to his own theory. See his "Another 'Great Debate,'" 963. Furthermore, in *Scientific Man vs. Power Politics*, it is clear that "science" is linked with "utopianism."

In defending himself from critics Morgenthau makes clear the historiographical character of his principles: "When a historian tells us that the balance of power is not a universal principle of politics . . . it is incumbent upon him to tell us how we can dispose by means of theory of the historic data."[25]

Then, after "disposing" of some of the historic data Morgenthau states: "Nothing more needs to be said to demonstrate that facts do not support a revision of American diplomatic history."[26] The alternatives Morgenthau is comparing, it must be repeated, do not constitute a choice between two social scientific theories, but a choice between two different conceptions of the national interest—two different principles for selecting out the historical theme in the construction of a socially useful myth.[27] That was the function of power in his models, not the construction of international theory.

The Function of Balance of Power

In addition to understanding the forces of international relations, Morgenthau wanted to understand how peace could be preserved. In this aspect of his approach, the power-seeking principle functions neither as an explanandum event (consequent) nor as the theoretical part of the explanans (major premise), but as an initial condition in the explanans (minor premise). In this case the explanandum event, the event to be explained, is how the presupposed struggle for power could be limited. Because of his failure to self-consciously incorporate the motivational standard, Morgenthau's balance of power concept cannot explain whether balancing is an intended or unintended consequence.

According to Morgenthau, there existed two mechanisms to limit the aspiration for power: one consisted of normative limitations; the other consisted of "the self-regulatory mechanism of the social forces, . . . that is, the balance of power." Demonstrating the relevance of the basic standards is best served by concentrating on the possible explanatory value of the balance of power as a theory of peace. In this respect there are two different types of explanation that are possible.

It should be obvious that a wide explanatory gulf exists between a statement that a limit to the drive for power is an unintended consequence of individuated actors each striving to gain power, versus a statement that the limit is a self-conscious attempt on the part of a balancer to maintain the relative positions of all the essential actors in the system. In the former case the behavior of some coral fish can be used as a model,[28] whereas in the latter case a self-conscious, role-functioning actor is central. Morgenthau is quite inconsistent on this point, which is the fulcrum upon which any explanatory theory must hinge. On the one

---

25. Morgenthau, "Another 'Great Debate'," 963.
26. Ibid., 965.
27. Ibid., 971-978.
28. See Lorenz, *On Aggression*, 12-22, but especially 35-38.

hand, he denies the relevance of motives and ideologies; on the other, he occasionally talks about the objectives of the balancer.[29] Clear headedness searches in vain for any meaningful notion of objectives that does not entail motives.

In fact Morgenthau has little if any basis for the role of a self-conscious balancer. In addition to his rejection of motives, he stated that: "It will be shown in the following pages that the international balance of power is only a particular manifestation of a general social principle to which all societies composed of a number of autonomous units owe the autonomy of their component parts; that the balance of power and policies aiming at its preservation are not only inevitable but are an essential stabilizing factor in a society of sovereign nations."[30]

Of course Morgenthau never does show that the balance of power is a particular manifestation of a general social principle. He merely selects other thinkers who have used a concept of equilibrium or balance in their treatment of various subjects. Moreover, there is no analysis or explanation showing the inevitability of balancing. Because the examples drawn from the Federalist Papers or the American economy are not considered with respect to the size of systems, we do not know if the concept of hidden-hand inevitability or oligopolistic coordination is the proper explanatory theory. In the former, the explanation derives from unintended consequences of atomic individuals (as it does in the coral fish), in the latter from self-conscious understanding of the collective system. We will return to this topic in greater detail in chapter 4. However, as Morgenthau uses it, the balance of power is merely a label in search of an idea.

The Function of Morgenthau

Morgenthau's subordination of all foreign policy decisions to principles of power nonetheless had certain consequences. Superficial as it was, Carr's approach was somewhat praxical and tried to take account of changing conditions of world order. Moreover, in Carr's framework, political thought did not require first or main principles. It isn't even clear that Carr's realism required any principles, because reality was aligned on the side of facts, empirical analysis, and relativity of thought. This alignment was juxtaposed against principles, arguing that principles were a sort of superstructure used to justify interests.

Morgenthau placed far greater emphasis on the doctrinal statement of universal principles of politics, and thus substituted an anti-utopian principle, allegedly based on historical facts, for a utopian principle allegedly based on *a priori* reasoning. Part of the rationale for this was to embellish the importance of

---

29. Morgenthau, *Politics Among Nations*, 194.
30. Ibid., 167.

power considerations on the American mind-set. One effect on the discipline, however, has been to confuse theory with thinking.

The political thinking of Carr and Morgenthau focuses on the orienting principles of international actors. These principles attempt to concentrate all of political reality into two ultimate orientations, two world views that can then be used to select facts in the creative exposition of a story. A theory, however, is a logically coherent system that we use as a tool to explain aspects of the world that humans live in. A good theory should help clarify our ideas about how international politics functions under different initial conditions. Thus, it should provide answers. Political thinking winds up with unproductive and interminable squabble between two camps, each of which tries to justify its principles.

The justification of principles is a commonplace of human existence. It is standard practice in the history of ideas. The use of methodological devices like the state of nature—which is really what the realism-liberalism dichotomy is all about—can be manipulated to suit the philosopher's purpose, and it is instructive that the state of nature is no more real in Hobbes than it is in Rousseau.[31] Morgenthau was a traditional diplomatic historian who considered power and the national interest to be first principles of international politics. As a polemic designed to rally the nation behind clear thinking about the dangers of missionary zeal, the doctrine had some utility. As a social scientific theory designed to explain international politics, Morgenthau's theory of national interest is incapable of generating falsifiable propositions. And the approach cannot be transformed into a social science. If one were to add some new principles to the supposedly first principle(s), it would not add explanatory scope. In political thinking the statements are unbounded by initial conditions; the logical relationships between assumptions and conclusions are ignored; the coding criteria for statements are unspecified; the focus is on individuated actors rather than the various types of systems in which the actors are or could be embedded; motives are universally presupposed as dichotomous; and time is not incorporated in the analysis.

AN ALTERNATIVE HISTORIOGRAPHY

The main alternative to realism is found in those who believe that they are widening the scope of international relations. Writers such as Stanley Hoffman and Richard Rosecrance have built investigatory frameworks that do not presuppose that all of international relations is a struggle for power. The descendants of these approaches include some neoliberal institutionalists. The next chapter analyzes the contribution of this approach to the development of

---

31. In Locke, it is an actual condition defined as the condition that exists whenever men are not living under a common power. But Locke claimed that the state of nature was governed by a natural law: to seek peace and follow it. This is arguably at least as arbitrary as Hobbes' position.

theory in international politics or international relations. These writers have embraced many ideas that Morgenthau explicitly rejected, and have conceived international relations as having as many outcomes as it has diverse factors that feed into the production of those outcomes. Whereas this chapter has covered orienting principles, the tradition of historical sociology represented in the following chapter provides an investigative framework for the study of international relations. Such frameworks also need to be appraised in terms of the basic criteria stated in chapter 1.

3

Investigative Frameworks

An alternative perspective for analyzing international relations was proposed by historical sociologists. Partly in opposition to the presupposition of a universal power-seeking principle, historical sociologists attempted to impart a wider scope to the study of international relations. Like Carr, they included the possibility of a cooperative principle, though they put greater weight upon it. They moved away from universalist principles on two levels. At the level of the international system they focused on behavior that varies, using categories such as "diplo-matico-strategic behavior" or "regimes." Second, they generally believed that domestic factors such as goals or values were relevant for analysis. They partly succeeded in widening debate to include these factors. However, as I will argue below, they have not formulated a specialized explanatory apparatus. Instead, they have simply provided a wider matrix of categories. These categories are so wide and, from the standpoint of a theory of international politics, so contingent, that we are left with merely an investigatory framework. That framework does provide an alternative historiographical principle, one that emphasizes the different principles that emerge in international relations. But it is an historio-graphical principle nonetheless. Some writers who are currently identified as neo-liberal institutionalists are descendants of this approach to international relations. Other approaches focused on historical contingency, such as foreign policy analysis,[1] exhibit similar theoretical limitations. As paradigmatic examples, however, this chapter examines the approaches of Stanley Hoffmann and Richard Rosecrance.

---

1. See, for example, Valerie M. Hudson, with Christopher S. Vore, "Foreign Policy Analysis Yesterday, Today, and Tomorrow," *Mershon International Studies Review* 39 (1995): 209-238.

STANLEY HOFFMANN

Scope and Method

Stanley Hoffmann thought that attempts to formulate international theory were premature. That presupposition limited Hoffmann to a very tentative research agenda; one based on a set of core questions designed to uncover differences in a system's "principle of order." These core questions were a conceptual framework that would "allow us to organize our knowledge, to orient research, and to interpret our findings." Hoffmann stated that this conceptual framework should direct research towards empirical theory, by which he meant causal theory. He stated that it is general empirical theory that tries to account for major parts of the field and is lacking.[2]

In addition to the many problems associated with the relationship between empiricism and causality, problems dating back to at least David Hume, Hoffmann's position made clear that he would not employ deductive theory and its associated methods of establishing initial conditions and explicit coding criteria. The failure to meet these standards resulted partly from a failure to focus on system-types.

Instead of a well-bounded international focus, historical sociologists have placed most of their theoretical efforts in widening our conception of national interest.[3] This wider conception merely incorporates the possibility of coopera-

---

2. Stanley Hoffmann, *Contemporary Theory in International Relations* (Englewood Cliffs, NJ: Prentice-Hall, Inc., 1960), 7-10. This tradition developed greater sophistication over time. In the United States Stanley Hoffmann is often cited as the historical progenitor of this approach. Robert O. Keohane and Joseph S. Nye stated that their own approach resembles that of Hoffmann, their former teacher. See *Power and Interdependence: World Politics in Transition* (Boston: Little, Brown and Co., 1977), viii. Although they still had what is here termed a framework they refined the approach in some ways. They did, for example, focus more clearly on analyzing relations, especially in their model of international organization. This latter framework warrants greater development. Nonetheless, much of the criticism leveled against Hoffmann applies to this book as well, but Hoffmann's position amplifies the distinction between frameworks and explanatory theory in a more obvious way and is, therefore, useful in clarifying the basic standards of analysis.

3. In one book, Robert Keohane, for example, stated as his central argument "that cooperation can under some conditions develop on the basis of complementary *interests*, and that institutions, broadly defined, affect the patterns of cooperation that emerge." [Emphasis added]. See his, *After Hegemony: Cooperation and Discord in the World Political Economy* (Princeton: Princeton University Press, 1984), 9. But who would deny this statement? Or the following one: "Institutionalist writers have always stressed that cooperation can be fostered by institutions." Ibid., 66. Despite the use of sophisticated tools of rational-choice theory, this proposition is very close to Carr's belief that territorial-unit bases of power were not the only possible form of international authority. But the theoretical question is what kinds of institutions produce what kind of cooperation

tive and institutional alternatives to power-seeking. However, it has not demonstrated much capacity to go beyond conceptions of interest and foreign policy. As we will also see in chapter 5, this problem results from all attempts to treat international relationships as an outcome; that is, as an aggregate product of unit behaviors or values. Hoffmann made this unit focus an explicit part of his approach: "An international system is a pattern of relations among the basic units of world politics, characterized by the scope of the objectives pursued by those units and of the tasks performed among them, as well as by the means used to achieve those goals and perform those tasks."[4] From this perspective, international relations theory became a question of what combinations of national conditions lead to a characteristic style of international action. This position is very common-sensical, but incapable of systematic application. Thus, the debate between historical sociologists and universalists simply became a question of deciding what was the common style—cooperation or conflict—to describe international relations. Whatever analytical apparatuses were then used were pressed into service only to vindicate one possibility or the other.

The Inductive Road. Instead of starting research by adopting typological hypotheses, Hoffmann expected to encounter types along an inductive road to theory. He articulated three stages of theory development: the description of different international systems, comparisons between different types of international systems, and comparisons between types of domestic and international systems.[5]

Only the first stage was originally thought attainable, largely because Hoffmann wedded his mind to a *tabula rasa* version of inductive method. If such a notebook approach can be called a methodology, it is largely an intuitive one in which the logic of explanation is only an afterthought. The major problem with Hoffmann's approach is that without basic knowledge (theory) of a particular subject matter (system), the researcher doesn't know what evidence supports an explanation (confirmation). Let us examine this approach further to drive home its difference from that employed in a scientifically focused typology.

Hoffmann believed that four "sets of data" had to be correlated in order to "define" different international systems. No procedures for such correlations were specified. Given the complexity of Hoffmann's categories that would have been very helpful. The first three sets each included ten questions. These sets were labeled "structure" (broadly: the units and distribution of power),

---

under what kinds of conditions. There is no evidence that the use of a framework is capable of answering this question. As a metaphor it can be noted that a sound engineer attempting to analyze a piece of high-fidelity equipment does not tell his audience that good sound may be possible, but explains the characteristics of the sound as a function of the structure of the system across various conditional ranges, such as volume or distance.

4. Stanley Hoffmann, *The State of War: Essays on the Theory and Practice of International Politics* (New York: Frederick A. Praeger, 1965), 90.

5. Hoffmann, *Contemporary Theory*, 174-175.

"forces" (broadly: the technology of conflict), and "foreign policy" (broadly: the factors affecting, and the goals of the units). The fourth set entailed the "outcome" (broadly: the overall power configuration) of the interrelationship between these three sets. At times Hoffmann recognized that such an outcome could also be an input into foreign policy formulation. For instance, he spoke of how the types of "'power configurations' . . . reshape, condition, and command foreign policies." But he did not develop a typology of power configurations. Instead, outcome never meant more than characterization.[6] Hoffmann attempted to specify criteria for this last set in *The State of War*. In that book another series of questions was erected in order to determine whether the category of international system exists in reality.

Accidental Outcomes. An international system existed for Hoffmann if there were regularized inter-unit relations, if the units were aware of their interdependence, and if it could be specified what was within the system and what was without. "Within" presumably meant domestic affairs; "without" meant trans-unit relations.[7] These conditions implicitly recognize, albeit vaguely, the conditional, motivational, and—very generally—coding standards. There are two major problems with this formulation of international conditions. First, the codings are much too weak. There are still no empirical referents specified for terms such as "regularized," "aware," "domestic," and "trans-unit." Second, the focal presupposition is reversed: Hoffmann treats the international system as a foreign product, an outcome of the first three sets.

In addition, Hoffmann thought that two other criteria were necessary to identify the existence of an international system: location and temporal limits. The location of an international system is primarily an empirical question. It is therefore not central to this analysis. But temporal limits is an important concept; it implicitly recognizes the durational standard. Hoffmann thought this problem was "the most difficult of all."

According to Hoffmann, the problem of temporal isolation required researchers to answer the first three sets of questions. New international systems emerge when the basic structure of the world changes, when a basic change in the technology of conflict occurs, or when the goals and purposes of the units change. This formulation vaguely incorporates the conditional presupposition. But since there are no coding criteria, and no types from which departures are to be compared, the formulation remains vague. This problem is compounded by the failure to incorporate explanatory standards. Hoffmann nonetheless believed that combinations—undefined—of these answers imply a fundamental distinction between revolutionary and stable international systems. Unfortunately, there is no calculus that computes these combinations. The characterization of systems as revolutionary or stable is just a descriptive characterization of outcomes. Hoffmann's position is that a stable system is one where relations

---

6. Ibid., 179-182.
7. Idem, *State of War*, 91-92.

among the units are marked by moderation in scope and means; an unstable system is one where moderation disappears.[8]

Hoffmann's other criteria for deciding whether an international system exists are also problematic. Deciding what is inside and outside an international system cannot be answered empirically. That puts the cart before the horse. You need boundaries in order to code the data. And as I have argued above, the existence and awareness of regularized external relations among units does not specify a type of international system. If each researcher can decide independently if an international system exists, and how to characterize it, then very little theoretical guidance has been supplied. It is in this sense that Hoffmann demonstrated a real ambivalence with respect to the focal presupposition. Even if real, his international system was not an ideal type but an unintended consequence of contingent combinations. An analogous formulation would require an observer to wait for car wrecks at a busy intersection in order to determine if an unstable vehicular system existed in reality. If it seems to the researcher that many wrecks have occurred, the system would be characterized as unstable. If it seems that few have occurred, the system would be characterized as stable.

It is of course impossible to isolate a system by descriptive methods alone. When, for instance, does the car wreck example become an unstable system? Is it at the point of impact? Is it at the point when corrective action becomes impossible? Is it when the rain fell on top of the oily asphalt? Is it at the point that one of the drivers finished his seventh cocktail at the local pub? Or is it only during major holidays, such as New Year's Eve? This point cannot be determined unless the researcher specifies what system is under investigation. If one is investigating the physical characteristics of tires, then oily asphalt is the explanation of instability. If one is investigating human reflexes, alcohol is the relevant explanation. In the real wreck it may be a combination of factors that determines the instability. However, without basic knowledge of each theoretical subject matter, the researcher doesn't know what constitutes evidence.

The theoretical problem here is that comparisons prior to the specification of explicit "idealized" patterns are like comparing why some doors in a house stick without understanding the concepts of square and plumb, which may be applied to doors either by an analysis of Euclidean geometry or by the use of a carpenter's level, square, and plumb line. Only the idealized, deductive pattern of Euclidean geometry is theoretical—that is, explanatory. The carpenter operates at the level of praxical assessment, moving from one elementary part of the door system to the next. And he is just as likely to explain the sticking as a result of the house settling as he is from the fact that the geometry of the door is no longer in harmony. But because good carpenters understand the geometry (at least implicitly), they know how to fix the problem. It is not generally wise to hire a carpenter who talks about about all the conditions that might result in the possibility of a well-functioning door. Hoffmann's approach

---

8. Ibid., 92-96.

was more like that of the educated homeowner than the professional carpenter. Hoffmann's sets of questions were a framework that permitted characterizations of international events and processes, but necessary relations and standards of explanation were not present to guide research.

Thus, Hoffmann's usage of inductive method failed to satisfy the second basic standard, that of explanatory theory. There were no conditional premises upon which conclusions could rest. Nothing can be learned by starting with the facts alone because it is impossible to select relevant facts unless a problem is before the mind. Such problems, generally speaking, can be constrained only if the focus of inquiry—the subject matter—is limited to a particular type of order.

All aspects of the explanatory enterprise begin with hypotheses. The first of these is about the homogeneity of the class of entities under investigation. Thus the hypothesis that "all satellites travel in elliptical orbits" relates satellites (an entity) to elliptical orbits (a property). Induction—that is, sampling—is useful in establishing as probable the material truth of such propositions. It is necessary to start, however, with an entity, with a system as system. At the international level this requires identifying what constitutes the common framework which all actors of a class are deemed part of. Thus, bipolar systems, confederal economic organizations, hierarchical military subsystems, and democratic human rights organizations are likely to have different theory sketches to explain their action patterns and the range of conditions under which they exhibit stability.

Science and Social Studies. Hoffmann's unwillingness to incorporate the explanatory presupposition resulted partly from his misunderstanding of science. As a result Hoffmann did not adequately use the focal presupposition to identify international types of relationships (systems). Influenced by Raymond Aron, Hoffmann always separated the natural from the social sciences. If not inviolable, this separation was treated largely as insurmountable. Hoffmann dismissed social scientists who searched for laws capable of accounting for the behavior of states. But in doing so he seems to have dismissed the entire scientific enterprise, as if anyone not searching for empirical laws is automatically not engaged in this enterprise.[9] Although it is true that physical scientists have discovered covering laws, such discoveries have not been true of other branches of science. The theory of evolution, for example, does not function through the employment of covering laws.

In effect, Hoffmann dismissed scientific procedures without adequately presenting those procedures. His "science" was a straw man designed to justify a different kind of theory, namely, that of historical sociology. That justification is unnecessary. There are no insurmountable barriers to the integration of historical sociology and scientific procedure. Historical sociologists aspire to develop ideal types. Ideal types are necessary for any (social) scientific theory.

---

9. For examples, see Stanley Hoffmann, *Contemporary Theory*, 41-42; *Janus and Minerva: Essays in the Theory and Practice of International Politics* (Boulder, CO: Westview Press, 1987), 14-15; and *The State of War*, 124.

Indeed, it is the absence of developed typological schemes that historical sociologists have failed to address. In the absence of well-formed typologies, social science is abandoned in favor of social studies. For the discipline in question, international theory is abandoned in favor of international studies. Like area studies, international studies is a consequence of poorly formulated or non-existent typologies, which inevitably devolve into issue specific investigations.[10] Such approaches clearly fail to embody focal presuppositions.

In science, distinguishing among types require a language of classification that is based on observable *internal* characteristics of the systems under investigation. That language is based on all members of the class having identical properties—not similar *external* behavior. Whale Sharks and Blue Whales both swim in water, eat plankton, and have docile behavior with respect to other animals, but they are not the same type of animals: whales are mammals; sharks are fish.

This is not to rule behavioral elements out of court: one of the significant properties of mammals is that they bear their young live and nurse them.[11] These properties are behavioral in some senses of that term but these properties are invariably associated with other properties of mammals—vertebration, mammory glandulation, warm-bloodedness—all of which are constitutive of mammals, and all of which are not, for example, constitutive of birds. Classificatory schemes based exclusively on behavioral outcomes have a tendency to result in superficiality; such as the old childhood fable that mammals live on land, fish live in water, and birds live in the air.

Although historical sociologists did attempt to employ ideal types, they employed a classificatory language based largely on the external behavior of the units rather than the internal (international) relationships that order the units into system types. The problem of superficial classification is easily illustrated. One could, for example, conceive of an international system in which all the national actors were fascist, racist powers that cooperated at the international level and had high levels of interdependence, in which there were many transnational actors, in which there were tacit and formal rules that were observed, in which regularized procedures existed for managing their economic and financial systems, and in which there were common norms—especially the norm of maintaining racial superiority. By the standards common to historical sociologists, this system—like the one which it is hoped contemporary international politics will increasingly resemble—would be characterized as moderate, or cooperative, or as exhibiting conditions of complex interdependence. But surely there is a problem with a typology that cannot in principle distinguish between these fundamentally different forms of international system. The norms (action patterns) maintaining the racist and liberal versions of complex interdependence

---

10. Marcus Kreuzer suggested this comparison to me.

11. In any classification scheme there are usually borderline cases that do not fit as well as the main body of cases. At the lower end of the evolutionary ladder, for example, there are a few mammals, such as the platypus, that do not bear their young live.

would be radically different. The scope of acceptable trading partners, for instance, would probably be radically different. To call both stable systems, or stable regimes, is to offer a generality, not a generalization.

It is highly unlikely that any historical sociologist would have argued that the racist version fits the meaning of complex interdependence, and given the context within which they wrote their meaning was generally clear. However, nothing in their methodology restricts such a characterization.

The use of categories across the entire field of international relations—which Hoffmann's questions exemplify—precludes the possibility of formulating a theory of types. We are simply not smart enough to integrate such wide range of information into coherent explanations. In the racist system, for instance, the cooperative behavior could be a function of institutional features in the international system (a racially-based economic cartel). It could be the result of cultural identification among publics and elites forged in the transnational racial policies of the regime. It could result from a transnational political alliance designed to control governments and the subordinated parts of the populations (a supranational party apparatus). We need not multiply examples. Whichever possibility (or possibilities) explained the particular case would have to be explained in terms of a particular theory—international, cultural, transnational alliance, etc.—or combination thereof. But we cannot explain the international aspects of the case without an international theory, one which starts with types. The racist and liberal versions of complex interdependence imply two different types of systems. This kind of distinction is analogous, for example, to the classical distinctions between monarchy and tyranny, aristocracy and oligopoly, or democracy and republic.

Hoffmann's sets of questions were consistent with a research program that tried to describe the world more systematically—his first stage—and with greater attention to diversity and change. But the approach did not facilitate theoretical explanation or comparison of different international systems. That should not be surprising. Because so many unordered questions were involved, a researcher could do little more than describe what constituted the main characteristics of arbitrarily selected historical periods. Hoffmann employed no criteria to move from questions to types of international systems. He instead presented a vague notion that some factors, either internal or external to the units, were causing outcomes.

This approach requires some further examination. Richard Rosecrance also traveled this long, inductive road to theory. He, too, attempted to start with facts and then construct a typology. There were, of course, differences. Rosecrance paid a bit more attention to international regulatory mechanisms, and even considered the analytically challenging regulatory concepts of W. Ross Ashby. With a healthy dose of imagination, one can almost envision an international theory somewhere further ahead. But this distant vision occurred after Rosecrance had already traveled a great distance on Hoffmann's long road. An examination of his progress along this road should, therefore, prove instructive.

RICHARD ROSECRANCE

The Unbounded System

Richard Rosecrance applied a similar research program, one which character-ized historical periods of international relations as stable or unstable.   The general argument which Rosecrance attempted to develop was that the interaction of international, environmental and actor elite factors leads to stable or unstable outcomes.   These outcomes were thought to vary as a function of major changes in the constitution of disruptive and regulative influences.   For Rosecrance, "system" meant this entire complex, and the study of international relations entailed virtually anything that affected outcomes.   This usage was an oddly broad conception of international system.   If compared to concepts such as economic system, the difference is stark: economists do not usually consider everything that effects economic relations—earthquakes, riots—as included in the economic system.

Rosecrance offered three stages of analysis, each of which purported to represent a form of explanation. Each stage had a different analytical basis.   The first stage was based on traditional historiography, the second on systematic analysis of the categories necessary for differentiating international systems, and the third on the basic determinants of stability and instability.   I examine each of these stages in turn.

Traditional Historiography.   In the first stage Rosecrance produced nine historical systems based on "traditional divisions of historical scholarship."   He believed that these historical divisions indicated that the modes, techniques, and objectives of diplomacy changed at these crucial junctures.   As a result, each system had a characteristically different style.   Rosecrance described these differences and changes of style and characterized each period as either stable or unstable. Europe during the mid- to late-eighteenth century (1740-1789), and during the Concert of Europe (1814-1822) serve as examples of stable systems. Europe during the periods of the Napoleonic expansion (1789-1814) and imperialistic nationalism (1890-1918) was characterized as unstable.   For Rosecrance, it is clear, that "unstable" meant "chaos, breakdown, and war."[12]

Each period Rosecrance examined was sketched by drawing upon factors such as the intellectual and cultural background of elites, their international orientation with respect to both international relations and the constitution of other actor-systems (factors that vaguely incorporate the motivational and valuational standards), the mobilization potential of the instruments of violence, the ideological attachments of the masses (a regime characteristic), and the existence of international institutions—such as the Concert—or of mechanisms of regula-tion—such as shifting alliances.[13]

---

12. Richard Rosecrance, *Action and Reaction in World Politics: International Systems in Perspective* (Boston: Little, Brown and Co., 1963), 10-11, 231.

13. Ibid., 5-7, with a more precise specification presented on 224-230.

From the perspective of explanatory theory, the main problem with these historical divisions is that there were no formal analytical controls governing the selection of evidence. There can be little doubt that Rosecrance's information was generally relevant to the decisions which were actually made, but it is not possible to assess how all these factors should be integrated into a theory of international relations or international politics. At this stage of his analysis, it is impossible to conceive the international system as relatively independent from any other parts of the social and cultural environment. As with Hoffmann's failure to employ the focal standard, in Rosecrance there was no focus on international political relations.

Systematic Analysis. In the second stage Rosecrance formulated categories in order to explain how changes in these categories account for changes in his nine systems. Success at this stage would presumably account for the specification of system outcomes as stable or unstable. In his words, he "endeavors to systematize the historical analysis into categories in terms of which the separate systems may be specified." That is, he wanted to derive the analytical components implicit in the traditional historiography in order to justify the classification of the nine historical systems. Then, by showing variations in the supposedly derived categories Rosecrance hoped to account for the different international systems; that is, to show "how changes in the components make for changes in the international system."[14]

Rosecrance had three primary components that he employed to account for changes in his international systems. These components were actor inputs, regulative influences in the international system, and environmental constraints. Actor inputs were treated as a source of disturbance to the international system, and regulative and environmental factors were treated as limiting or barrier influences.[15] The environment, however, dropped out of the analysis because it was treated as a fixed constraint. That left two analytical components: disturbances (actor inputs) and regulative influences.[16] However, the relevance of this framework in explaining the outcomes of each system is completely dissipated, because ultimately Rosecrance stated that the determination of stability depends on whether "outcomes fall within limits generally 'accepted' by the major participants in the system." This factor, however, was not at all linked to the ratio of actor disturbances and regulatory influences.[17]

It was at this point that Rosecrance moved right to the brink of a theory of international politics as a distinct disciplinary enterprise. Three concepts placed Rosecrance at this brink: the use of regulatory influences such as the Concert or shifting alliances, the recognition that these different mechanisms might function

---

14. Ibid., 10, 220, 275.

15. Note the similarity to Morgenthau, whose metaphysics divides into the "struggle for power" and "limitations to national power."

16. It is unclear how it happens that variations in this factor never occur within the temporal limits of Rosecrance's systems.

17. Rosecrance, *Action and Reaction*, 231.

differently in regulating the national actor-systems, and the notion that inputs arising from the national actors could be disturbances to the international regulatory system. Had Rosecrance employed a typology and specified optimal action patterns for each type, it would have allowed him to envision a theory. Instead, he fell back after a brief glimpse, and chose to rely on the acceptance of the major participants as the standard to judge international stability. But that criterion simply reduces to the concept of national interest.

Rosecrance was trapped between two conceptions of international relations: a traditional conception that saw international action as a sort of unintended outcome of clashing national interests and a developed scientific conception that was capable of seeing a macrosystem as an entity with its own internal code of behavior, imminent in the structure of existing relations. Like most social scientists in the twentieth century, Rosecrance's conception was traditional. Rosecrance could not really sustain a system conception in other than atomistic terms—a problem left over from the breakdown of Greek science following the rise of modern physics.[18]

This problem is related to the notion that individuated humans are located in one social system. Under such a presupposition it is counterintuitive to conceive of the terms "internal" or "decision-maker" as applicable to international levels-of-analysis. But once the presupposition that decision-makers have a fixed location in either the international or national system is dropped and one recognizes how they function in each of them, depending on their motives, the difficulty disappears. Then a macrosystemic explanation can start with the type of relationships in the system, and the hypothesized action patterns necessary to maintain those relationships.[19]

Of course, the problem Rosecrance encountered in explaining stability was magnified when he considered system change, and he fell right back into foreign policy analysis. System change was understood as a function of transformations in the subcomponents. There was, however, no clear purpose behind this effort. Rosecrance explicitly denied that changes in the components necessarily lead to changes in the patterns of stability and instability. Thus, the explanatory focus of this second stage shifted from explaining the transformation of outcomes to explaining the grounds for distinguishing among the nine systems. However, Rosecrance was then in the unenviable position of explaining change for its own sake.[20]

Although he offered none, Rosecrance was searching for a theory of the regulatory process that would explain how changes in the capacity of a system would affect outcomes, and he relied on W. Ross Ashby for formal assistance. As Rosecrance understood Ashby, the stability of a system depended on

18. On the origins of atomism, see Harry Prosch, *The Genesis of Twentieth Century Philosophy: The Evolution of Thought from Copernicus to the Present* (Garden City, NY: Doubleday, 1964).
19. See chap. 6.
20. Rosecrance, *Action and Reaction*, 224, 231.

increasing the variety of regulatory responses to the proportion of disturbances.
Rosecrance attempted to map Ashby's principles onto his international systems.
He stated, for example, that in the postwar bipolar system: "regulatory influences
temporarily increased in variety while disruptive influences temporarily lost
variety. . . . The environmental table gained in variety, and it was able to exert
a greater regulative impact than previously. A tenuous stability emerged."[21]

One, however, must assume that this assessment is based on the absence of
major war in the bipolar system. Because Rosecrance could not possibly count
and weight the actual variety of disturbances to the variety of the regulator,
Ashby's principle—as Rosecrance applied it—lost all mathematical meaning, and
thus, all precision. This inapplicability of mathematical concepts is probably
inevitable in empirical analyses of this sort, though they may be applicable in
computer models.[22] However, no qualitative coding scheme was offered either.
The only accomplishment in this stage of analysis was the reinterpretation of
previous conclusions in terms of a more abstract sign system. Thus Rosecrance's
failure to adopt a coding scheme which could be meaningfully associated with
the world constituted a failure of the coding standard. His reinterpretation was,
therefore, ad hoc and arbitrary.[23]

Basic Determinants. The third stage "aims at a still broader view"—as if one
were needed—by a further abstraction to four basic determinants (direction,
control, resources, and capacity) of stability and instability. There is however,
little analytical difference between this stage and the previous one, since these
determinants were employed merely in the service of summation. In his
conclusion, Rosecrance used his determinants only as labels that impinge on
stability and instability. He could not use these categories to assess the stability
or instability of macrosystems *qua* systems.

Rosecrance did not believe he had developed a theory and it is not appropriate
to criticize him on these grounds. He appropriately called his approach
"systematic," and claimed that it provided a link between "general organizing
concepts" and "detailed empirical investigation" by incorporating "a considerable
fund of factual information in a theoretical approach which aims at a measure of
comprehensiveness."[24] This systematic approach is consistent with Stanley
Hoffmann's notion that there would be a "long road to international theory."

Lessons on the Long Road

With respect to demonstrating the usefulness of the basic standards, Rosecrance's book raises two questions. First, how well selected was Rosecrance's
framework from the perspective of illuminating the subject matter of international

---

21. Ibid., 261-262.
22. See chap. 8.
23. Rosecrance, *Action and Reaction*, 261-267.
24. Ibid., 267.

politics?   Second, what distinguishes the characterizations developed in Rosecrance's framework from the type of propositions derived in an explanatory model?   These questions refer, respectively, to the focal and explanatory standards.

Although Rosecrance employed both an international and an actor framework, the latter had much greater weight in his analysis.   There were, for example, three subcomponents of actor inputs, and ten parts made up the subcomponents. In and of itself the number of formal categories in a model does not necessarily imply the relative weights of those categories.   But in the third stage of his analysis, all the determinants of stability and instability were focused on the individuated actors. International regulative factors were basically divided into two subcomponents—institutional and alliance mechanisms—and they were conceived as a constraint on actor disturbances.   The analysis was focused methodologically and substantively on how the actor-systems behave as a function of their direction, their control of resources, and their quantity of resources.   Even regulative factors were often treated as a function of actor direction.   Therefore, Rosecrance's study is really an analysis of foreign policy formation and its implications on the international system.

There can, however, be little question of the importance of both international and national actor-system analyses in explanations of either foreign policy or international politics.   The question is primarily which to treat as system and which as parameter.   In simple terms it is a question of subject matter. However, Rosecrance's systematic framework characterized the real world in a style which cannot be characterized as explanatory.

An explanation is successful to the extent it can derive propositions about behavior from a set of definitions, axioms, propositions, and theorems in an analytical system. (These analytical elements need not be *a priori* elements). Such success requires at least a partially deductive system.   On the other hand, the categories or variables employed in a framework operate exclusively on the level of assessment between concepts and the world of initial conditions, and thus lead only to description.   Rosecrance was, in fact, focused exclusively on an exhaustive classification of initial conditions, which trapped him in a veritable hornets' nest of complexity from which he could find no explanatory exit.   The joint failure to incorporate a deductive model and explicit coding criteria assured meager results.   It was what might be called a sort of notebook approach to understand the world.   With a notebook, the determination of relevance, identification, and truth is arbitrarily based on the skill and intelligence of the researcher.   Although the statement was dubious, Rosecrance even claimed that category selection was distilled from traditional history.   Although he offered no reasons or standards to support the relevance of the chosen categories, they bear such an obvious relationship to Hoffmann's approach that it would be folly to ignore the link.   However, those categories also were constructed without coding criteria.   They may evoke similar feelings in the minds of researchers, but there is little guarantee that this will amount to very much knowledge.   Even well-coded qualitative categories lack the fine precision of mathematical language.

With ill-coded qualitative categories, scientists are left with hypotheses which, like the Copernican hypothesis before Brahe, are merely disputatious. Such research projects do demonstrate one result, namely, the bankruptcy of studying the facts before understanding the focus of inquiry.

A framework can characterize or interpret events or processes in terms of selected categories. Explanation requires differentiating the relevant elements of a subject matter into functioning types with optimal action patterns. If the type of system has been specified, actors who are rational with respect to that system should conform to hypothesized action patterns. Because of the absence of well-specified types, Rosecrance can offer no systematic reasons why actors make decisions.

The problem with a framework, no matter how systematic, is that only by accidental means can the approach place us on a road towards explanatory theory. We are not smart enough to produce a theory from categories that range across the entire field of international relations. With only a framework, it is likely that the long road to theory will become an infinite road. There is nothing inherently wrong with frameworks unless one wants a theory. If so, a theory of international politics must first specify what variables are relevant to behavior in international systems *qua* international systems. Although the various factors that these approaches employed are each potentially relevant in explaining a particular international event, such explanations are unlikely to illuminate those behavioral patterns which result more or less directly from international factors or the consequences of those patterns on future states of the international system. It is impossible for a framework to explain systematically the manner in which the state of an international system affects behavior or whether actors are behaving rationally with respect to the international system.

Although correct, Hoffmann seems unjustified to state that Rosecrance's study "suffers from the author's neglect of the problem of delimitation between systems." Hoffmann could differ with Rosecrance's assessments of system identification, but he himself lacked internal standards to govern the truth of specific identifications. Neither the world in all its contingent complexity nor a set of questions, nor the so-called inductive method can provide the means for a "rigorous selection of . . . the essential features . . . to define each system."[25]

---

25. Hoffmann, *The State of War*, 18n.

4

Anarchy

Anarchy is a widely used concept. Many writers apply it to all of international relations, and conclude that balances of power result under conditions of anarchy. This idea tends to presuppose that all of international relations is of a type. During the 1980s this idea was most closely associated with the work of Kenneth Waltz. This chapter examines his neo-principled approach to international relations.

KENNETH WALTZ

A Neo-Principled Approach

Kenneth Waltz recognized the vast research difficulties that arise from complex international relations. His contribution to the profession focused on his belief that, in order to cope with these difficulties, the aim of theory is: "to try to find the central tendency among a confusion of tendencies, to single out the propelling principle even though other principles operate, to seek the essential factors where innumerable factors are present."[1]

Perhaps Waltz, like Morgenthau, seems dominated by a search for a *principium politica* that underlies the phenomenal world. But it would be inappropriate to treat Waltz with Carr and Morgenthau. Waltz clearly placed his later work

---

1. Kenneth N. Waltz, *Theory of International Politics* (Reading, MA: Addison-Wesley Publishing Co., Inc., 1979), 10.

under the label "science." Moreover, he stated unequivocally that scientific theories have an explanatory purpose.[2]

In fact, this incorporation of scientific concepts is perhaps Waltz's greatest contribution to professional developments in the field of international relations. It is true that none of the scientific concepts he used were new, and that he did not develop these ideas systematically. But their very incorporation in a traditionalist research program was a major departure from previous traditionalists. Morgenthau, for example, refused to recognize that the behavioral revolution had occurred. Waltz, however, set his position in a scientific context. And that implies that his arguments must stand or fall according to the canons of science. If his arguments fall, as the following analysis shows, the reader should not lose sight of the courage it must have taken for a traditionalist to open his analysis to this line of criticism. It is hoped that future generations of social scientists can benefit by the more widespread use of scientific reasoning that Waltz promoted.

Reductionism. On some of the simpler concepts of scientific procedure, such as the relationship between laws and theories, Waltz presented the standard consensus adequately. However, he showed little comprehension of the meaning and function of explanatory conceptions. For example, his criticism of other authors, who in his terms are "reductionists," was not well argued. For a scientist to state that a reduction has occurred has little to do with locating causes at the level of units. Statements such as these are analytically unregulated spatial metaphors.[3] In practice, successful reductions are a desirable objective.

Those who study in depth the logic of explanation use reduction in a technical—not a pejorative—sense. For example, theory "T" is said to be reduced to a theory "T*" if, and only if, the laws of "T" can be derived from "T*". Thus, Kepler's laws of planetary motion were reduced to Newton's laws of motion and gravitation, and Newton's laws are reducible to a parameter substitution in Einstein's theory of relativity.

In his critique Waltz was certainly correct, as the previous section has indicated, that Hoffmann and Rosecrance tended to locate causes at the level of the units and thus largely conceived the international system as an outcome. There is, however, nothing scientifically inappropriate about such an objective in general. The problem is that it does not seem logically possible to accomplish such an objective in international politics, because there is no calculus capable

---

2. Ibid., 5, 69. With respect to scientific explanation, Waltz cites Ernest Nagel. However, in a section not cited by Waltz, Nagel makes it quite plain that the Aristotelian requirement for first principles as the basis for scientific explanation is untenable in light of modern science. See Ernest Nagel, *The Structure of Science: Problems in the Logic of Scientific Explanation* (Indianapolis: Hackett Publishing Co., [1961], 1979), 45-46.

3. Waltz, *Theory of International Politics*, chaps. 2 and 3, are replete with this concept of reductionism. This notion originates in his earlier book, *Man, the State, and War: A Theoretical Analysis* (New York: Columbia University Press, 1959).

of transforming the diverse factors feeding from the units into general statements about the international system.

By contrast, consider the situation in which statistics can be employed. In epidemiology or demographics, statistical techniques can be used to transform unit information into system information because there exists, practically, a one-to-one correspondence between the integer series and the number of elements in the system. Therefore, some behavioral characteristics of the whole system—such as population growth—can be measured by aggregating elements of the system and comparing their variation to an aggregated scale in the environment, such as food supply. Because the number of units is very large, and because there are potentially many populations to study, possibilities exist for controlled and natural experiments, and there is potential for meaningful interpretation. Within current methods and techniques, these conditions are not present for most problems in concrete macrosystems analysis.

Thus, a reduction of international politics to aggregated features of national politics seems foreclosed in principle. But in a formal sense it is just as "reductionist" to deduce a particular phenomenon from a macrosystemic theory. Whichever direction such reductions proceed by, they represent the hallmark of fertile scientific research.

A Bounded Realm

In any event, Waltz attempted to develop his own theory. He claimed that a successful theory had to show how international politics was distinct from economic, social, and other *international* domains [emphasis added]. He then stated that making the field distinct required showing how political structures would allow international politics to be conceived as a distinct system. He defined "structure" as a unit-positional concept—one referring to the arrangement of a system's units.[4] In order to understand this concept Waltz referred to domestic political structures, and then attempted to provide criteria for the meaning of "structures."

Arrangement. Arrangement of units was first defined as a principle of order.[5] According to Waltz, domestic politics is hierarchically ordered, because there are relations of super- and subordination among the units. Second, the units are formally differentiated; that is, their distinct functions are "specified."

As far as this definition goes, it is clearly meaningful. But it doesn't go very far. Both the United States and the Soviet Union had, by this definition, hierarchical orders, but the manner in which the parts of their political systems were arranged was markedly different. This type of definition is best characterized as an exercise in empty formalism. Waltz is supplying categories, not a

---

4. Waltz, *Theory of International Politics*, 79-80.
5. Ibid., 81.

specification of different types of structures. Specification of type entails the
relationships among the categories.

Both of Waltz's definitions of structure are really focused on some vague
notion of law and legitimacy: "By 'specified' I do not mean that the law of the
land fully describes the duties that different agencies perform, but only that broad
agreement prevails on the tasks that various parts of a government are to
undertake and on the extent of the power they legitimately wield."[6]   It is,
however, precisely on this point that Waltz's position constituted a failure of the
first basic standard: to focus on international political relations. And his position
failed even against its own standard: to mark off international systems from other
international systems. His approach, in fact, marked off "international political
systems from other international systems" by defining *domestic* structures.[7]
Thus, it did not accomplish its own objective. Although in his sixth chapter
Waltz claimed that chapter 5 served the purpose of marking off international
politics as a "bounded realm,"[8] the bounded realm he chose never resolved his
original problem, that of distinguishing among different international systems.

Waltz was nonetheless able to find a feature common to both international and
domestic structures. A third definition of structure was stated: the relative
capabilities of the units. "The relation of Prime Minister to Parliament and of
President to Congress depends on, and varies with, their relative capabilities."[9]

As Waltz applied his three definitions to the international system, he reached
what must have appeared to be a startling conclusion, namely, that most
definitions of domestic structures do not apply to international politics! In
international politics the principle of order was called anarchy, because none of
the units are entitled to command.[10]   Unit functions were called coordinate
rather than supra- and subordinate.[11]   The only definition found in domestic
structure that Waltz found relevant to international structure was that concerning
capabilities.

Stipulated differences between international and domestic structures are not
an Archimedean point for building international theory. The payoff of that

---

6. Ibid. The two definitions may in fact be only one, since formally differentiated units
seem to be related to the hierarchical order and the at least partial legitimacy of the law
of the land.

7. Note that this is precisely the approach used by Hoffmann: to mark off international
politics from domestic politics. Although few writers ever overcame this distinction—which is usually known as the fallacy of false alternatives—and despite the outright
kidnapping of terms such as "system" and "science" by its practitioners, all traditionalists
adopt this focus for the study of international politics.

8. Waltz, *Theory of International Politics*, 116.

9. Ibid., 81.

10. Ibid., 88.

11. If in the post-1945 bipolar system a researcher were to compare the relations among
the Soviet Union and its satellites—Czechoslovakia and Hungary, for example—it would
be a little difficult to square this definition with reality.

approach tends to result in myths of international conflict. As an historiographical principle, this is perhaps a convenient myth by which to select relevant facts
in the writing of an international story. However, alternative myths, which select
evidence of cooperation, economic intercourse, or common interests are equally
valid conventions for the writing of a story. In particular historical periods, one
or the other may provide a more economical myth, but there is no clear way to
adjudicate among such competing perspectives.[12] The key question, however,
is how can it possibly be asserted that this approach resembles a scientific
theory?

Waltz's Meaning of Theory

Waltz's conception of theory bypasses the explanatory presupposition. Waltz
seemingly believed that a stipulated definition of subject matter was logically
equivalent[13] to the construction of a theory, because he stated that his chapter
on political structures constructed a systems theory of international politics.
Moreover, it was further claimed that balance of power theory was a development of that theory.[14] However, note his meaning of theory: it merely
stipulates that international politics is largely different from domestic politics,
except for one variable. To use a similar approach to distinguish humans and
birds, we would come to the conclusion that humans can be defined as
featherless bipeds. Like Waltz's definition, this one is true. But it is not a
terribly powerful biological theory.

The so-called structural theory was based on premises or presuppositions about
legitimacy and authority in domestic political systems. That line of reasoning
established only what Waltz deemed relevant—the distribution of capabilities—for the subject of international politics. However, a presupposed definition
of subject matter is not much of a scientific theory. Astrophysicists and
geologists limit their research domains in terms of stars and rocks, but that
provides only the most trivial theory of rocks and stars. The concept of anarchy
doesn't explain anything beyond the trivial about international politics. Anarchy
is simply the absence of functionally specified government, a mere definition of
Waltzian structure employed to isolate the distribution of capabilities. The
distribution of capabilities was a category or, possibly, a variable, but certainly
not an explanatory theory. Nor did theory develop in chapter 6, where the
balance of power was discussed.

---

12. Willard Hutcheon, "Reason in History and its Rationale," in Martin Tamny and
K.D. Irani, eds., *Rationality in Thought and Action* (New York: Greenwood Press, 1986).

13. There is some sense in which a definitional conception of theory is true. But
theoretical definitions are not merely stipulative. They relate the elements in a system.
Thus "straight line" is defined differently in the various geometries. In the pragmaticist
tradition of Charles Sanders Peirce, definitions are left open for continual revision in the
light of new experiments and evidence.

14. Waltz, *Theory of International Politics*, 123.

Balancing. Waltz fails to employ the motivational standard in his conception of balancing. He claimed his balance of power theory was analogous to the theory of the economic market. He assumed self-interested competition among a system's units, which can be characterized as arational.[15] Waltz sought to explain from this assumption a result; namely, the recurrent formation of balances of power. "Balancing" and "bandwagoning" were distinguished: bandwagons occur when most of the states in a system get behind one member. Waltz believed that because survival is their minimal goal, states could bandwagon only if their security was not threatened, a goal which would be threatened by attempting to maximize power.[16] However, as with Morgenthau, a state's purposes made no difference to Waltz; whether states sought balance or sought domination a balance of power would tend to result. However, if motives are irrelevant in explaining balance, then why does balancing result? Waltz asserts that the system "induces" it.[17]

It is at this point that the entire Waltzian system was sundered from reality. Waltz did not conceive the system level as incorporating actors who were embedded inside and motivated by a continually varying international structure. For Waltz to include actors and their motives as part of the international system, he would have had to completely revise his understanding of levels-of-analysis. Whatever the reason, he did not.

Levels of Motivation. The failure to incorporate the motivational presupposition tends to result in a failure of the valuational standard as well. Although the exclusion of motives is often based on levels-of-analysis considerations, a mature view of system levels must include motives. These motives may be self-conscious, conscious, or preconscious, but they must be included. The question Waltz could not address was which system level was motivating a specific international actor in a specific situation. In any specific decision, an actor is confronted with a trade-off among values. An actor could be motivated to increase armaments spending either because an opponent was increasing its

---

15. Waltz's units are arational with respect to the macrosystem, which is to say that the units are self-interested rather than system-maintainers.

16. For a sophisticated analysis that includes this subject, though one which constitutes difficult reading, see Arthur Lee Burns, "From Balance to Deterrence: A Theoretical Analysis," *World Politics* 9 (1957): 494-529.

17. Waltz, *Theory of International Politics*, 89-92, 126; on motives see 107, 119-121. Waltz was inconsistent and, as he moved towards more applied propositions, he could not maintain his position on motives. In the first place he assumed that states seek security—a truism, but a goal nonetheless. Waltz generally meant that states seek their own individual survival rather than some system-motivated goal. However, in discussing the stability of an oligopoly he is led to numerous statements that smaller number systems affect the members incentives and their stakes in the system to the point that their members are "better able to manage affairs for their mutual benefit." See ibid., 135-136. Duncan Snidal and Hein Goemans persuaded me that it was incorrect to accept Waltz's denial of motives at face value.

armaments (the system level), because it is good for the Keynesian economy (the state level), or because an actor's ego needed to achieve dominance over others (the personality level). Waltz, however, has a system without any human parts—decision-making without any decision-makers. Because he boxed himself into a corner by accusing others of being reductionists when locating causes at the national or individual level, he could not admit motives and values when he needed them, and could not conceive the individual as a matrix of motives resulting from the variety of role functions that are performed—any one or number of which could, in an actual situation, be motivational.

As a result of these failures to meet the motivational and valuational standards Waltz's results began to flow mysteriously from anarchy. Why does the absence of government "induce" a survival motive, and why does survival lead to balancing behavior? No argument is ever developed. Of course, no answer is necessary from the perspective of international politics. All animals have a survival "motive" and they have it whether or not they are part of an anarchical system. Humans generally flee burning buildings despite the existence of functionally specified and hierarchically organized fire departments. Many of the advanced species tend to employ collective survival patterns, a process which seems to be related to group identity. Perhaps animals that have a survival motive have an evolutionary advantage over those which lack this capacity?

The entire result of Waltz's "theory" was the proposition that in all (anarchical) international systems balances of power will tend to form. This proposition is formally equivalent to saying that in all meteorological systems, fair weather will tend to form. In all fairness to Waltz, both these propositions—about weather and about balance—may be said to be true, but a meteorological theory can only be considered successful to the extent that it can tell us from what system of variables and relations, what kind of weather will form, and why. A theory must answer questions about why or how a specific result can be accounted for, understood, or explained.[18]

The balance of power concept, as Waltz used it, was little more than a metaphor, a mere neo-principle which differed from Morgenthau's only by virtue of not assuming its origin[19] in human nature. Of course, the use of metaphor was consistent with Waltz's view of theory as "creative idea"—as simplification somehow beyond both deduction and induction, which cannot be judged independently of the assumptions an author makes.[20] Because there was no

---

18. In fact, this position is explicitly adopted by Waltz. See ibid., 69.

19. This is probably a distinction without a difference. Morgenthau certainly believed that the international system lacked government, and that a balance of power would result from independent, interest-seeking actors.

20. Waltz, *Theory of International Politics*, 10-12. Waltz's view of theory is usually characterized as the descriptive view of scientific theories. The descriptive view, however, contrary to Waltz's assertion that his theory is explanatory, claims that theories do not explain anything but merely describe a world of sense experience, either one derived from primitive "impressions" or "gross experience." Thus, the enterprise hinges

difference in the equilibrium (balance) regardless of the type of system[21] (multipolar or bipolar), it remained unclear what behavioral variations were being explained. Finally, because motives were ruled out of court, it was unclear how it could be known whether a particular balance was an intended or unintended consequence. A fair appraisal must conclude that the central theoretical chapters (5 and 6) in Waltz's *Theory of International Politics* fail to meet the focal, explanatory, motivational, and valuational standards.

Economic Analogies

The Invisible Hand. In this section, I show that Waltz also misuses economic theory. Instead of supporting his argument, his analogy increases his distance from the explanatory standard. He omits the role that rationality plays in economic theory, specifically confuses the relationship between free and oligopolistic markets, and thus confuses the relationship between numbers of actors, interdependence, and stability.

The closest Waltz came to a deductive explanation of balance was through an analogy to microeconomic accounts of the market. His market was, however, used only as a metaphor that resembled balance. How do they resemble each other? Both are "invisible."[22]

The classical economic market is not, in fact, analogous to Waltz's balance of power. In marketplace theory a price mechanism adjusts the behavior of individuated actors in a way which regulates their willingness to supply and demand goods and services. Actors may not be aware of the macro-results of

---

on translating every theoretical notion into an observation term. The view was somewhat more popular during the late nineteenth century among physicists who were unhappy with the atomic theory of matter and in the work of Carnap. Waltz uses Ludwig Boltzmann as his authority on the meaning of theory, going back to an article from 1905 as his source. The position has been jettisoned by almost everyone because there are no convincing reasons to believe that the translatability thesis is actually practiced by scientists or even possible in principle. In fact, Boltzmann apparently did not accept this view of theory. On this point see Nagel, *The Structure of Science*, 117-129, 128n. Waltz's belief, however, that he is defining this or that, that theories depict reality and are contrivances, and that assumptions are peculiar to a theory and not capable of being true are statements consistent with the descriptive view—and somewhat the instrumental view—of theory, and in my judgment largely account for his inability to explain anything. The alternative to these views of theory is realism (which is not "political realism").

Waltz seems to change his position in a later essay by stating: "Realism's approach is primarily inductive. Neorealism is more heavily deductive." See Kenneth Waltz, "Realist Thought and Neorealist Theory," in Robert L. Rothstein, ed., *The Evolution of Theory in International Relations: Essays in Honor of William T. R. Fox* (Columbia, SC: University of South Carolina Press, 1991), 33.

21. The bipolar-multipolar fallacy is treated in depth in chap. 5.
22. Waltz, *Theory of International Politics*, 89-92.

their atomistic decisions, but they are certainly thought to be aware of prices, which are macro-given data for each individual actor. Waltz cited Alfred Kahan, who called this phenomenon the "tyranny of small decisions."[23] However, microtheorists are aware of the relationship between macroeconomic prices and microeconomic decisions, that is, between system and actors. Microtheory holds only if those individuals act "rationally" with respect to macro-given prices, a concept absent from Waltz.[24] On the other hand, Waltz's balance of power was merely an empirical generalization predicted to occur in all anarchic systems. No mechanism, direct or indirect, accounts for balancing. The internal and external mechanisms that Waltz does employ are used in his discussion of stability. The problems with that discussion are examined below. These mechanisms do not, however, account for Waltz's empirical generalization about balancing. Throughout much of the history of science, empirically generalizable predictions were common knowledge, but theoretical understanding remained distant. Everyone knows that aspirin reduces fever, but that is not a theory of fever reduction.

Waltz's "balance" was quite unlike microeconomic theory, for even if he were correct about balancing—and how could he be incorrect?—the most he could claim was constant conjunction, à la Hume, and then assert circumstantial support through his market analogy. Unfortunately, it turned out that his metaphor was no substitute for deductive argument, because Waltz would not have been justified in making such a claim. Waltz's omission of rational motivation led to increasingly ambiguous and contradictory statements.

Oligopoly. Because of the failure to incorporate the motivational standard, Waltz does not adequately distinguish the competitive free market from oligopolistic markets. Due to the absence of this standard, Waltz also omits that the free market results in optimal prices only for large numbers of actors, where none has a big enough share to disturb the market. A hidden-hand market mechanism works—if it works at all—only by assuming this macrotheoretical condition at the outset. Perhaps this accounts for Waltz's examples? In the relevant section of his "theory," all of his examples utilize hundreds to thousands of actors.[25] Paul Samuelson indicates how market size determines the effectiveness of invisible mechanisms: "[W]hen one's grain, merchandise, or labor is large enough in size to produce appreciable depressing or elevating effects on market prices, some degree of monopolistic competition has set in, and the virtues of the INVISIBLE HAND must be that much discounted."[26]

Although Waltz occasionally distinguished between perfect competition and oligopoly[27] he tended to conflate the two systems: "States facing global problems are like individual consumers trapped by the 'tyranny of small

---

23. Ibid., 108.
24. Ibid., 109.
25. Ibid., 91-92.
26. Paul A. Samuelson, *Economics*, 11th ed. (New York: McGraw-Hill, 1980), 39.
27. Waltz, *Theory of International Politics*, 93-94.

decisions.'"[28] This is clearly false for many international problems. Oligopolies can engage in price wars or collusion, for example, in order to regulate the behavior of opponents, strategies that Waltz at other times recognized.[29]

In terms of explaining why states balance, Waltz's shift to an oligopolistic analogy provides no rationale. Because hidden-hand mechanisms are inappropriate metaphors in oligopolistic markets, they cannot account for Waltz's theory of international balancing. When Waltz did examine the question of small n systems, he was no longer attempting to explain balancing. At that point he shifted from explaining balance to explaining the stability of balancing.

Waltz considered oligopolies in the first part of chapter 7, which "carries the theory further." There he looked at the effects that numbers of units have on "economic answers." "Economic stability," he claimed, "increases as oligopolistic sectors narrow. Other effects also follow." To sum up these other effects: large established firms survive best; bargaining costs fall and incentives to pay bargaining costs rise as firms become fewer; enforcing and making agreements, and surveillance are easier with fewer firms. According to Waltz: "These . . . points strongly argue that smaller is better than small. Smaller systems are more stable and their members are better able to manage affairs for their mutual benefit.[30]

In order to explain the stability of balance Waltz departed further from simple economic logic. Waltz stated that economic interdependence loosens as systems become smaller. However, that conclusion cannot be said to follow from his propositions. A single actor can easily disequilibrate a small system by lowering prices. Such behavior leads to destabilizing price wars unless the actors learn to behave appropriately.[31]

Although a price mechanism regulates the behavior of price-rational actors in an oligopoly of firms, that mechanism operates differently than it does under perfect competition. This has a great deal to do with the more complete state of information that exists in a small system. Economists have developed increasingly sophisticated models of oligopolistic prices. For example, many

---

28. Ibid., 110-111.

29. Ibid., 133-134.

30. Ibid., 135-136. In fact, Waltz's position is in direct conflict with Morgenthau's, which indicates an arbitrariness of reasoning from principles alone. Morgenthau states: "This reduction [since 1648] in the number of nations that are able to play a major role in international politics has had a deteriorating effect upon the operation of the balance of power. . . . These developments deprived the balance of power of much of its flexibility and uncertainty and, in consequence, of its restraining effect upon the nations actively engaged in the struggle for power." See Hans J. Morgenthau, *Politics Among Nations: The Struggle for Power and Peace*, 3rd ed. (New York: Alfred A. Knopf, 1963), 346ff.

31. For an excellent introduction to oligopoly pricing see F.M. Scherer and David Ross, *Industrial Market Structure and Economic Performance*, 3rd ed. (Boston: Houghton Mifflin Co., 1990), chap. 6.

models now incorporate how pricing is effected by the "lumpiness" of goods. But for my present purposes, the simple version of oligopolistic pricing is sufficient to explain the relationship between small numbers and interdependence. Unlike the competitive free market, if a firm lowers its price to increase market share, other firms will follow suit, but if it raises price the other firms will maintain prices in order to increase their market share. Thus, no firm has an incentive to depart from common pricing, which tends toward the monopoly price. Thus, there is a price equilibrium, "just like" the free market. But in the free market you do not need to consider information or self-conscious strategies in the same way. Small n systems are necessarily more interdependent than large n systems.

Uncertainty. Waltz then translated his thoughts about numbers and economic answers to military affairs. In military affairs, Waltz also analyzed stability largely in terms of number of actors. He somewhat skated away from that argument by stating that differences in numbers and stability are not the defining difference between bipolar and multipolar systems. The defining difference is that between internal and external mechanisms of balance. He did, however, imply that bipolar systems are more stable than multipolar systems because there is less uncertainty about how to manage the balance. Certainty increases because the internal bipolar mechanism is more "reliable and precise."[32]

If different mechanisms of balance are devices to explain stability, (and these are the only candidates), then two problems stand out. First, how is uncertainty a politico-structural account of behavior? It seems to be a psychological account of international political stability. Why do we need this concept in a world governed by an invisible hand? How is uncertainty calculated in a world without rational actors? Is this reductionism? Does this mark off international political systems from other international systems? Second, even if we grant Waltz his mechanism and overlook its partly psychological character, why does it work the way he suggests? The price mechanism is based on a reasoned account as to how actors will behave if those decisions are motivated by a utility schedule that directly corresponds to increasing increments of fungible units of exchange. But how can Waltz claim that less uncertainty accounts for greater stability? Why would uncertainty work the way Waltz suggests, even if the concept of rationality is smuggled in unnoticed? Why would a self-interested, manipulative, security-seeking or power-seeking political actor react to less uncertainty by balancing of any sort?

The most transparent answer is that it would not be rational to upset a system in which an actor felt reasonably secure. However, Waltz was never capable of embracing the role of rationality in the social sciences, because in international relations during the twentieth century, the idea of rationality evoked strong

---

32. Ibid., 161-162, 168. Burns provides a seminal analysis of uncertainty. See "From Balance to Deterrence," 494-529.

emotional ties of identity to one of the two camps. For many, to admit its function into an explanation was tantamount to treason. So much for science!

THE POWER OF MYTH

Thus the main problem with Waltz's theory was that because balance occurred without reason, there was no explanation whatsoever. Bipolar and multipolar systems were ultimately conceived as variations of this single anarchical, balance of power international system. As with previous orienting principles these variations in the distribution of capabilities resulted in no macrosystem variations. Balance of power is the purported tendency in all cases. This conception of international relations is a continuation of the natural law tradition of the seventeenth century. It is a very powerful myth that balances result as if by a hidden-hand. But it cannot be maintained in light of our knowledge of oligopolistic behavior and collective action problems. Such efforts clearly fail to meet the focal, explanatory, motivational, and valuational standards.

The only basic standards which Waltz seemed to employ were the conditional, coding, and durational standards. But they are presented in truncated and often arbitrary form, problems examined in the following chapter. The combination of those failures and the ones presented in this chapter demonstrate that the Waltzian approach missed the mark. This is particularly evident when we try to apply Waltz's principles to the life and death of the post-1945 bipolar system. The next chapter examines the applicability of bipolar-multipolar concepts to empirical evidence. There it becomes clear that the bipolar-multipolar dichotomy is a dismally underspecified approach to the international system. Not all writers examined in that chapter share Waltz's general position. But all writers who use the bipolar-multipolar dichotomy are merely waltzing with theory.

5

Paying the Piper: Applied Theory

In the previous chapter I criticized Waltz's approach on theoretical grounds. In the exact sciences theoretical failures are often sufficient to send the logically flawed theorist back to the drawing board. But in the social sciences logical rigor is not as strictly applicable. The relationship between theoretical propositions and empirical applications should be explored even when the reasoning is less than rigorous.

UNDERSPECIFICATION

In this chapter I examine the empirical applicability of the bipolar-multipolar dichotomy. My appraisal shows that even relatively simple macroproblems cannot be explained with this dichotomy. As previous chapters have indicated, most approaches to theory in international relations, and particularly to bipolar international politics, suffer from underspecified conceptual models.

I examine the problem of underspecification in Waltz, the correlates of war approach to international politics, and some derivative applications of these underspecified concepts. This chapter is consistent with the conclusions of the previous one. The problem of underspecification results largely from failures in the focal, conditional, motivational, and valuational standards. Failures in these standards also result in dysfunctional coding criteria.

This chapter also clarifies some other theoretical concepts relevant to a theory of international politics—including the relationship between system size and uncertainty, the role of the decision-maker in international analysis, the difference between type-based analysis and those based on a single continuous system, and the objectivity of decision-making analysis.

The bipolar-multipolar dichotomy presupposes that the number of great powers should be a major determinant of behavior in the international system. The number of powerful actors in a system is certainly one international relationship necessary to explain optimal action patterns. However, the conditional standards employ other relationships as well. The role function of the actors, informational factors, the regime characteristics of the international actors, and the actual action patterns of actors are also relevant. Another problem with the dichotomy is that the codings used for "great power" are generally drawn across the entire range of international relations, in an unbounded sense akin to Morgenthau's expansive conception of power.

This dichotomy cannot explain important and obvious macroproblems directly relevant to the post-1945 bipolar system. A few examples include the sudden death of the bipolar system, the pattern of crises in postwar bipolar politics, the existence of the North Atlantic Treaty Organization and Warsaw Pact, and the great levels of uncertainty that were generated sporadically throughout the system's life. Some of these and other failures will be illustrated below. These illustrations will clarify that I do not mean that this dichotomy failed to predict these events.

In international politics it is premature to expect correct and accurate diagnoses and prognoses, though on occasion this may be possible. But theoretical approaches should be expected to achieve at least postdictive theoretical consistency regarding general system patterns and major transformations. The sudden death of bipolarity mandates an autopsy. Even the preliminary autopsy results supplied in this chapter demonstrate that postdictive consistency is too demanding a standard for underspecified, bipolar-multipolar conceptions. During the course of this analysis the problems characteristic of stipulated definitions—arbitrariness, overgeneralization, imprecise classification—should also become clear.

Kenneth Waltz

The previous chapter noted that Waltz does incorporate some initial conditions. From those conditions Waltz sought to formulate substantive hypotheses about bipolar systems. There were three major hypotheses about bipolar systems that covered system change, the mechanisms of balance, and uncertainty.

System Change. Waltz hypothesizes that anarchic systems transform only by changes in organizing principle or by consequential changes in the number of principal parties. If neither entity changes, then a given international system is stable.[1] On empirical grounds, this hypothesis evaporated with the sudden death of the bipolar system. The international system remained anarchical and, in most of Waltz's measures of power, there were no consequential changes in number. Moreover, according to Waltz, most is good enough.

---

1. Kenneth Waltz, *Theory of International Politics* (Reading, MA: Addison-Wesley Publishing Co., Inc.), 161-162.

On Waltz's grounds it cannot be claimed that the Soviet economy grew so weak that it was no longer a consequential actor. His idea of consequential power is based on how individuated states score on diverse factors such as population, territory, resource endowment, economic capability, military strength, political stability, and competence. But he states that these capabilities "cannot be sectored and separately weighed."[2]

Without sectoring and weighting, the Soviet Union and the United States remained the two most consequential actors, particularly in military capabilities. Therefore, the hypothesis failed to explain bipolar system change. Waltz clearly lacked a sufficient number of categories and hypotheses to explain transformation. Though the initial conditions that he specified as necessary for transformation were false, transformation nonetheless occurred.

Internal Balancing. Waltz also hypothesized that bipolar systems balance by internal means because the poles rely on themselves for security.[3] On theoretical grounds, it has already been argued in the previous chapter that interdependence rises in an oligopoly. And unless one arbitrarily selects data, it is very difficult to find much empirical support that bloc leaders "relied on internal means" of balancing. In coding "internal mechanisms," Waltz used only unsophisticated indicators of spending and manpower.[4] These indicators exclude many obvious and important action patterns of postwar bipolar history. From the earliest days of the cold war the United States relied on a global network of bases in order to place its bombers within range of the Soviet Union. The Soviet Union viewed its satellites as a strategic buffer. Other major postwar events also are excluded: the Marshall Plan and Cominform, NATO and the Warsaw Pact, Berlin, Korea, the European Defense Community, the Cuban missile crisis, the multilateral force, and the Soviet invasion of Czechoslovakia. Even nuclear weapons did not obviate the need for external means of balancing: both blocs were jockeying theater nuclear weapons during the 1970s and 1980s. Finally, if alliances (external means) are unimportant in bipolar systems because the allies cannot protect the bloc leader, then the United States and Soviet Union must not have understood that the bipolar mechanism of balance is "more reliable and precise." For they invested major resources in their alliance relationships. Of course, if we look only at who "paid" for these actions, then perhaps even these events can be collapsed into Waltz's category of internal balance. That collapse might provide consistency but only at the expense of accuracy.

---

2. Ibid., 131. Waltz is correct that it is difficult to make variables truly independent in the social sciences, though he grossly overstates the case here. The difficulties require greater care in the selection of coding criteria, which are necessary both for sectoring and weighting.

3. Waltz, *Theory of International Politics*, 167-170.

4. On the function of definition in scientific propositions see Morris R. Cohen and Ernest Nagel, *An Introduction to Logic and Scientific Method* (New York: Harcourt, Brace and Co., 1934), 223-244.

Uncertainty. Waltz also stated that calculations are easier to make in a bipolar system. Unless researchers arbitrarily select data or substitute their own assessment of certainty for the judgments of decision-makers, it is difficult to argue that calculations were necessarily easier to make in the bipolar system. The bomber gap, missile gap, Berlin crisis, and Cuban missile crisis illustrate the difficulty. These uncertain situations were not resolved because of the small number of great powers. Without the great informational availability that existed in the post-1945 system, it is highly plausible that these and similar events would have led to great instability. That capacity was largely a result of technological factors rather than the number of great powers. In order to investigate its function in the system, we need a separate variable for informational transparency, as specified in the basic standards.

Bipolarity also does not account for greater certainty after strategic parity was achieved. That certainty is more accurately tethered to the development of stable nuclear second-strike capabilities than it is to the presence of two great powers. As with informational availability, an explanation of certainty after the late 1960s is partly a result of technological factors. And even then the system often exhibited high degrees of uncertainty. Fears of a window of vulnerability and the 1984 Soviet defense review, which recommended putting the Soviet Union on a total war footing, are two clear examples. That an actor has only one primary opponent is only one of many information factors that feed into the certainty of decision-making.

A very persuasive argument has been made that the relationship between certainty and system-type is multidimensional. The only factor which increases certainty in a very small *n* system is that the number of alliance combinations are restricted. In a dyarchic system the combinations are, in fact, fixed, because there are no other actors to ally with. However, the certainty of other factors falls dramatically in a dyarchic system. Because the actors are of great relative size, any conflict can be devastating. Second, the chance of third-party correction of an imbalance is nonexistent, because there are no other essential actors in the system to throw their weight behind the weaker party.[5]

Intellectual Anarchy. The three hypotheses examined above constitute Waltz's most specific statements about bipolarity. There is, however, no good empirical evidence for those hypotheses. Unless we explain away the obvious, only gratuitous empirical support exists for his hypotheses about system change, internal balancing, and uncertainty. Waltz's failure to hit any targets is not surprising. In contrast to the basic standards Waltz based his approach on anarchy. So, he generally failed to focus on international political relationships. That failure resulted in dysfunctional coding criteria and underspecified conditional propositions that are not sufficient for even postdictive explanation of obvious historical action patterns. Underspecified initial conditions and the

5. See Arthur Lee Burns, "From Balance to Deterrence: A Theoretical Essay," *World Politics* 9 (July 1957): 494-529.

use of arbitrary, ordinary language, and stipulated definitions completely invalidated Waltz's attempt to explain the action patterns of concrete international systems.

Isolated structural-numeric factors cannot explain action. Political actors do not act only as a function of isolated structural-numeric factors. The wider range of initial conditions specified in the conditional presupposition are important determinants of optimal action patterns. Actors play different roles in different systems, their effectiveness depends on information factors, and their regime characteristics partly control their operational codes. A model without these elements can only produce anarchy.

J. David Singer

The approach associated with J. David Singer also employed a bipolar-multipolar dichotomy. I will show that his approach failed to meet the focal, explanatory, conditional, motivational, and valuational standards. Singer explicitly attempted to derive international relationships from the random interactions occurring in the international system. These efforts were based on two major presuppositions: that the international system is in some sense equivalent to the structure of these interactions, and that variations in these structures are, at the macrolevel, probable determinants of war and peace.

This agenda motivated what came to be known as the Correlates of War (COW) project, and by all accounts, including those of the researchers,[6] the bipolar-multipolar dichotomy has not yielded any systematic knowledge about the causes of war. So perhaps Singer's general philosophical presuppositions should be revisited and appraised. These presuppositions were most succinctly captured in a paper written in the early 1960s.[7]

Objectives. Singer's article mentioned that an analytical model included descriptive, explanatory, and predictive functions. With respect to the explanatory function he stated that a model should exhibit "a capacity to *explain* the relationships among the phenomena under investigation."[8] Although he acknowledged that the primary purpose of theory was explanatory rather than descriptive, in doing so he added a qualification. It was not sufficient that models treat causal relationships in a fashion that was valid and thorough; it was

---

6. Or as one researcher stated: "Unfortunately, the extensity of the literature on this subject is matched only by its indeterminacy." See Alan Ned Sabrosky, ed., *Polarity and War: The Changing Structure of International Conflict* (Boulder, CO: Westview Press, 1985), 3. See also J. David Singer, et al., *Explaining War: Selected Papers from the Correlates of War Project*, with a Foreword by Bruce M. Russett (Beverly Hills, CA: Sage Publications, 1979), 11.

7. J. David Singer, "The Level-of-Analysis Problem in International Relations" in Klauss Knorr and Sidney Verba, eds., *The International System: Theoretical Essays* (Princeton: Princeton University Press, 1961), 77-92.

8. Ibid., 79. Emphasis in the original.

also required that these models be "parsimonious." According to Singer, this injunction was often overlooked despite the fact that its research implications were "not inconsequential." And in a footnote he described these consequences by referring to the problems of non-parsimonious decision-making models. Singer alluded to one critic of these models, who pointed out: "that no single researcher could deal with all the variables in that model and expect to complete more than a very few comparative studies in his lifetime."[9]

The evidence suggests that this rationale constituted a chief motivating factor both in Singer's formulation of the level-of-analysis problem and in the general research agenda of the COW project. Thus, the COW project was in part designed to permit the rapid and extensive production of publishable studies. Those studies were designed to uncover correlations on a longer road to deeper causal analysis. This rationale and the hidden-hand tradition of international relations, which denies the necessity of motives, were undoubtedly influential in Singer's version of the levels-of-analysis problem as well.

Levels-of-Analysis. Singer's formulation of the level-of-analysis problem fails to meet the focal and motivational standards. Singer split international relations into two gross categories: the international, and the nation-state levels. The decision-maker was placed exclusively in the category of the nation-state level, as were all the possible differences in the world. On the other hand, the international system encompassed:

the totality of interactions which take place within the system and its environment. By focusing on the system, we are enabled to study the patterns of interaction which the system reveals, and to generalize about such phenomena as the creation and dissolution of coalitions, the frequency and duration of specific power configurations, modifications in its stability, its responsiveness to changes in formal political institutions, and the norms and folklore which it manifests as a societal system.[10]

It was claimed that this approach had some difficulties, especially in exaggerating the impact of the "system," and in the postulation of uniform foreign policy operational codes for all the actors. If this seems to have some resemblance to Morgenthau's approach—which denied motives in favor of a focus on the uniformities inherent in all pluralistic systems—it did, and Singer explicitly referred to Morgenthau when he specified the systems level. Singer also explicitly linked this methodology to stimulus-response psychology and its reliance on "black-boxes." But the purported greatest difficulty and purported greatest potential benefit were captured in the following statement: "And though this may be an inadequate foundation upon which to base any *causal* statements, it offers a reasonably adequate basis for *correlative* statements. More specifically, it permits us to observe and measure correlations between certain forces or

---

9. Ibid., 79.
10. Ibid., 80.

stimuli which seem to impinge upon the nation and the behavior patterns which are the apparent consequence of these stimuli."[11]

After remarking that the causal links would have to be investigated after an apparent pattern was found, Singer returned to what he viewed as the two greatest—at least short term—benefits: "Moreover, by avoiding the multitudinous pitfalls of intra-nation observation, one emerges with a singularly manageable model, requiring as it does little of the methodological sophistication or onerous empiricism called for when one probes beneath the behavioral externalities of the actor . . . [and second] the systemic orientation should prove to be a reasonably satisfactory basis for prediction. . . ."[12]

This general approach is a radical alternative to that proposed by the basic standards, for it clearly eliminates motivated actors from the international system. (That entails a violation of the valuational standard as well). It also violates the focal standard. Although COW researchers ceaselessly mention the systems level, none of them have ever found systems (types of relationships). As mentioned above, Singer stated that the international system encompasses the totality of interactions that take place within the system and its environment. Whereas the focal presupposition demands that researchers start with international political relations, Singer's statement[13] never mentioned a system of relations within which interactions take place. A system cannot be defined as a something, an "x", which occurs within a system. This formulation is equivalent to stating that there is *a system* within *the system*, without ever specifying what *the system* is.

System as Outcome. It is fairly clear from the subsequent research projects that the COW project was focused on the system as an outcome, in a fashion conceptually, if not methodologically, similar to that of historical sociologists. This inductive approach clearly violates the explanatory presupposition. By analyzing the possible interactions resulting from the external behavior of nation-states, the international system would be conceived in a sense similar to the way physicists conceive the behavior of a volume of gas. But the big difference between the physical scientist and COW researchers was in the specification of initial conditions. Lacking a proper focal standard, COW researchers failed the conditional standard as well.

Consider gas molecules interacting inside a balloon. With a small number of molecules there is a correspondingly small number of interactions. However, if either the number of molecules is increased or the volume of the balloon is decreased, the interaction pattern (pressure) in the system is increased. A question for physicists might be: "At what pressure does the balloon explode?" This is analogous to the kind of question a COW researcher might ask: "What kind of international interactions (pressures) lead to wars (explosions)?" By

---

11. Ibid., 82.
12. Ibid., 82.
13. See the passage that precedes footnote 10.

conceiving the international system as interaction outcomes, it was a small step to conceive various system sizes, or levels of polarity, or distributions of capabilities, as ranged along a continuous scale—akin to high and low pressure. That scale could then be correlated with a continuous scale about the amount, duration, or propensity for war—akin to explosion. But the difference between the physicist and COW approaches is that the former would expect different correlations in different types of "balloons." The correlation between pressure and explosion would vary under different initial conditions, such as whether the balloon was a hot-air balloon or a child's balloon. In this sense COW researchers were unlike physical scientists: they had no balloons, no systems.

Alliances, Capabilities, and War. One laborious effort to test the relationship between such randomized structural factors and war followed a paper which Singer coauthored with Karl Deutsch. It was in that paper that Deutsch and Singer focused on the bipolar-multipolar dichotomy. They hoped to demonstrate that as the bipolar international system became increasingly multipolar, the frequency and intensity of war would diminish.[14] This hypothesis led to two widely noted papers. One paper attempted to measure the relationship between alliance aggregation and the onset of war but discovered a contradiction. The authors found that the inflexibility (due to reduced interaction possibilities) that an alliance introduces into a system has a high correlation with the onset and amount of war in the twentieth century and a negative correlation in the nineteenth.[15]

Another study tested two models of stability. In that study, the "preponderance and stability model" stated that wars would increase as systems move away from high and stable concentrations of capabilities. That is, as systems moved from bipolarity to multipolarity, war would increase. On the other hand, their "parity and fluidity model" held that wars would decrease as systems moved away from high and stable concentrations. That is, as systems moved from bipolarity to multipolarity, wars would decrease. In this study the authors found that the preponderance model held for the twentieth century while the parity model held for the nineteenth.[16]

The authors recognized that their results were inconclusive. There are, of course, two contradictions. There is the contradiction that occurs across centuries in each study; in addition, the two studies are intuitively inconsistent about the relationship within each century. In the first study, the nineteenth century is characterized by the claim that rigidity (alliance aggregation) does not lead to

---

14. Karl Deutsch and J. David Singer, "Multipolar Power Systems and International Stability," *World Politics* 16 (April 1964): 390-406.

15. J. David Singer and Melvin Small, "Alliance Aggregation and the Onset of War, 1815-1945" in *The Correlates of War*, 2 vols. (New York: The Free Press, 1979): 225-264.

16. J. David Singer, Stuart A. Bremer, and John Stuckey, "Capability Distribution, Uncertainty, and Major Power War, 1820-1965," in *The Correlates of War*, 2 vols. (New York: The Free Press, 1979): 265-297.

war, whereas in the second study, the claim is that fluidity (lower concentrations) does not lead to war. With respect to the twentieth century, the first study claims that rigidity does lead to war and the second study that rigidity does not lead to war.

There are a number of reasons for these contradictions. The vast web of factors feeding into "amount" of war—logistic, economic, technological—could never be captured simply by "alliance aggregation." One cannot code behavioral properties by arbitrary definitions or postulated equivalences with other properties, but must instead specify relevant properties of a subject-entity. No predicates—and "are war-prone" is a predicate—can be analyzed without being bound to a subject-class (system-type). For any subject-class there are particular factors involved in war; terms such as "amount" and "high and stable," are too system-dependent and context-dependent to have any general merit.

This is to say that the authors never specified two systems—bipolar and multipolar—for comparative treatment, opting instead to conceive of systems as directly related to increases or decreases in a particular property. If behavior varies in a system, then one must identify the conditions necessary for the existence of such systems. Bipolarity never occurred in the period between 1815 and 1945, which is the main period investigated. Blocs and bloc leaders as forms of international political organization—with organizationally consolidated identities and consolidated security arrangements—did not exist, and capabilities were not heavily concentrated around two actors.[17] The bipolar-multipolar dichotomy fails to identify proper initial conditions. That failure results from theoretical constructs that start with individuated national actors, from which the authors attempt to aggregate international relationships. And that approach fails to meet the requirements of the focal presupposition, namely, to focus on international political relationships. There is also a logical problem with the bipolar-multipolar dichotomy. A continuous conception of the international system means that the axioms for both bipolarity and multipolarity must be logically equivalent. If this presupposition is wrong, as it seems to be, then the explanatory value of any results is completely dissipated. The following two sections clarify the differences between continuous and type-based international systems.

---

17. It is on these grounds that we disagree with characterizations of the pre-World War I period as bipolar. The argument is not merely that the alliances happened to last a long time. The pre-World War I alliances were bilateral, were based on clauses that differentiated the conditions under which the alliances would operate, and did not include public and institutional commitments. The post-World War II alliances were institutionalized and based on three-musketeer organizing principles: "all for one and one for all." This is not an exhaustive list of differences but is sufficient to indicate the boundaries between the two kinds of alliance relationships. To characterize an actor as a bloc means that we are dealing with a fundamentally different animal when compared to "balance of power" type alignments. See also chap. 7.

Outcomes as Continuous. These studies by Singer and his associates are part of a widespread belief that bipolar and multipolar systems can be placed on a continuum. This belief diverges from the focal presupposition, entails indefensible commitments to certain kinds of axioms, and leads to dysfunctional coding criteria. Their notion that a system can be "closer to pure bipolarity" illustrates this belief. The bipolar-multipolar conception presupposes that these forms are subtypes of a single international system with a continuous range. That presupposition is implausible. Most other social sciences identify *types* of entities as presuppositions for analysis. Types employ qualitative thresholds (non-equivalent axiom sets) that do not range across systems. Such systems are not aggregated from a set of primitive elements, they are concatenated as a set. Psychology distinguishes between neurotic and psychotic types and further distinguishes within these classes; comparative politics among democratic, authoritarian, industrial, agrarian, socialist, and corporate systems; economics between free market and command systems. A skillful practitioner may identify "mixed" or hybrid types, but there is no continuous transition among these entities.

In formal terms, a type is basically a set and sets include members. What distinguishes types of systems are the properties of a system's axioms. One cannot find continua between international systems because of the type of sets that constitute continuous series. If a set has a continuous range, such as one finds in the set of real numbers, then a foundation exists for coding practices that place a system on a continuum. We do, of course, perceive continua all the time—between boy and man, across historical events, and perhaps even between our behavior and our moon rising in Aquarius. However, only when there is a one-to-one relation between a continuous divisible scale and a set of corresponding elements—such as exists for the measurement of spatially extended bodies by the addition of rigid measuring rods (units)—can continuity be defined precisely.[18] That divisibility must in principle be an infinite divisibility, or at least a reasonable approximation, given the problem at hand. Some economic and voting systems may be meaningfully analyzed as sufficiently resembling the system of numbers to render behavioral continua meaningful if a particular system-type has been specified.[19]

If bipolar and multipolar systems are on a continuum, they must have logically equivalent axiom sets. This is to say that all the theorems and axioms of each type must be either a theorem or axiom of the other type. Logical equivalence

---

18. Or as M. R. Cohen related this point: "[t]he divisibility of continuous space does not lead to discreteness, but, on the contrary, defines definitely what is meant by continuity . . ." See his *Studies in the Philosophy of Science* (New York: Henry Holt and Co., 1949), 119-120.

19. This argument does not imply that, where relevant, quantitative studies are sufficient to fully understand social phenomena at all levels of investigation, but only that there exists a meaningful continuum—for example, between total Democratic and total Republican Party electoral dominance in the two-party U.S. political system.

permits transformations (deductions) to occur in both directions. Efforts to deduce different system types from the distribution of capabilities or alliance aggregation assume precisely such equivalence. However, no convincing case has ever been made that the distribution of capabilities, or any other attribute, is a sufficient condition for system change, and the axioms scientists choose must be relevant to the worlds they attempt to interpret.

Types and Subtypes. All international systems must be concatenated as qualitative sets in order to analyze their particular properties. All attempts to find structural transitions between types demonstrate a misunderstanding of this problem.[20] Even in cases where class attributes may be meaningfully represented as continuous variables, as in demographic or epidemiological systems, if the system is complex, its characteristics (such as the rate of births or infections) may nonetheless oscillate in qualitative nonlinear fits and starts if a parameter value crosses a critical threshold.[21] In such cases, thresholds mark off subsets rather than distinct types, but only because a common logical subsystem exists.[22]

It is difficult to conceive why anyone would believe that a type can be derived from the behavior and interactions of elements. It would be like trying to determine the relationship between a husband and a wife by adding up and correlating their total interactions with other individuals. Obviously it is not necessary to count all the interactions of all individuals in order to determine the existence of a nuclear family. That approach makes the identification process dependent on arbitrary definition. In international politics we surely know by now that NATO is a different animal than the pre-World War I Triple Entente and Triple Alliance.

Objectivity and Decision-Making. For all the supposed differences between Waltz's approach and Singer's approach, both reached the apotheosis of their dogmas about polarity in their fervent desire to rid international politics of human beings—those pesky creatures who keep messing up the models. If it can be shown that there are causes outside the statesman, forces acting upon the decision-maker, then it becomes unnecessary to have human beings whose freedom of action and motivated choices get in the way of a science of politics. In so doing the "objective" features of reality can be investigated rather than the "subjective" features.

---

20. In addition to Waltz and the COW-inspired efforts, another example is found in Richard Rosecrance, "Bipolarity, Multipolarity, and the Future," *Journal of Conflict Resolution*, 10 (September 1966): 322.

21. James Gleick, *Chaos: Making a New Science* (New York: Viking Press, 1987). On the distinction between the predicate and propositional calculus see Irving M. Copi, *Introduction to Logic* (New York: The Macmillan Co., 1961), 302ff.; and Samuel D. Guttenplan and Martin Tamny, *Logic: A Comprehensive Introduction* (New York: Basic Books, Inc., 1971), 149ff.

22. See, for example, my seven subtypes of bipolarity, Andrew P. Dunne, *The Life and Death of Bipolar Systems* (Manuscript).

The confusion in this position should be obvious. First, it confuses who is supposed to be objective, the observer or the observation. It is an objectively true statement that Ronald Reagan was partly motivated by anti-communism. It is also an objectively true statement that Jimmy Carter was motivated partly by Christian values and human rights. This is not to suggest that all their actions were dominated by such single-mindedness. In various actions each was also motivated by the structure of bipolarity. But the fact that these statements are objective—albeit elliptical in these illustrations—underlines that it is the responsibility of the social scientist to make the objective statements, rather than justify research strategies behind a cloak of pseudo-objectivity based on objective-subjective dichotomies.

Once human motivation is sundered from social systems, real causality is removed from the system. The social scientist is then incapable of deciding the truth and falsity of propositions. In fact, the terms of the propositions lose all meaning. Consider again the concept of certainty. If human motivation is not part of the international system level, what could "uncertainty" possibly mean?

There are three problems with most views of the relationship between certainty and system level. First, certainty about what? There is no such thing as generalized certainty or uncertainty. If it is certainty about security that is at issue, then the number of actors controls at least three different uncertainty factors. The number of alliance combinations is only one of these factors. As Arthur Lee Burns argued, the number of actors also affects momentousness (weightiness) and predictability (time urgency). For Burns, momentousness means that all of an actor's bullets are in one basket (earmarked against one opponent), and thus any miscalculations entail the most weighty consequences. Predictability of balancing is reduced because there are fewer alliance partners in the event of conflict. Therefore, decisions are more time-urgent. As numbers are reduced, the uncertainty arising from these dimensions has a tendency to increase an actor's insecurity level. The insecurity arising from these two factors is especially high in the two-actor situation. Moreover, Burns presupposed that the actors were rational, and that they could understand the system in which they were embedded.[23] That approach fundamentally differs from one that presumes that forces are causing behavior, and do so in systems that lack conscious or self-conscious actors!

THE EVOLUTION OF NONACTOR MODELS

Polarity, Offense-Defense, and Scarcity

These conceptions of a continuous international system based exclusively on the number of actors have done great damage to research agendas. Such conceptions are too far from the focal presupposition. One exchange in

---

23. Burns, "From Balance to Deterrence."

particular illustrates the damage. The exchange took place in an article by Ted Hopf, a comment by Manus Midlarsky, and a response by Hopf.[24]

Bipolarity: Hopf and Waltz. Hopf's original article argued that Waltz's polarity does not explain stability during sixteenth-century Europe. Hopf accepted Waltz's definition of polarity—based on numbers of great powers—even though he denied Waltz's hypotheses. By stability of the system he meant peace; war is the measure of instability. Instead of Waltz's hypotheses, he wished to substitute "a comprehensive definition of the offense-defense balance" in order to explain the instability in the "multipolar Europe of 1495-1521 and bipolar Europe of 1521-59." However, Hopf apparently did not consider that Waltz's definition of polarity cannot be empirically applied. As stated above, one problem with Waltz's book is that it is based largely on arbitrary, stipulated definitions rather than propositions, and thus, it cannot be tested at all.[25]

The difference between a stipulated definition and a proposition is that the latter may be judged true or false. However, it cannot be claimed that Waltz does this, because to say that a state's status as a pole is based on size is to say very little. Hopf follows this thicketed path by treating the bipolar-multipolar distinction as "defined" by the distribution of capabilities. There is, however, no formula[26] in the Waltzian system—or any other system based on aggregating unit-indices[27]—which can meaningfully adjudicate the choice of bipolarity and multipolarity. Hopf, therefore, found it necessary to employ ad hoc standards in order to decide when to call one historical period bipolar and another multipolar. These standards entailed comparisons: among the two "top" states and the total distribution of power, between these two top-dogs and the next most powerful, and between the two top-dogs and the Soviet-American system.[28]

To state that a system is bipolar must be to claim that the propositions which make it bipolar are true. However, the definitions offered by Waltz could not distinguish between the East-West bipolarity of 1952 and the fact that, in 1989,

---

24. Ted Hopf, "Polarity, the Offense-Defense Balance, War," *American Political Science Review* 85 (1991): 475-493; Manus Midlarsky and Ted Hopf, "Polarity and International Stability," *American Political Science Review*, 87 (1993): 173-180.

25. For instance, Hopf's characterization of the Europe of 1521-1559 as "bipolar" is exceedingly arbitrary. As one basic history text puts it: "There were approximately three hundred significant political entities in Germany on the eve of the Reformation." See Eugene F. Rice, Jr. and Anthony Grafton, *The Foundations of Early Modern Europe, 1460-1559*, 2nd ed. (New York: W.W. Norton, 1994), 128.

26. Waltz explicitly rejects segmentation and weighting. See *Theory of International Politics*, 131.

27. Some social scientists have been aware of the difficulty of measuring all the factors that go into the balance of power since at least the 1930s. For example, see Harold D. Lasswell, *World Politics and Personal Insecurity* (New York: Whittlesey House, 1935), chap. 3.

28. Hopf, "Polarity, the Offense-Defense Balance, and War," 480.

the Soviet Union and the United States were still the greatest military powers on earth, with a great disproportion of total military capabilities, territory, population, and resources.

A remark made in connection with Stanley Hoffmann may again be repeated: comparisons prior to the specification of explicit idealized patterns are like comparing why some doors in a house stick without understanding "square" and "plumb." There is nothing necessarily distinct about a system of many actors—two of which are disproportionately large—and one in which many equal-sized actors exist. In both cases it is consistent with the system's structure for any actor to form an alliance with any other actor. Although by no means the only consideration, it is this kind of distinguishing feature—one based on the way actors are related to each other—that separates "balance of power" from bipolar systems. Bipolar systems are characterized by long-term, collective alliance relations. They are three-musketeerish rather than bilateral.[29]

Stability. Hopf also uses a "definition" of stability that is arbitrary and only indirectly related to the international macrosystem.[30] Although it could be argued, convincingly, that increases in the frequency, duration, magnitude, and severity of war increase the instability of human lives, such a proposition has no necessary relation to the stability of a specific international system. The question which must be asked is whether the elements that constitute a particular type of international system continue to exist when disturbed—and war is one kind of disturbance. But the question cannot be answered by arbitrary definition.

Arbitrary definitions might, for example, treat increases in viruses, electoral conflict, and inflation as respective causes of instability in life, the U.S. presidency, and the U.S. economy. Clearly, those propositions miss the mark. Systems that have the capacity to overcome those disturbances are stable. Thus, the presence of an immunological subsystem in the living organism is what determines its stability, not merely the amount of viruses or even the amount of cell-destroying viral infections.

In these examples it is again presupposed that instability is a continuous variable that can be correlated one-to-one with another continuous variable, the absence of which is logically equivalent to stability. There is no evidence for such propositions in any concrete social macrosystem. Even in the macroeconomic example, the inflation rate would have to be sufficiently high that it caused changes in other parts of the economy. In hyperinflationary periods, such as Germany in the 1920s, the wealth of creditors is completely wiped out. However, during modest inflation—or deflation—economic systems exhibit no instability, though particular groups are likely to see a real change in their proportion of real income.[31]

---

29. See footnote 17.
30. Hopf uses Jack Levy's definition of stability.
31. Paul A. Samuelson, *Economics*, 11th ed. (New York: McGraw-Hill, 1980), 255-259.

To understand the problem in international politics, consider a series of hypothetical wars fought between the Soviet Union and China in a period prior to the fall of the Soviet Union. Assume that technology favored the offense because a vast array of enhanced radiation weapons had been developed, there were no other nuclear weapons, and all other states declared their neutrality. Assume further that each war is fought for a long duration, the magnitude of interpolar conflict is some constant (depending which arbitrary definition of polarity is selected, it will either be 1, .67, or .5), and assume severity (battle deaths) is twenty percent of Soviet population and fifty percent of China's population. Under these assumptions, it is at least plausible that after such a series of wars the international system would be more stable.

Though only plausible, the reasons are fairly obvious. The characteristics of enhanced radiation weapons are such that capital would not be destroyed in a catastrophic fashion. The battle death victims might include a disproportionate share of groups that each government was least dependent upon, or in fact, preferred eliminating. In the case of China, it is at least conceivable that the economy would function better at a less bloated population level. Although such a war would be extremely unstable with respect to human life, in the macro-system the postwar structural and action pattern might closely resemble the prewar period, without any loss of players and with robust economic potential for all actors.

Moreover, it cannot be argued that this is an unlikely outcome, for the question is not about outcomes or prediction. The question is about the meaning of stability, and if a case—rather than a stipulation—can be made that even very powerful indicators of war are not logically relevant to the meaning of international instability, then there is something seriously wrong at the level of theoretical concept formation rather than the empirical level.

Thus both Waltz's arbitrary definition of polarity and Levy's arbitrary definition of instability that Hopf used are incapable of illuminating the phenomena which are ostensibly within their scope.

The Offense-Defense Balance. Hopf is conceptually on somewhat firmer ground in his use of the offense-defense balance. Such a factor is clearly acceptable within the scope of the international system. He does not, however, provide adequate coding criteria for this concept, and thus his evidence is based purely on ad hoc judgments. In this context it might have been expected that Hopf would have introduced, at least as a metaphor, a discussion of the cost-exchange ratio, a concept which can be meaningfully quantified, even if the coding of the concept would have presented difficulties in his historically chosen cases.[32]

---

32. Simply stated, the cost-exchange ratio is the ratio between the cost of a defensive system and the cost to offset it. If "R" symbolizes this ratio, then R = offset cost/defense cost. If $R < 1$, offense is favored; if $R > 1$, defense is favored. See William Schneider, Jr., et al., *U.S. Strategic Nuclear Policy and Ballistic Missile Defense: The 1980s and*

A meaningful usage of offense-defense balance would tether that concept to the particular balance existing along each actor's front. Instead, Hopf presents some ethereal characterization for the "total" system. However, this is uninformative; with this formulation even if the concept were a good predictor it would be impossible to ascertain whether it was an epiphenomenal or systematic predictor.

One meaningful theoretical analysis that includes the offense-defense balance, "From Balance to Deterrence," was written in the late 1950s by Arthur Lee Burns. Unlike practitioners of the "total" characterization, Burns' approach was analytically specified. He formulated a model that incorporated each actor's specific relationships to all the other actors in the model, how their decisions were interrelated and based on a rational assessment of their long-range and short-range alternatives, how the play of a war cycle might increase the propensity to reduce the number of players, how the number of players might affect the relationship between certainty and security, and how technological changes (nuclear weapons) might transform the optimal strategy in a given system due to changes in the offense-defense (cost-exchange) ratio. But unlike common efforts to analyze "poles," Burns' system was comprised of actors who had neurological systems. Burns later made clear that the offense-defense concept is not very useful in the absence of a third axis. One also needs a measure of the absolute costs of war; otherwise the offense-defense relationship applies indifferently to systems in which the weaponry is based on cavalry and those in which it is based on nuclear weapons.[33]

Midlarsky's Comments. Midlarsky adopts a different line of argument with respect to Hopf's article. In his "Comment," Midlarsky accepts Hopf's use of historical materials, statistics, dimensions of comparison, and measures of instability. He also accepts Hopf's conclusion "concerning the absence of a relationship between polarity and stability for his time period of investigation." It seems that Midlarsky also did not consider that Waltz's polarity and Levy's instability cannot be meaningfully applied. In any case, Midlarsky wants to argue that the reason Hopf's polarity produced no observable differences in war stability is because the relationship is "contingent on a third variable . . . the scarcity of international desiderata." He further claims that his own studies support this conclusion.[34] Moreover, Hopf, in his response, sees "no obstacle

---

Beyond (Philadelphia: Institute for Foreign Policy Analysis, April 1980), 8, 23-24. It is doubtful that the offense-defense concept can be directly applied to entire international systems.

33. Arthur Lee Burns, "From Balance to Deterrence,"; idem, *Of Powers and Their Politics: A Critique of Theoretical Approaches* (Englewood Cliffs, NJ: Prentice-Hall, Inc., 1968), chap. 6.

34. Midlarsky and Hopf, "Polarity and International Stability," 173. The study to which Midlarsky referred was published previously as a chapter in his book, *The Onset of World War* (Boston: Unwin Hyman, 1988).

at all to a most productive marriage between Midlarsky's research program and my own."[35]

The previously stated problems with respect to polarity are sufficient to assure that any children resulting from such a marriage will be dysfunctional. With respect to Midlarsky's particular study a few additional problems may be noted.

The first problem is that "international desiderata" is defined too broadly. In the presentation of historical evidence Midlarsky uses this concept to capture anything that might remotely lead to "envy" among states. "Scarcity" can thus include a lack of colonial territory, domestic territory, agricultural production, religious adherents, international resources, or self-esteem by a statesman.[36]

Also, in his "Comment," Midlarsky employed other evidence to show how a period might be characterized as one of abundance, thereby framing out the opposite boundary of scarcity. Some of these included upgrades in the infrastructure, state building, increases in government revenue, increases in civic beauty, and imperial expansion. Hopf, in his "Response," states that Midlarsky's variable needs to be tightened up, which is surely an understatement.[37] And although Hopf is correct that a generalized economic growth variable for the system as a whole—or, for that matter, any other generalized variable—provides no theoretical guidance, Midlarsky's problem is deeper still. The above examples of scarcity cited from the book make it clear that Midlarsky is not focused on economic scarcity, but, rather, anything that causes envy.[38]

The problem in Midlarsky's approach to scarcity is identical to Morgenthau's approach to power. The category is so expansive that it includes anything which one can remotely call scarce. Such unbounded analytical enthusiasm is related to how Midlarsky chooses to build his models.

Modeling Outcomes. Midlarsky's work is preoccupied with the concepts of equality and war. This rarefied conceptual environment leads directly to reification, where abstract concepts such as "hierarchical equilibrium" and "international desiderata" take on a life of their own. The problem here is common to all approaches that begin their analysis with outcomes. Because an outcome can be characterized by a common label—war, peace, cooperation, stability—does not in the least imply that it is governed by equivalent axiom sets. Were this the case, then the stability of the solar system—based on Newtonian mechanics—and the stability of a baseball pitcher's ERA over time—based on discipline and training—would be identical.

Although war seems to limit analysis to a common phenomenon in a way which the solar system and baseball pitching do not, it does so in an arbitrary, misleading (overgeneralized), and insufficient (imprecise) sense. It is arbitrary in the sense that "common" cannot be determined by stipulated definitions,

35. Midlarsky and Hopf, "Polarity and International Stability," 177.
36. Midlarsky, *Onset of World War*, 52-65.
37. Midlarsky and Hopf, "Polarity and International Stability," 178.
38. Cf., Midlarsky, *Onset of World War*, 11.

especially definitions stipulated about an attribute. Thus the term "red" does not denote red things because it is stipulated as the name of things that look like fire engines and apples, but because it denotes a particular range of wavelengths in the electromagnetic spectrum. Otherwise a science of optics would be impossible. It is misleading in the sense that it implies there are general causes of general attributes when in fact, no scientist has ever found one. And it is insufficient in the sense that it does not—and cannot—distinguish among the types of social systems that are more or less likely to go to war.

Midlarsky's focus on the systemic war is a systematic example of such reification. By page three of the book he has decided that because systemic wars have been repetitive features of international life, decision-makers cannot be the decisive factor; thus, he too believes he can dispense with human beings. Instead, the "hidden features" of structure drive the system towards war. Like Waltz's "invisible" explanations of markets and balance, Midlarsky begins his analysis in the world of the occult.

This process will eventually lead to the construction of what Midlarsky calls "hierarchical equilibrium theory." He tells his readers that this scheme emerged from consideration of dispute length and the likelihood of dispute buildup. He then stipulates that a requirement for the absence of systemic wars is the "avoidance of an accumulation of serious disputes." The stipulated definition of this term is that there is an "average equality in beginnings and endings of disputes." However, Midlarsky does not make it obvious how disputes are coded. The term simply reappears in a periodic, seemingly stochastic distribution, untethered to anything meaningful.

Midlarsky has two reasons why disputes should not be permitted to accumulate. First, it is asserted that such accumulation increases the probability that more countries will become involved in the disputes, which will widen the scope of a conflict. Second, the existence of protracted disputes may serve as a model that other governments will imitate. Apparently these relationships are expected to hold regardless of the type of dispute, its intensity, the countries involved, their operational code, or their estimates of the expected value of continuing the dispute versus settling it.

Nonetheless, Midlarsky wants to reduce these disputes. So, in order to achieve an "average equality in the beginning and ending of disputes" he invokes the "hierarchical equilibrium structure."[39] He claims that this is the only structure that will meet the "minimum entropy requirements" of stable and durable coalitions. Analyzing this property of the hierarchical equilibrium structure is beyond the scope of this argument. More central is to consider how such a model could possibly be applied.

---

39. It should be noted that the structure Midlarsky builds is a very poor replica of Kaplan's loose bipolar model. It is strange that Midlarsky attributes this structure to Waltz.

Midlarsky applies this model in the same manner as he applies the concept of international desiderata—with unbounded enthusiasm. Thus without any significant analysis, the mere existence of this structure in 1962 is proposed as an explanation of why the Cuban missile crisis was settled.[40] Of course, having disposed of decision-makers on page three, Midlarsky doesn't have to consider the messy implications of these creatures on page eight. Did Khrushchev ignore Castro, his ally, because of their power differential? Could it also be because of Soviet style? How about the existence of nuclear weapons and the vast superiority which the United States enjoyed in 1962? How about the predominance of the U.S. Navy in the Caribbean Sea? Midlarsky's theory offers no guidance as to how a researcher should weigh these diverse motives feeding into dispute resolution.[41]

APPRAISING NONACTOR MODELS

It is perhaps useful to reconsider the origins of COW-like techniques. All of these studies were in general designed to eliminate human action from international models. The rationale for this, proposed in Singer's level-of-analysis article, was "parsimony." That criterion was apparently necessary because decision-making models incorporated too many variables, and therefore, a researcher would be unable to complete more than a few comparative studies in the course of a lifetime. The COW project certainly avoided this problem, since many books and articles are now available.

The reason to accumulate so many studies was to find patterns, which could then serve as the basis for causal analysis. But the patterns haven't been found. Given the general breakdown of the positivist approach, it is unlikely that they will be found through stipulated definitions applied across the entire range of international relations. The positivist program for turning all events into atomic statements has long been deemed bankrupt, in all but a few social science approaches, of which these are a dimming example.

The exclusion of decision-makers from the so-called international level-of-analysis is itself the result of an arbitrary definition of being. It assumes that the decision-maker is located somewhere in the analytical schemata of a social scientific theory. This is nothing more than an unregulated spatial metaphor. It confuses the meaning of concrete location—which is based on principles of physical conservation—with the meaning of analytical function—which is not spatial at all. Decision-makers can make decisions on the basis of information arising in any functional system. The international, national, and personality systems are merely the grossest of these possibilities. It is the task of the

---

40. Midlarsky, *Onset of World War*, 7-8.

41. For an analysis of decision-making in the Cuban Missile Crisis see Michael C. Desch, *When the Third World Matters* (Baltimore: Johns Hopkins University Press, 1993), chap. 4, especially 113.

international theorist to illuminate the logical relations in the international domain as if that were the only basis for decision, which requires well-specified international models. Then in the actual world it can be determined whether an actual decision-maker followed one theory or another and whether the decision was based on the reasons proposed in the theory. The fact that this is hard work does not justify a research program designed to avoid the problem.

PART II:

. . . And Beyond

6

Macrotheory:
Levels, Embedment, and Reason

Although all theories require perspective, not all perspectives can develop into international theory. The scientific spirit strives to control the processes of inquiry so that orderly patterns in the world may be discovered and explained. The goal of finding order is tempered by a correlative disposition that recognizes that different types of systems exhibit characteristically different orders.

In previously considered authors, there have been two tendencies. One is to conceive international relations as a study of actors' pursuits of goals or interests, which are then limited either by international mechanisms or some other factors such as international law or the environment. The weight of these arguments rests on these goals, generally conceived as spatially internal to the actors' domestic systems. Second, there have been efforts to study the stability of systems exclusively from some structural characteristics, such as the numbers of units or alliances or the distribution of capabilities. The weight of these arguments rests on factors conceived as spatially external to the actor-systems. In both approaches, the weight of argument is placed on purportedly dominant factors—conditions—either internal or external to the actors. These factors are thought to cause behavioral outcomes. Of great interest to the social scientist is that actors in these approaches are really residual entities, and their behavior is largely epiphenomenal.

MORTON A. KAPLAN

In the international theory of Morton Kaplan, this deification of conditions is not encountered. What fundamentally distinguishes Kaplan from his contemporaries, and what forms the key to understanding why his approach was so ill understood and misrepresented by both proponents and opponents, was his insight into the role of the individual in the course of historical macropolitics.

Whereas others could write of the levels-of-analysis problem with characteristic disdain for the role of the decision-maker or with characteristic inflation of the subjective in human affairs, Kaplan sought to unite the decision-maker in the manifold diversity of the macrosystem. In this context, it is best to conceive Kaplan's approach to the problem not as an effort to find the causes of international action, but to understand how the international system would function in the minds of self-conscious, rational decision-makers. In Kaplan, the term "level-of-analysis" as it is customarily used, literally has no place. It is not even clear that the term "levels" has the appropriate connotations. Instead it is essential to understand his macrosystems as one of many "sets-of-motivation" that are processed by decision-makers.

The Academic Background

Kaplan's conception was quite radical given the immediately preceding academic background of international relations. Within the social scientific tradition, the two greatest books in the field had been Quincy Wright's *A Study of War* and Harold Lasswell's *World Politics and Personal Insecurity*.[1] In their books, both writers had studied international relations from the perspective of individuated actors.

Focal Presupposition: The Individual. In Wright's book the term "levels of analysis" is indexed only once, and the entry characterizes the concept in a very simple fashion. Wright first distinguished between two kinds of studies about war: those of particular events and periods, and those of general trends and relationships. He then stated that war could be observed from "many distances" and analyzed at "many levels." There were three levels: that of the immediate observer, that of the philosopher, and that of the social scientist and historian. Wright, of course, was particularly concerned with the level occupied by social scientists and historians.

Historians and social scientists could study war from one of three perspectives: the historical, the analytical, or the practical.[2] The analytical level is of direct concern, because it is here that Wright took up the question of causality, which is the central problem which the concept of levels-of-analysis was later designed to represent and which has been assessed above in connection with Singer.

Wright treated causality from so many perspectives that it is impossible to attribute a single meaning to the term.[3] Causality was conceived differently

1. Quincy Wright, *A Study of War*, 2 vols. (Chicago: The University of Chicago Press, [1942], 1965), and Harold D. Lasswell, *World Politics and Personal Insecurity* (New York: Whittlesey House, 1935).

2. Wright, *Study of War*, 14-16.

3. Ibid., 727-739, 1284. This problem of specifying causality was partly the function of the origin of the book, which was an outgrowth of the Causes of War project at the University of Chicago. The project produced an enormous amount of research and Wright opted to present the results of this research in his voluminous book. The book

depending on whether one adopted a scientific, historical, or practical perspective. Because Wright's greatest influence was among social scientists engaged in international relations, his conception of science and causality is highly relevant.

Wright conceived of science as a search for "timeless" propositions: "Science strives for generalizations which accord not only with the observations upon which they were based but also with all future and past observations unknown at the time the generalization was made."[4]

Although this statement is not wrong, in contemporary parlance one would state that the ideal of the exact sciences is to formulate covering laws.[5] The basic problem Wright faced is that he could not conceive what it would mean to have timeless propositions about human warfare: every particular war is different; all the conditions that lead to war are changeable; variables cannot be isolated from historical and practical aspects of causal processes.

In dealing with social activity, historic time can never be entirely eliminated as an unmeasurable factor, cause-and-effect relations cannot be entirely separated from means and end relations, constants cannot easily be divided into disciplines within which specialized methods may be emphasized. The presence of contingency, of purpose, of universal change, and of universal interrelatedness . . . renders the application of scientific method to human and social problems exceptionally difficult and frequently unproductive.[6]

But what would a cause be in such a case? To determine a cause of war, Wright thought it would be necessary to investigate possible changes in the meaning of the concepts by which war was defined. There were as many meanings as perspectives, but among "scientifically minded" individuals, war had been attributed to one of four individuated entities: the government, the state, the nation, or the population.[7]

---

is in many ways a detailed, annotated bibliography of the history of ideas about war. But the problem is also the result of the book's "subject matter." Wright is trying to understand a general phenomenon—war—which is a property of a system, not a subject. To investigate a property, however, requires the specification of a particular type of system, or one runs the risk of reifying.

4. Ibid., 681.

5. See in chap. 2 the treatment of covering laws as applied to the principles of Hans Morgenthau.

6. Wright, *Study of War*, 683.

7. Ibid., 720, 19, and chaps. XX, XXIII, XXVI, XXX. The respective causes of war for each entity were the unmeasurabilty of political and military forces in interstate relations; the lack of effective sanctions to maintain international law as a standard to regulate state interests; the need nations felt to identify themselves as an exclusive group; and the difficulty of making "peace" a more important symbol in world public opinion than symbols that favor "war." See also 733.

Both in his formulation of levels of analysis—observers, philosophers, and social scientists—and of the different well springs of causality, Wright remained tethered to the notion of an individuated actor with a particular perspective. But Wright could not reconcile this attachment to human diversity with his notion of science, which he viewed as timeless and general.

General Causes and Manipulation. Prior to his departure to Yale, one of Wright's colleagues at The University of Chicago was Harold Lasswell. Lasswell's heavy emphasis on psychology was undoubtedly a strong influence on Wright, particularly Lasswell's psychological conception of change: "A more active attitude toward the rearranging of reality is taken up when the emphasis is upon ways and means of obtaining transformations in the familiar patterns of reality. By casting analysis in manipulative form, and specifying the "principles" of management, new possibilities frequently come to the attention of the thinker."[8]

This statement about rearranging reality may be compared to Wright's notion of causality as a scientific concept. Wright conceived the general causes of change in a variable to be changes in another variable: "In the scientific sense the cause of the changes in any variable is a change in any other variable in a proposition stating the relations of all the factors in a process of equilibrium."[9] In Wright's view this conception of causality led scientists to have particular conceptual preferences. And Lasswell's influence is imminent in the argument: "They prefer concepts which denote things which can be manipulated and experimented with, though this is often difficult in the social sciences."[10]

When combined with the strong emotional revulsion that war evokes, these presuppositions lead the social scientist onto shaky ground. If scientists seek timeless propositions and prefer to manipulate variables, and if the analysis of war is processed through a scientific perspective, then there is a two-step process to eliminate the causes of war. The first step was purportedly necessary if social scientists were to avoid intellectual isolation: "The social scientist, seeking to retain contacts with both the practical and theoretical workers, centers attention upon the isolation of measurable or at least recognizable factors, useful for predicting or capable of manipulation for controlling the future."[11]

---

8. Harold D. Lasswell, *World Politics and Personal Insecurity* (New York: Whittlesey House, 1935), 5. Lasswell's career began with a psychological emphasis. His earliest work analyzed the role of mass persuasion during World War I. See his *Propaganda Technique in the World War* (New York: Alfred A. Knopf, 1927). He later went on to employ Freudian methods in the analysis of political personality structures. See his *Psychopathology and Politics* (Chicago: The University of Chicago Press, 1930).

9. Wright, *Study of War*, 728-729.

10. Ibid., 732.

11. Ibid., 16. Practical workers—journalists, diplomats, military thinkers, and historians—conceived causes according to the particular motives and purposes existing in their individual situations. Theoretical workers—by which Wright meant philosophers and theologians—conceived causes from a level "so thoroughly outside the immediate

The second step was purportedly necessary because the causes of war were the product of diverse individuated perspectives: "Fictions, while necessary in the natural sciences, are the essence of the social sciences. The social scientist must create a structure of assumptions and use a language which is at the same time symbolic and emotive. Unless he can establish his assumptions by successful propaganda, it is hardly worth while to make hypotheses or to investigate their validity."[12]
And from this standpoint, unpredictability was an opportunity to be exploited.

While it would be difficult enough to predict the future occurrence of war if the criteria for deciding what war is were constant, the solution becomes indeterminate when these criteria are changing. . . . This very changeability of the criteria, however, makes war even more controllable. The problem can be attacked from two sides: by changing the facts which have been called war and by changing the concepts which required that certain facts be called war.[13]

To make war a function of what things are called entails a very heavy dose of nominalism. Perhaps this was a characteristic view of the twentieth century, the first real Age of Anxiety. And again, note the imminence of Lasswell's psychological presuppositions in Wright's position.

Lasswell's approach was focused on the political psychology of actors, who were conceived either as individuals or a distribution of individuals in a nation. The world was focused into symbols associated in mental configurations. Most humans identify, either positively or negatively, with symbols closely tied to economy and place. Symbols such as "American," "urban-dweller," "labor," and "management" are evocative symbols. From this presupposition it followed that changing the symbols of mass society was equivalent to changing the distribution of values in mass society. And these latter changes are tantamount to changing the international system. If, for example, the loyalties of individuals—especially elites—throughout industrial societies could be transformed from "nation" to "class" concepts, such as a devoted Marxist would hope, then a new dominant social system would come to replace the nation-state as it has historically existed.[14]

The ideas of Wright and Lasswell represented a long succession of ideas that began in the 1600s—not too long after the Peace of Westphalia—with the rise of modern science and its attendant conception of individuated bodies in motion. But even as they wrote, these ideas were undergoing eclipse as a result of

---

situations in which war and peace recur that they can seldom give advice . . ." According to Wright, theoretical workers focused on the fundamental values of society towards good and evil. See also 14-16, 734-738.

12. Ibid., 683.
13. Ibid., 719.
14. Lasswell, *World Politics and Personal Insecurity*, 7, 29-51.

relativity theory and quantum mechanics. Individuated entities and causal connections were soon only parts of our scientific knowledge.

Wright and Lasswell were committed to science as science. But the hallmark of science is perhaps captured in Peirce's principle of fallibilism—that knowledge is always subject to revision. The incongruities between their individuated conceptions and the focal presupposition are fundamental.

In terms of the focal presupposition, the individuated approach to international politics commits three major errors: the fallacy of misplaced concreteness, the fallacy of simple succession, and the suppression of macrosystem objectivity.

The individuated approach implies the political variant of what Whitehead claimed was wrong with seventeenth century science: the fallacy of misplaced concreteness. Whitehead has argued that this fallacy derives from the conception that individual bodies can be described on the basis of simple location.[15] The political variant, mentioned in various parts of this book, is to conceive of decision-makers as occupying a fixed location, usually a national one. To be sure, individuals make decisions—political or otherwise—on the basis of the information they have. Their physical location and primary group relations are certainly major parameters determining the processing of that information. But to turn location into fixed individual information, to render it the only decision-making reality, is to take an abstract concept—individuality—and think of it as a concrete entity. But no individual is purely individuated. To presuppose that individual human beings, or individual states, are atomic building blocks out of which all social or international phenomena are aggregated is to embrace a standpoint that is as unnatural as it is hostile to understanding the relationships which form the order of any system.

The fallacy of misplaced concreteness leads to what might be characterized as the second fallacy, in which causality—and hence explanation—are conceived as simple succession. When coupled with the notion of timeless truths, it was this fallacy which led Wright into nominalism and the manipulation of fictions. If one thinks of individual decision-makers as simply located, and thinks that their behavior simply follows from their beliefs in a simple cause-and-effect sequence, then all individual decision-makers are subject to the same causal laws. And if that is the case, then the way to "cause" peace is to manipulate symbols until a change in behavior comes about.

Theories in the exact sciences, however, are in no simple sense timeless or based on simple causal succession.[16] Scientific theories are conditional, the first condition being the homogeneity of the class of systems to which the universal propositions are meant to apply. Thus Newton's "universal" laws of motion and gravity do not apply to the motion of electrons around an atom or the motion of light around a planet. Given the specification of boundary conditions, a theory

15. Alfred North Whitehead, *Science and the Modern World: Lowell Lectures, 1925* (New York: The Macmillan Co., 1925), 49-58.
16. An analysis of causality and conditions appears in Appendix B.

or law applies across time and space if, and only if, the same subject matter is under investigation. War or social identity—like motion—are not subjects at all but properties of particular systems. Similarly, individual decision-makers manifest different mind-sets depending on the social and international systems in which they are embedded. They are not decision-makers at all except with respect to the particular role function(s) they embody. When treated as a summation of individuals, however, the international system concept loses all meaning, just as adding up individual identities in a family does not make a family. One must start with the family. Conflict—a property—will manifest and be intelligible in radically different ways depending on whether the "family" is the Charles Manson family or the Cleaver family of which "Beaver" was part.

Despite the aspiration of Lasswell and Wright to conceive of the total system, individuated reasoning created enormous intellectual difficulties. It became impossible to conceive of anything whole, because one must instead rely on the aggregation of units to achieve a "whole." However, because not all agree on any particular symbol, the whole is always a fraction. The entire conception is, of course, mechanical, an outgrowth of Newtonian science.

Finally, a small sacrifice was necessary—and has remained necessary—to apply these presuppositions to international politics. Social scientists were required to unfetter themselves from any conception of truth. What instead becomes important are causes which, ultimately individuated, require appropriate manipulation. Thus, the objective features of a system are suppressed, international politics becomes a field without real relationships, and decision-makers abandoned on instrumental grounds are later denied a hearing on ideological principles. But this is a small price to pay to achieve noble purposes—sort of like eliminating oxygen to prevent fires.

Little wonder that few have crossed the brink that separates international relations from a theory of international politics. When a sense of wonder and curiosity about the external world is abandoned in the service of social utility, when science and scholarship attain status only through a capacity to affect public policy, and when the goal of social science becomes the manipulation of public opinion, then serious scholarship is an endangered species and the social sciences become merely another myth. Whether such a "science" serves as a myth of the state or as a myth of the enemies of the state is—from the standpoint of rational discourse—a trivial characteristic only.

The Embedded Decision-Maker

In this context, Kaplan offered a different approach to the understanding of international politics. Four major differences distinguish Kaplan's approach from the predominant presuppositions in international relations. First, the presupposed focus was that the relevant actors were decision-makers who were embedded in an international system of relations. Second, it was presupposed that these relations are structured and that strategic action is a function of the particular structure in which the actors are embedded. Third, it was presupposed that a theory had to state explicitly the actions that were optimal for the specific system of relations in which the actors were embedded. Finally, the confirmation of theory in historical cases depended on whether the specific actions of real actors was motivated by that strategic structure, rather than psychological or domestic motives—for that alone would provide an explanation rather than a mere description.

However, it was so inconceivable for students of international relations to conceive of decision-makers in any way other than psychological atomism, that they could never really understand the book. And this predisposition to atomize was augmented by a naive and dogmatic attachment to empiricism and nominalism.

Naive empiricism and nominalism were used to vindicate the use of stipulated, arbitrary definitions. Psychological atomism was used to describe the location of the statesman. When Kaplan introduced the macrosystem into discourse, the only way to save these dogmas was to eliminate the decision-maker from the international macrosystem. Unlike Wright's attempt to manipulate decision-makers, what Singer and Waltz did with their levels was to capture decision-makers, to kidnap them and tuck them away in a realm where they believed they could be effectively controlled—inside the domestic political system. Here they would cause no harm in the international system by doing anything "rational"—a treasonable offense—but would merely represent a national or subnational interest.

Kaplan's approach to the problems left over from seventeenth century science guaranteed at once an original approach and one which would be incomprehensible to all those steeped in the former dogma. Whereas all his predecessors and most of his contemporaries were focused on the spatio-temporal location of the decision-maker, Kaplan's actors were minds that were conscious of the systems in which they were embedded. His systems were not outcomes of random aggregations—whatever that might mean; they were theory sketches of the rational mind engaged deeply in a specific, bounded realm, a realm marked off from other realms in order to understand the logic and character inherent in the structure of relevant relations.

The Legend of Billy Dee. Consider a simple illustration of these differences in approach. Billy Dee is sixteen years old, somewhat insecure, and lives in an inner-city ghetto. Two gangs, the Reds and the Blues, each control thirty percent of neighborhood territory. Billy Dee lives in the forty percent remainder. In his daily routine, Billy Dee never wears blue or red clothing, avoids making any signals that could be identified with one of the gangs, avoids certain locations that are disputed territory, and so forth.

One day Billy Dee learns that the Reds have claimed his city block as part of their turf, and almost certainly have the capabilities to maintain their prize. He also knows that Blue will contest this move. Moreover, he knows with a very high degree of probability that neither gang is likely to recognize his neutrality. Billy Dee joins Red.

A few months later Billy Dee's mother, Annie Mae, earns a promotion, and she and Billy Dee move to a modest but comparatively secure suburb. There are no gangs, and Billy Dee goes to the local park regularly. Annie Mae tells him that in the new environment he will not be accepted socially unless he learns to cooperate with his peers. There are a fairly large number of peers, but Billy Dee tends to associate with a group that ranges from five to seven in number. Boys will be boys and there are arguments, jealousies, rivalry for girls and esteem, and so forth. Billy Dee, however, seldom takes the same side in these disputes. In fact, he becomes the leader of the group because he generally accommodates himself to diverse positions, often switching allies from day to day. He usually does not take the side of a subgroup that is exerting dominance over the other members.

From an atomistic perspective, a number of explanations may be offered to explain Billy Dee's behavior. Billy Dee is insecure and seeks security. Thus, he does not take a firm stand on issues, always acting out of expediency. In fact, his behavior is consistent with this principle throughout his history. He didn't join a gang until he had to, and as soon as it was in his interest, he joined Red. A variant of this explanation would add that Billy's insecurity is not merely consistent with, but is a function of his changing history. This school would of course recognize that Billy Dee is insecure. But when he moved to the secure suburb—when his history changed—his interests changed. The institutional setting provided by the park and the suburb, and Annie Mae's invocation of suburban values, constitute a regime in which cooperation is possible.

However, a macrosystem theorist must offer a fundamentally different explanation. That is what Kaplan's international system models were designed to do. A macroexplanation of Billy Dee's behavior would hold that his actions are strategic, and attempt to optimize his values in the context of the macro-system of values in which he is embedded. It may be added, parenthetically for the moment, that Billy Dee plays a different role in each system.

The three systems which Billy Dee lived in might, with some poetic license, be called a loose bipolar, tight bipolar, and "balance of power" system. When he lived in the no-man's land of loose bipolarity, he acted as a neutral. The rule was to subordinate the interests of both gangs to his interest in keeping his area neutral. When Red conquered Billy's block, starkly reducing the probability of maintaining neutrality, Billy joined Red. The rule for someone seeking to optimize from this position of weakness was to identify (integrate) his interests with those of Red. When Billy moved to the suburbs, where the system was a function of shifting alliances, the rule was to keep open his options with all the members of the group.

Thus, macroexplanations of Billy Dee's behavior are strategic, not descriptive. Changes in Billy's situation account for changes in his strategic actions—that is, *if* Billy Dee's strategy is motivated by macroconsiderations.

In each of the three explanatory accounts—insecurity, changing history, macrosystemic—nothing more than a different descriptive interpretation has yet been offered. Each of these interpretations is forged from a different perspective: constant interests, changing interests, macrostrategic. Throughout the book it has been argued that the use of principles and frameworks can grasp only such an historiographical standard. If this is where the macrosystemic approach ended, it would constitute merely another historiographical standard, a different way to select facts in the creative exposition of a story or characterization of events.

The objective, however, was to explicitly state hypotheses of optimal behavior, for specific types of international structures. If an international actor would be motivated to optimize in a specific international system, how would the actor behave? As in economic theory, an answer to this conditional question is impossible unless one presupposes the analogues of economic rationality and market structure: namely, international rationality and a particular international structure.

Rationality assumptions are necessary to reach conclusions in all social theory, but what prevents them from becoming arbitrary, like the assumptions of Hobbes and Rousseau about the state of nature, is to state the particular concrete system in which actors are embedded. The particular system can, of course, be a possible system as well as a concrete system, but it should be a potentially possible system.

Different systems constitute different systems of value. In the absence of a system of values, it is impossible to confirm propositions. Billy Dee could have been motivated by any number of value systems, not merely the macrosystem. He may just as well have acted for atomistic reasons as for macroreasons. The answer to that question is what determines if the theory applies to Billy Dee's changing history. Perhaps Billy Dee was not optimizing. Perhaps he was so fearful of making any decision that all of his decisions were actually ad hoc adjustments to circumstances. Perhaps Billy Dee had an idiosyncratic need to be dominated, and under loose bipolarity he couldn't choose which gang he wanted to be dominated by. In tight bipolarity the decision was made for him, and when he went to the suburbs he was dominated by Annie Mae's advice about cooperation and drifted back and forth from one group to the other depending on which subgroup was dominant at various times (the opposite pattern from the original specification that he always joined the nondominant group). In such a case the macrotheory would not apply. This, however, is an empirical question, not a theoretical one, and one needs the theory to illuminate the problem. The very meaning of self-interest changes depending on whether Billy Dee is motivated to optimize based on a theory of his external relations or optimize based on his need to be dominated. "Self-interest" is merely a label unless it is bounded by the particular system in terms of which it is judged.

In the above formulation, the legend of Billy Dee implicitly includes each of the basic standards: the explanation uses the macrotheoretical relationships among the actors as the focal presupposition; the account is—at least in principle—partly deductive; there are three distinct types of systems (initial conditions) specified in terms of theoretical variables; those variables, such as the number of actors, their role function, their capabilities, and information factors have been described in terms of coding criteria (implicit in the illustration); the criteria for verification are based on the actor: Billy Dee's motivation to act is based on the macrosystem or his psychological needs; Billy Dee's motivated choices indicate which system of values are being maintained; and the implication that there is a pattern of action in each type of system incorporates a temporal standard rather than a timeless one. Although this legend is merely illustrative of Kaplan's theory sketches, the models of the international system which he developed employ these standards as well.

Reason in Theory and Action

If the general spirit of Kaplan's systems can be discerned from this legend and from the concept of the embedded decision-maker, the deeper structures of his theory cannot. These structures cannot be grasped in metaphor alone but must include a more detailed language, one which is specific enough to assess the truth of propositions.

That language, however, was shaped by the problem that the theory was designed to address. *System and Process* was written during the mid-1950s in reaction to the alliance policy of the Eisenhower Administration. As Secretary of State Dulles made an effort to expand the system of alliances to which the United States was committed, Kaplan began to formulate a theory of how differently structured systems of international politics would exhibit characteristically different patterns of action. The problem is analogous to other problems in the social sciences, such as how different market systems (free, oligopolistic, monopolistic) lead to different supply and demand equilibria, or how different social structures (extended or nuclear families) lead to different norms and child-rearing practices.

All such social scientific theories are dependent on some conception of rationality, but each is dependent on a specific system of values towards which one is supposed to be rational. The relationship of reason to theory and action is the beach upon which most shipwrecks occur in the social sciences. If the rudder of reason is misunderstood in theory, it becomes impossible to understand how to set course across the turbulent intellectual currents of the future; and if it is misunderstood when applied to historical actions, it becomes impossible to assess whether the captain was simply overwhelmed, lucky, or skillful in the navigational outcome of which he was part. In all of the previously considered works, it is the failure to understand the proper relationships of reason to theory and action that lead to the shipwrecks which result, though the immediate causes are captured in failures of the basic standards. But reason is the master standard.

It is a natural habit of the human mind to generalize. And to orient themselves, most people seek an ultimate orientation. In the twentieth century that orientation has often been considered historically. For Marxists, history moves toward the Classless Society; for Christians, it moves toward the Second Coming; for liberals, it moves toward Civil Society; for so-called institutionalists, it moves toward the Cooperative Outcome, and for so-called realists, it moves in recurring cycles of clashing interests. There is, however, no evidence for any of these positions: history is written, it doesn't move at all.[17]

Kaplan's position differed from these in that he maintained a deep faith in reason, without necessarily expecting to find it in the world of action. In this view, all systems have potential for good and bad, stable and unstable, equilibrial and disequilibrial, or progressive and regressive patterns. It is the task of the theorist to explain what leads to one type of pattern or the other. That task entails explaining how and why the internationally rational actor would act in a particular system structure, how and why the other actors would act if deviant or stupid actors were present, how that system structure would transform if the deviant actor could not be controlled. It is the task of the historical researcher to determine whether an actual system is consistent with a particular system structure, and if so, whether the action pattern is equilibrial or disequilibrial and, if so, whether the actors behaved according to the reasons proposed in the theory.

Thus, international rationality functions differently in theory and action. In theory, rationality is a presupposition necessary to determine optimal behavior. In the assessment of historical action, it is a proposition that must be supported with evidence. The former function is scientific in the formal and deductive sense, the latter in the experimental and case-study sense.

It is impossible to analyze things without holding the vastness of the universe constant while allowing a very small number of things to change. A theory of human health must operate within some broad boundaries that are constant: an environment that is not hopelessly irradiated by nuclear war, an earth that remains on a stable orbital trajectory, the nonexistence of a viral strain that cannot be defeated by immunological or pharmaceutical systems. Given these boundaries, one can start to examine variations in diet, or exercise, or stress to determine human health.

However, writers in the field of international relations—and the tobacco industry—often write as if a change in the boundary conditions constitutes a weakening of a theory. This is akin to the common sense view that because John Smith was flattened by a speeding truck, it just goes to show that all that theory stuff about smoking doesn't explain anything. And just as a theory about smoking cannot predict either the actual behavior of John Smith or the actual reasons for his health or lack thereof, a theory of the international system cannot predict that statesmen will follow it, or the actual reasons that a particular international system remained stable or unstable. No particular event can overturn a theory. This is true in the exact sciences as well. How then is it ever possible to confirm a theory of international politics?

Kaplan's research agenda entailed two lines of research that may be pursued in the confirmation of a theory, depending on whether the theory is treated as basic or applied to historical action. A truncated version of his position may

17. See Willard Hutcheon, "Reason in History and its Rationale," in Martin Tamny and K. D. Irani, eds., *Rationality in Thought and Action* (New York: Greenwood Press, 1986).

guide the reader through the following two chapters: the ideal of basic theory would constitute a deductive and deterministic model. In this sense, confirmation of a theory is tied to its internal logical consistency. If the ideal could be achieved in the latter, it would find historical cases—natural experiments—which resemble the initial conditions of a theoretical model and assess whether decision-makers acted in accordance with the theoretical hypotheses and were motivated by the macrostrategic system or some other system of values. If they were not so motivated, then the focus of inquiry is more likely to shift to questions of stability and transformation.

In the following chapter, the use of theory in concrete historical inquiry is explored, followed in chapter 8 by explorations of Kaplan's basic theoretical language and deterministic computer modeling. In particular some problems in Kaplan's usage of theoretical language are uncovered. The chapter resolves these problems by stating a set of formal protocols that make less ambiguous the concepts of equilibrium, stability, and transformation in terms of the logical relations among action, structure, and regime characteristics.

7

Applied International Macrotheory

This chapter analyzes the concrete applicability of the "balance of power" and loose bipolar types of systems. It also analyzes the unit-veto system. There are three analytical foci—sets of initial conditions—to Kaplan's models: an action pattern, an international political structure, and the regime characteristics of the international actors. Employed as analogs in the previous chapter were Billy Dee's action pattern, the structure of the group and gang relations in which he was embedded, and his psychological characteristics. Billy was a part of systems classified as "balance of power" and loose bipolar types. Although similar terms have been used by others, Kaplan reserves the term "balance of power" for a particular type of system, "bipolar" for a different type. To indicate its special meaning, Kaplan's conception of "balance of power" is bounded by quotation marks. Thus, unlike traditional approaches, these systems are not necessarily conceived as derivatives of a single axiom set. This entails the construction of different theory sketches for different international systems. Such a research project rejects the fundamental tenets of general systems theory. This innovation becomes further pronounced when we consider the unit-veto system.

The analysis of political types is a standard of maturity in much of science. It is, for example, basic to comparative politics, psychology, biology, and ethology. Although it is also the basis for much of physics, the success of physics has in part obscured this message. That success was already profound when the modern state system was still in its infancy.

I first discuss the relationship between Newtonian conceptions of physics and traditional conceptions of international relations. Newton's success established what seemed to be a universal metaphysics. The traditional approach was strongly influenced by those conceptions, despite the fact that traditionalists have often defined their work in opposition to science. The discussion of Newton sets the context for a presentation of Kaplan's comparative models, which are not

Newtonian-like. I then analyze how Kaplan's "balance of power" system[1] has been modeled and applied in comparative case studies, analyze the applicability of his loose bipolar system, and then briefly present the unit-veto system to show the onerous requirements for its stability.

MONOTYPICAL INTERNATIONAL RELATIONS

As previous chapters have indicated, most writers employ a monotypical conception of international relations. Many do believe that there are different types of outcomes (stable and revolutionary), or different subtypes of a balance of power system (bipolar and multipolar). But those writers believe that these variations occur within a single type of system. In broad terms, this monotypical conception of international relations is a system of sovereign, independent states. That formulation presupposes the problem of explaining political order on the basis of individuated entities. From this individuated presupposition, writers have attempted to explain the theoretical problems of war and peace, stability and instability, or political order and change in general.

This presupposition of analyzing individuated entities is so dominant that it is seldom examined. It is a product of the early history of international relations, beginning in the sixteenth century, and extending through the rise and coagulation of the modern state system. Despite the many differences among students of international relations, the individuated conception of political analysis, which violates the focal presupposition, is shared virtually by all. One of the significant reasons for these conceptions was the success of Newtonian physics.

Isaac Newton was born in 1642, shortly before the Peace of Westphalia. By 1700, Newton's science was being disseminated in tandem with the early development of the modern state system. Newton's influence among educated elites throughout Europe was enormous. It has become a major part of our

---

1. In the comparative analysis of Kaplan's "balance of power" model, I have used the basic data, framework, and most of the arguments presented in the original studies of the Italian city-state and Chinese warlord systems. I have added some basic factual details—names, dates, geographical, demographical, and historical—that clarify the presentation. Most of these details have been added in the Italian case. But the order of presentation has been adjusted, the arguments fine-tuned, and the general form of the arguments clarified. The more consistent use of the regime, structural, and action categories should prepare the reader for the formal protocols presented in the following chapter. These studies also set the context for the application of the theory to European state system. I re-present Kaplan's argument that the "balance of power" model is not disconfirmed in post-1870 European international politics. In fact, I think somewhat stronger claims can be made for the model as applied to this period. The departures of the actual from the theoretical initial conditions lead to departures from the essential rules that are consistent with the logic of the theory as well as with the other comparative studies. In my judgment, that consistency seems unlikely on the basis of chance and should therefore be treated as partial corroboration of the theory.

political inheritance. Most conceptions of causality, levels-of-analysis, and balance of power are framed in popularized variants of Newtonian language. Two of Newton's contributions are of particular note in this regard: the laws of motion, and the theory of gravity. Newton's thought divided over the question of the realism of these laws.[2]

Newton believed that the principle of inertia was a "real" cause of motion and rest. Inertia was conceived as a universal force inherent in the nature of physical bodies. This inherent quality is what made inertia real. Newton also presupposed that it was necessary to "deduce" generalizations from the phenomena—that is, from the independent bodies in motion. The resemblance to the traditional approach to international politics is obvious. The political analogues of these physical bodies have become states, and the analogue of inertia—the *principium politica*—interests.

On the other hand, Newton did not believe he had established his laws of gravity as a real cause. Unable to conceive a physical mechanism to explain the force of gravity Newton had to settle for a mathematical or formal relationship to describe a planet's acceleration about the sun. In international politics, the analogue of gravity has been the balance of power concept. Most of those who have attempted an explanation of this concept have proposed one of two causes of the balance of power. Either some hidden hand causes balance to result from the independent bodies in motion, or some form of consciousness is necessary, perhaps a self-conscious balancer.[3]

If one adopts the consciousness conception, only a short step is necessary to argue that a (completely) different kind of consciousness will lead to a (completely) different kind of system. In extreme form, this leads to utopianism. In more reasonable versions, it implies the analysis of institutions, regimes, intersubjective meaning, and cooperation theory. In one way or another, these latter ideas presuppose the necessity of conscious actors.[4]

---

2. An excellent introduction to Newton's thought is John Herman Randall, *The Career of Philosophy* (New York: Columbia University Press, 1962), vol. I: 563-594. Randall mentions that by 1789 over seventy-three popularizations of Newton's *Principia* had been published, including Count Alogrotti's *Newtonianism for Ladies*. Ibid., 571.

3. Morgenthau, for example, never resolved this problem, on the one hand denying that motives are relevant, on the other, talking about the objectives of the balancer. See *Politics Among Nations: The Struggle for Power and Peace*, 3rd ed., (New York: Alfred A. Knopf, 1963), compare 167 and 194. It was these kinds of contradictions that were reviewed in Robert Tucker, "Professor Morgenthau's Theory of Political Realism," *American Political Science Review* 46 (1952): 214-224. Morgenthau dismissed Tucker without answering him in "Another Great 'Debate': The National Interest of the United States," *American Political Science Review* 46 (1952): 962n.

4. See Stephen D. Krasner, ed., *International Regimes* (Ithaca: Cornell University Press, 1983), particularly John Gerard Ruggie, "International Regimes, Transactions, and Change: Embedded Liberalism in the Postwar Economic Order," 195-231; and Robert Jervis, "Security Regimes," 173-194. Jervis' distinction between a regime (e.g., The

It is this search for the cause of the balance of power—or other international outcomes—that sets up our modern levels-of-analysis problem. Singer's approach, as well as Waltz's, located causes in either systemic or subsystemic levels.[5] The latter was arbitrarily defined as the decision-making level —presumably to avoid the difficulties of "onerous empiricism." The systemic level was defined in terms of interactions, which in effect meant aggregate outcomes. Debates in international relations often reduce to this question of whether the actors and their motives matter, or whether they do not. Recent efforts to resolve the agent-structure problem are an outgrowth of this Newtonian-like division that identifies states as bodies in motion. The prognosis however, is not good: the Newtonianism is still rampant. In all approaches that adopt this framework, the very notion of causes draws the analyst to the state as cause.[6]

As a result of these ideas there have been two dominant ideas of the balance of power. These ideas have been covered in earlier chapters. One idea is the automatic conception of balance. This conception presupposes that any system comprised of independent actors will tend towards balance. This conception is often linked, explicitly or implicitly, with the quaint notion of a hidden hand. Each actor's struggle to maximize self-interest results in a balance or a stability among them. The actors need not be conscious of the macrosystem in which they are embedded, and need not take into account the implications which their actions or inactions will have on the macrosystem. Thus motives, rationality,

---

Concert of Europe) and a balance of power system hinges precisely on the distinction between consciousness versus hidden hand explanations. See also Jervis' "From Balance to Concert" *World Politics* 38 (October 1985): 58-79, and "Systems Theories and Diplomatic History," in Paul Gordon Lauren, ed., *Diplomacy* (New York: The Free Press, 1979), 183-211. Conceptions based on "constructivism" are similar but aspire to incorporate practices as necessary concepts in explanation. See Rey Koslowski and Friedrich Kratochwil, "Understanding Change in International Politics," *International Organization* 48 (spring 1994): 215-47, and Alexander Wendt, "Anarchy is What States Make of It: The Social Construction of Power Politics," *International Organization* 46 (spring 1992). But these approaches still offer at most a framework. Moreover, in the light of relativity theory it is extremely difficult to comprehend intersubjective meaning unless the actors have a second-order frame of reference and a logical language. Only in the context of an objective world can scientific meaning be communicated.

5. J. David Singer, "The Level-of-Analysis Problem in International Relations," in Klauss Knorr and Sidney Verba, eds., *The International System* (Princeton: Princeton University Press, 1961); Kenneth N. Waltz, *Man, the State, and War: A Theoretical Analysis* (New York: Columbia University Press, 1959).

6. For example, Alexander Wendt states: "In effect I am suggesting for rhetorical purposes that the raw material out of which members of the state system are constituted is created by domestic society before states enter the constitutive process of international society . . ." See footnote 4, 402n. On the same page Wendt explicitly employs state-of-nature reasoning.

ideology, and other regime characteristics of international actors can be dismissed, because all decisions are a function of the self-assertion of self-interest. This is the most traditional conception of the balancing process. It is prominent in Waltz and Morgenthau, though no writer in international relations maintains this conception consistently. Morgenthau, it will be remembered, also has a balancer, a role that certainly entails consciousness.[7]

The second view entails a self-conscious conception of balancing.[8] There tend to be stronger and weaker variants of this theme. In the weaker version, at least some actors must believe that the maintenance of the macrosystem is a desirable objective. When they observe the system tending toward imbalance—because an actor is getting too powerful, for example—these status quo actors, (perhaps a self-conscious balancer such as Great Britain during the nineteenth century) must intelligently assess the situation and make adjustments to maintain the system.

The stronger variant requires that all actors share the values of balance. In this idea of balance, the actors must believe that self-restraint is necessary to maintain the international system. This conception is present among some historical sociologists, Robert Jervis' conception of security regimes, and various conceptions of constructivism and intersubjectivism.[9]

Consider the concept of motherhood in analogous terms. The automatic conception of balance would be akin to an instinctual conception of motherhood. All biological mothers will automatically produce good children. The consciousness conception would presuppose that the mother must have the proper ideas about good children. She would have to believe, for example, that violence and selfishness were bad values to instill in children. And the more mothers that have the proper ideas, the more good children that will be produced.

What both the automatic and consciousness conceptions of balance lack are the specific procedures or mechanisms necessary to maintain the balance (equilibrium). Without those procedures the concept of balance remains metaphorical. Kaplan's conception of an international system includes specific procedures. Those procedures—essential rules—are a central feature of his models. And those procedures are a fundamental reason for classifying his theory sketches as beyond the brink of international theory. Were Kaplan to formulate a conception of motherhood akin to his conception of the international system, Kaplan's "mother" would, for example, have to employ specific kinds of regulatory procedures to produce—or reproduce—the social system. Thus the ideal

---

7. See footnote 3 and chap. 2.

8. These two conceptions of balance conform to the seventh and eighth "verbal applications" of Ernst Haas, "The Balance of Power: Description, Prescription, or Propaganda," *World Politics* 5 (1953): 442-477. Haas' other conceptions are historically interesting but theoretically limited for a theory of international politics.

9. On historical sociologists see chap. 3; on psychological and constructivist conceptions see footnotes 4 and 6, this chapter. For a logically rigorous realization model that subsumes the weaker version, see the computer model in the following chapter.

conception of any social equilibrium entails self-conscious procedures, not merely consciousness.[10]

The previous chapter illustrated some of the major differences between this kind of macrosystemic approach and traditional approaches to international relations. There are two presuppositions that require emphasis. First, the macrotheorist focuses on the political relationships among the international actors, and presupposes that actors attempt to optimize their values in the context of the relationships in which they are embedded. It is more than plausible that differences in the number of actors, differences in their role functions, differences in the distribution of capabilities, and differences in informational transparency will crystallize into different types of systems that entail different maintenance procedures (basic theory). Second, the ideal of macrotheoretical analysis is to uncover those necessary procedures (rules, action patterns) that maintain the particular macrostructure under scrutiny. The specification of a particular type of macrosystem and particular strategies for system maintenance constitute a basic theory of international politics.

COMPARATIVE CASE STUDIES

The comparative analysis of international systems requires careful attention to the theoretical specification and empirical identification of a model's initial conditions. To explicate the meaning of this method, I focus first on Kaplan's "balance of power" model. This model is the most well-developed and carefully researched international system. I present the initial conditions of the model and then some historical cases that the model has been used to explain. I then analyze the applicability of his loose bipolar model. Finally, I briefly describe the characteristics of the unit-veto system.

"BALANCE OF POWER" SYSTEM

The balance of power idea can be used precisely if it is specified with reference to a particular type of system. The basic balance of power action pattern is one of short-term, instrumentally motivated, shifting alignments among autonomous actors in pursuit of self-aggrandizement. The basic theoretical problem of this pattern is: How is a stable order possible on the basis of these individual pursuits? And the basic answer is that there must be a balance of power.

---

10. The need to develop such mechanisms was generally recognized by Kaplan's contemporaries. Both Gulick and Morgenthau discussed the means or methods of balance. But neither offered more than a list of potential actions that might be used as balancing mechanisms. Such lists clearly serve only descriptive purposes. See Edward Vose Gulick, *Europe's Classic Balance of Power* (Ithaca: Cornell University Press, 1955), 52-91, and Morgenthau, *Politics Among Nations*, 178-197.

In order to make this general idea a theoretical system, it is necessary to formulate an analytically well-specified model that explains the ideal relationships among the international structure, regime characteristics, and action patterns of a "balance of power" system.[11] In the next section, I specify these initial conditions of the "balance of power" model. I first state the model's structural and regime conditions and then the essential rules (action patterns) necessary for system maintenance. In subsequent sections, I show how the model applies to two concrete historical systems, the Italian city-state system (c. 1268-1494), and the Chinese warlord system (c. 1916-1928).[12] I then turn to a particular permutation of the European "balance of power" system (1871-1914) to assess whether or not to treat the period prior to World War I as a bipolar system. In terms of fully specified "balance of power" and bipolar models, this characterization is ad hoc. The "balance of power" model provides a better fit with post-1871 Europe, even though France's loss of Alsace-Lorraine led to departures from ideal theoretical conditions. This will become obvious after we examine the other case studies, where departures also occur.

Initial Conditions

Applied macrotheory starts with a judgment about the correspondence between the initial conditions—particularly the structural conditions—of a macromodel and the actual conditions of an empirical case. The basic argument behind Kaplan's models is simple. The closer the fit between model conditions and empirical actuality, the more likely the action patterns (equilibrium) described by the essential rules will be manifest. If well specified, the manifestation of the essential rules are the procedures necessary and sufficient to maintain the system's structure. On the other hand, as the real world departs from the assumptions of a model, there should be a greater tendency toward disequilibrial action patterns (successful rule violations), or structural instability,[13] or both.

---

11. Kaplan refers to these as "three foci of equilibrium." See chap. 8, and basic standard number three in chap. 1.

12. Although greater research is required on these cases, that work is outside the scope of this book. The following analysis does not accept every theoretical interpretation of these studies. The bulk of the research on the Italian case was completed as a master's thesis. The research is excellent, but the author is still struggling with theoretical problems such as the relationship between individual actions (for example, particular efforts at rule violation) and system patterns (for example, successful rule violations). I tend to reinterpret the authors' results to correct this kind of theoretical error.

13. Cf. chap. 5 where the equivalence between war and instability is shown to be irrelevant to macroanalysis. Instead, instability is defined as the elimination of essential actors. Depending on the context, the concept can be interpreted to include those situations that undermine the capability of an actor to participate in the regulatory process.

The initial conditions of the "balance of power" system are divided into three sets of variables: international structure, regime characteristics, and action patterns.

International Structure. Structural variables refer to the number of actors, their role functions, their capabilities, and the availability of information. The "balance of power" model applies most extensively to a concrete historical system when those variables take the following values.[14]

First, the number of essential actors[15] is at least five. The theory states that the probability of successfully implementing balancing procedures declines in systems in which the number of actors falls below this number. In oversimplified terms, there is less room for miscalculation as numbers become fewer, and this increases the probability that an actor will be eliminated. Although there is probably an upper boundary beyond which the number of actors would make information costs too great for successful management of the balancing process, no convincing theoretical argument has been made that establishes this threshold. Kaplan believes the number is probably substantially less than twenty.

Second, the type of actors are functionally undifferentiated in a "balance of power" system. The role function of each actor is exclusively self-interested. There are no collective actors of any sort, no inter-actor institutional arrangements, and no supra-actor ideological identities. Although in any actual situation there will almost certainly be actors with nonessential role functions, the theory refers only to essential actors.

Third, the relevant capabilities in a "balance of power" system are primarily military capabilities. No single essential actor is predominant. Although real equality is too exacting and too unmeasurable a standard, there is some presumption that the closer the actors are to equal capabilities, the greater the stability of the system. The weaponry in the system is not nuclear. The theory also states that stochastic and unpredictable variations occur in the actors' capabilities (resulting from domestic, technological, or other factors exogenous to the international system). If security is to be maintained, the actors must take account of such potential variations.

Fourth, information is available about changes in the distribution of capabilities and alignment patterns. This informational transparency is necessary if the "balancing" procedures are to be implemented effectively.

---

14. These conditions are largely distilled from Morton A. Kaplan, *Towards Professionalism in International Theory* (New York: Free Press, 1979), 136-138. On these pages Kaplan presents the characteristics of the "balance of power" model in basic theoretical form, rather than its extension to concrete cases. This chapter emphasizes conditions that apply in extension, so that I do not discuss the model's restriction of military fronts to one for each essential actor. That assumption is employed in the computer model, the analysis of which is presented in the following chapter.

15. "Essential actor" is an undefined term in the theory. See Kaplan, *System and Process in International Politics* (New York: John Wiley, 1957), 22.

Regime Characteristics. With respect to regime characteristics the model specifies that the actors are internationally rational. This means that the values of the actors are focused on optimizing security, and no intra-actor factors interfere with this objective. The internationally rational actor prefers a high probability of survival to a moderate probability of achieving hegemony at the risk of elimination. To enhance survivability, all actors also desire future alliance partners. Thus, the internationally rational actor calculates its strategy on the basis of variations in the power relationships in the international system. That, after all, is the role function of an international actor in a "balance of power" system.

All sorts of domestic factors can interfere with this situation. Examples include revolutions, peace movements, corruption, stupidity, bad luck, and ideological rigidity. This complexity is excessive for theoretical analysis. But the particular regime characteristics of an actor can be considered theoretically. Regime characteristics refer to intra-actor organizational characteristics. These characteristics modify the international rationality of the actors. Security optimization strategies are most likely to be implemented by a state apparatus that is neither too directive and subsystem dominant (dictatorial) nor too nondirective and system dominant (democratic). Very dictatorial and very democratic regimes are less likely to exhibit consistently rational behavior.[16]

Action Patterns. Action patterns refer to Kaplan's essential rules. If both sets of conditions—structural and regime—are at stated values, then the action pattern which can be expected, and which is hypothesized as a theoretical optimum, is captured in a set of essential rules. Concrete historical systems that resemble the structure specified in the "balance of power" model are expected to have action patterns that resemble the essential rules. The essential rules of the "balance of power" international system are as follows:

1. Act to increase capabilities but negotiate rather than fight.

2. Fight rather than pass up an opportunity to increase capabilities.

3. Stop fighting rather than eliminate an essential national actor.

4. Act to oppose any coalition or single actor that tends to assume a position of predominance with respect to the rest of the system.

5. Act to constrain actors who subscribe to supranational organizing principles.

6. Permit defeated or constrained essential national actors to re-enter the system as acceptable role partners or act to bring some previously inessential

---

16. On the definitions of these terms, see Kaplan, *System and Process*, 16-18, 54-56.

actor within the essential actor classification. Treat all essential actors as acceptable role partners.

In the following case studies there should be stronger manifestations of the essential rules (equilibrium) in those cases where the initial conditions of the model most closely correspond to actual historical conditions. And there should be greater rule violations in those cases that depart from the initial conditions.

Italian City-State System

Winfried Franke analyzed the Italian city-state system as a "balance of power" system. His case study is divided into three equilibrium phases.[17] The first phase (1300-1425) departs from a number of the model's initial conditions and, as would be expected, also manifests the greatest amount of rule violations. The second (1425-1474) manifests the closest conformity of actual to theoretical structure, and correspondingly great conformity of actual and theoretical action patterns. Of the three, the theory best fits the second phase. Although the theory also fits the third phase (1474-1494), this phase departs significantly from some of the important requirements for equilibrium, particularly with respect to rationality. These departures decreased the regulatory capacity of the system and resulted in a high level of disequilibrial action. That incapacity proved fatal after 1494, when France invaded the Italian peninsula.

I begin with the second phase, when there existed close correspondence between the model's initial conditions and actual empirical conditions. Structural conditions are examined first, followed by regime characteristics. I then present the crises that could have led to successful rule violations and the evidence that they did not.

Next, the third and first phases are presented. There I show that departures from the initial conditions increase the disequilibrial tendencies and instability of the system. This order of presentation is designed to facilitate comprehension. It is easier to understand the use of the model when it more closely corresponds to an actual case, before undertaking the more analytically challenging use of the model in nonequilibrial situations.

---

17. Franke had five phases in all. The three equilibrium phases were flanked by formative and transformative phases. Franke's written work largely concentrates on the three equilibrium phases. By "equilibrium phases" he means that there was sufficient resemblance to the "balance of power" model to use the model as an explanation of the system's behavior. See Winfried Franke, "The Italian City-State System as an International System," in Morton A. Kaplan, ed., *New Approaches to International Relations* (New York: St. Martin's Press, 1968), 426-458 (hence, "The Italian City-State System") and idem, "The Italian City-States Considered as a 'Balance-of-Power' System" (M.A. thesis, The University of Chicago, March 1965), 1-163, (hence, "The Italian City-States").

The Second Phase (1425-1474). Franke demarcates the second phase from 1425, when Venice became involved in peninsular affairs. He argues that prior to this Venice concentrated its foreign policy east of Italy. This re-orientation began a process in which five essential actors—Venice, Milan, Florence, the papal states, and Naples—were increasingly active in regulating the peninsular system. After that time, all the structural conditions (for numbers, capabilities, role function, and information) of Kaplan's "balance of power" model are approximated in the actual system, (with some exceptions occurring in the early part of the phase). In terms of international role function, the actors were territorially independent and for the most part functionally undifferentiated.[18] Legitimacy was decentralized. No particular city, for example, was a legitimate, systemwide center. The actors were in military contact with each other, and the distribution of capabilities appears to have been such that no actor was strong enough to defeat any other pair of actors. During most of the phase all actors could offer, at minimum, a serious defense against any other essential actor.[19] Finally, because of the increasing presence of resident ambassadors—an invention of this period[20]—information was increasingly available. Other sources of information[21] were available from the commercial networks of Florence and Venice, and the religious networks of the papacy. This transparency facilitated diplomatic approaches to conflict resolution.

On the other hand, there was only partial correspondence between the regime characteristics in the Italian city-state system and the international rationality requirements of the model. In particular, the absence of institutionalized administrative structures undermined the capacity for international rationality. The Italian system existed prior to the rise of modern state bureaucracies. There existed no structures in the domestic systems of the actors that facilitated continuity of policy. This meant that international rationality was highly dependent on the personality system of individual rulers and the objective conditions in which they were embedded.

The second phase was nonetheless characterized by increasingly self-conscious regulatory activity on the part of the essential actors. This characteristic was partly the fortuitous result of skillful personality systems widely diffused throughout all five essential actors. This diffusion of skillful international actors in fact increased during the second phase.

There was also a common language, culture, and religion that may have amplified moderate goals and aspirations among the actors.[22] This factor is

---

18. The papacy was partly an exception, as it had a spiritually universal function as well as a secular one.

19. On some of the demographic features of these essential actors, see the figures provided for the first phase.

20. Garrett Mattingly, *Renaissance Diplomacy* (London: Cape, 1955).

21. See for example, Franke, "The Italian City-States," 120-121.

22. One indicator of this moderation is that none of the essential actors copied those advances in warfare that might have provided an actor a decisive advantage against

probably of only minimal importance. A common culture is also present in the Chinese warlord system, but that system was unstable. Moreover, the European state system exhibits significant behavioral variation that would be difficult to fit to a cultural parameter.

A brief examination of each actor-system indicates the increasing diffusion of rationality throughout this phase. At the outset of the phase, the regime characteristics of Naples and the papacy sharply inhibited their international rationality. The Kingdom of Naples had an advanced bureaucratic system in the thirteenth century that had in subsequent years relapsed into feudal disintegration. In addition to local factionalism, the papacy claimed the kingdom as an ecclesiastical fief, and two external actors, Anjou (French) and Aragon (Spanish), had dynastic claims to the kingdom. As a result, the mind-sets of some local barons were divided into Angevin and Arogonese identities. Throughout the reign of the childless and inept Joanna II (1414-1435), both Anjou and Aragon competed for her bestowal of legitimacy. Instead, a legitimacy crisis mushroomed during the post-Joanna succession struggle. The situation stabilized after the victory of Alfonso of Aragon (1442-1443), though it was renewed briefly following Alfonso's death (1458). His illegitimate son, Ferrante, was eventually successful. Only after this time was Naples ruled for the long term. Ferrante survived until 1492, often by resorting to tyrannical suppression of rebellious barons who were at times encouraged by the papacy.[23] Thus, during the second phase, Naples was a regime that often had to divide its regulatory focus between domestic and inter-Italian affairs. This problem was most prevalent in the early part of the phase whereas Naples was most internationally rational during Ferrante's reign.

---

opponents. In fact, observers have characterized the Italian style of warfare as "genteel" or as exhibiting a "highly refined style of etiquette." In contrast, the Swiss had developed the first modern infantry, a closed and disciplined tactical body that could accept a cavalry attack and then overwhelm the attacker in hand-to-hand combat. Kaplan attributes the non-incorporation of immoderate behavior to the stability of the city-state system, which provided no incentive to acquire such capabilities. Logistics made it difficult to strike at opponents, and the mercenary system placed constraints on immoderate forms of warfare. See Kaplan, *Towards Professionalism*, 161. A number of other objective reasons may account for why the Swiss system was not imported into Italy: possible uncertainty about the efficacy of the Swiss forces; Swiss restrictions on foreign employment; the large size and hence expense of the Swiss formations; and the extreme brutality of the Swiss style, which may have been incompatible with the mercenary system of warfare. And artillery, which required infantry support, was thus largely ruled out as well. The cannon used at the time were too cumbersome for effective use by the highly mobile Italian cavalry. Franke, "The Italian City-States," 93-94. On mercenaries, ibid., 58-63.

23. Franke, "The Italian City-States," 29, 52, 76-77, 82, 85-86, 104-105, 115, 118-120 135-136, 143, 146n; idem, "The Italian City-State System," 434-435, 442-443.

The papacy was also distracted. During the first phase the papacy had been racked by exile (1305-1377) and schism (1378-1414).[24] By the second phase the papacy had become more dependent on secular control of the papal states. Many of these states resisted control, an attitude often encouraged by the other essential actors in the system. Although Pope Martin V (1417-1431) began to consolidate the papal holdings after 1420, by 1434 a revolution in Rome had caused Eugene IV (1431-1447) to flee to Florence. Most of Eugene's subsequent international actions were motivated by his efforts to reconsolidate his domestic position. These distractions at first dampened the papacy's capacity to regulate international disturbances. Although by 1447, papal control of its region was again stabilizing, rapid turnover in popes undermined continuity of policy.[25] Nicholas V (1447-1455) was internationally conciliatory and cautious. Calixtus III (1455-1458) was not. But his tenure was sufficiently brief that he could not disequilibrate the system. His successors, Pius II (1458-1464) and Paul II (1464-1471) also manifested moderate and cautious behavior. Pius was preoccupied with reasserting papal authority (vis-à-vis a number of religious councils) and launching a crusade against the Turks, who had captured Constantinople in 1453. Paul was preoccupied with drastic reform of the curia, church affairs in Bohemia, and the continuing papal interest in a crusade against the Turks.[26]

The other three actor-systems were, however, led by particularly competent and skillful rulers who were replaced infrequently. This combination fostered continuity of moderate, internationally rational policies.

In Florence, Cosimo de Medici dominated Florentine politics from 1434 to 1464. Early in the second phase, Florence was at war with Milan and attempted to conquer Lucca (1429-1433). These efforts were so costly that it led to the overthrow of the Albizzi Oligarchy, and the rise of the Medici.[27] This

---

24. The "Babylonian Exile" removed the papacy to France, and during the schism there were at times three competing popes. Franke, "The Italian City-States," 51-52.

25. Ibid., 75-79, 82, 84-85; idem, "The Italian City-State System," 434, 435.

26. These personality fluctuations inside the papacy were stabilizing parameters. This would not have been true had other actors been sufficiently deviant that papal regulation was necessary. The papacy had great latent capacity that could have proved destabilizing if transformed into international capabilities. This danger was amplified by the spiritual function of the papacy, which in principle gave it a basis for widespread legitimacy. Disintegrative tendencies in the region under its secular control and frequent personality turnovers safeguarded the other actors from expansionary thrusts.

27. The social structure of the two parties was probably a factor in the Medici success. The Medici were more centrally organized, in a "spoked-wheel" configuration, whereas the oligarchs were densely interconnected and more egalitarian. The wars against Milan and Lucca triggered very high taxes that were wiping out family patrimonies. The rising commercial class—"new men"—were mobilized by the Medici. This party was more politically successful due to its superior organizational capacity. See John F. Padgett and Christopher K. Ansell, "Robust Action and Party Formation in Renaissance Florence: The Rise of the Medici, 1400-1434," (The University of Chicago, March 1992, Typewritten).

knowledge of war costs—both financial and political—must have contributed to Cosimo's internationally moderate policies throughout his life. And after the middle of the fourteenth century the Florentine economy was somewhat depressed, a factor that also would have moderated Florentine expansionary objectives. Cosimo appears to have fully understood the system and acted skillfully to maintain it. Finally, because the Florentine regime was a seat of legitimacy, Cosimo did not have to face any serious internal threats.

Milan, the most directive, subsystem dominant[28] Italian regime, was also internationally rational throughout most of this phase. Filippo Maria Visconti (1412-1447) and Francesco Sforza (1450-1466) had sufficient control of the Milanese Duchy to skillfully maintain or expand Milan's influence. Milan, however, was despotic and taxed heavily, which made it potentially unstable when rule was relaxed.[29] In times of succession (e.g., 1447-1450), Milan tended to become unstable. Dynastic claims by the French House of Orleans exacerbated this instability. Galeazzo Sforza (1466-1476) maintained internationally rational policies throughout the remainder of the second phase. Domestic discontent, however, led to his assassination in the early part of the third phase. That led to another succession crisis.

Venice, which had been aloof from peninsular affairs prior to the outset of the second phase, was increasingly involved in checking Milan after Foscari (1423-1453) became doge. The Venetian system was system dominant. Although the doge led the system, he was highly constrained by the Venetian political system. Personal diplomacy was not an option in Venice. Venice was moderate during this phase and maintained its regulatory focus when not distracted by Turkish threats to its overseas interests. Finally, the Venetian regime was legitimate and did not face dangerous domestic instability or feudal claims from external actors.[30]

Therefore, the second phase closely approximates the structural, and substantially approximates the rationality conditions of the model. It is also highly correlated with rule-consistent behavior. During this phase, six crises afforded the possibility of rule violation, but no successful violations occurred. The only violation that Franke considers plausible is whether there was a violation in the fourth rule: "Act to oppose any coalition or single actor that tends to assume a position of predominance with respect to the rest of the system." He considers whether the behavior of Naples and the papacy during the early half of the second phase constituted such a violation.

As a result of an expansionary policy during the first phase (1385-1402), Milan had almost achieved dominance (of the northern hemisphere if not the entire

---

28. In effect, this made Milan the most despotic regime in the system. See footnote 16.

29. Franke, "The Italian City-States," 50.

30. Cf. Scott Gordon, "Guarding the Guardians: An Essay on the History and Theory of Constitutionalism" (Indiana University, 21 September 1986, Typewritten), chap. 2. I thank Filippo Sabetti for directing me to this monograph.

system). Milan's efforts might have succeeded except that Milan's duke, Gian Galeazzo Visconti, died from plague (1402). In 1412 Filippo Maria, Gian Galeazzo's second son, rose to the lordship of Milan. He immediately began to re-establish Milan's expansionary policies. In these final years of the first phase, Florence was the only essential actor to oppose Milan.

In 1425 Venice reoriented its policy and an alliance was formed with Florence. The Florentine-Venetian League held Filippo Maria in check until his death in 1447. However, during this time Naples and the papal states did not participate in the balancing process. Their inaction is what Franke considers a possible violation of the rule to oppose actors that assume a position of predominance, but he dismisses this possibility. The major reason is that the Florentine-Venetian coalition was sufficient to constrain Milan, and it did so without threatening Milan's survival as an essential actor. Therefore, neither Naples nor the papal states were necessary to maintain equilibrium in the northern part of the system.[31] Franke's research makes clear that regardless of Naples and the papacy, none of the northern actors assumed a position of predominance during this phase. Also, according to Frank, there were no successful violations of the essential rules in the five other major crises during this phase.

In 1435 the death of Joanna II, the inept ruler of Naples, presented another opportunity for rule violation. Naples was subject to rival Angevin (French) and Aragonese (Spanish) claimants to the throne. Alfonso of Aragon eventually succeeded, and was recognized by the other essential actors in 1442-1443. Although Franke's treatment of this succession is limited, he points out that none of the other essential actors controlled or reduced Naples, and Angevin claimants, who would have posed a greater threat to the system then Aragonese claimants, were boxed out as a result. Naples maintained its role in the system despite the succession struggle.[32]

Second, when the death of Filippo Maria created a vacuum in 1447, the integrity of Milan's domain became unstable. Milan's losses would have mostly fallen to Venice, which raised the specter of Venetian predominance. Therefore,

---

31. Franke, "The Italian City-State System," 443, 457n7; idem, "The Italian City-States," 72n, 73n, 140-143. Franke also offers a second reason. These actors had domestic constraints that rerouted their regulatory activity. There were succession problems in Naples, and the election procedures of the papacy, coupled with instability in the region under its control, hindered their capacity to regulate the international system. Thus, their inaction cannot be interpreted as a deliberate violation of the system's fourth essential rule. Franke's second reason does not seem particularly important; that individual actors will consciously attempt to violate rules is not incompatible with the theory.

32. Franke, "The Italian City-States," 82; idem, "The Italian City-State System," 442, 448. The Angevin claimants were a greater threat because other French actors were involved on the peninsula.

all the essential actors, including the papacy and Naples[33] became involved in the succession struggle. Florence, under the leadership of Cosimo, developed a policy to install Francesco Sforza in Milan. Sforza was one of the ablest mercenaries and had a weak claim to the throne. This policy succeeded in 1450, with the tacit support of the papal states. Thus Milan was preserved as an essential actor, and thereby checked Venice. Sforza was so firmly established that an attack by Naples and Venice (which formed an alliance in 1452), could not dislodge him. The Peace of Lodi (1454) resulted in Sforza's recognition by the other actors.

Another possible rule violation occurred as a result of Neapolitan moves against Genoa. Almost immediately after the status quo had been confirmed in the Treaty of Lodi, Naples began pressuring Genoa, in particular over Corsica. This forced Genoa to submit to French protection (1458-1461). Genoa, however, was not an essential actor. In 1380 it had been reduced to nonessential status in a decisive naval battle with Venice.[34] Because the rules apply only to essential actors, this, too, fails to satisfy the requirements for successful rule violation.

Another succession crisis emerged in Naples with the death of Alfonso in 1458. Alfonso had selected his illegitimate son, Ferrante, to succeed him. A rival French claim was supported by Pope Calixtus III (1455-1458). Calixtus, however, died in the same year, and his decision was reversed by Pope Pius II (1458-64), who invested Ferrante with Naples. Florence also supported Ferrante, who was less of a threat than the French House of Anjou. After all, another French ducal house, Orleans, had a claim against Milan. Had Anjou succeeded to Naples, France would have had the capabilities to pressure Milan on two fronts. The choice of Ferrante thus preserved the independence of Naples. Again the rules were maintained.[35]

Cosimo's support of Ferrante marked the beginning of a Triple Alliance between Milan, Florence, and Naples. Cosimo forged the Triple Alliance in order to check Venice and the papal states inside Italy, and to forestall the realization of France's claims against Milan and Naples. This led to an unprecedented twenty-year peace.[36] The alliance was maintained after Cosimo's death (1464), and played a role in maintaining the system during the last crisis. In 1467 Venice tacitly supported an armed conspiracy against Florence, led by Bartolommeo Colleoni, a Venetian *condottiere*. But the Triple Alliance held fast and the conspiracy soon collapsed.

---

33. Naples' involvement was assured due to the stability of Alfonso and by the fact that Filippo Maria had named Alfonso his successor.

34. Genoa never recovered from the rout of Venice in 1379-80. Domestic unrest was subsequently amplified; there were ten revolutions from 1390-1394 alone. Rule by Milan and France became increasingly common. In the 132 years from 1396-1528, there were approximately 74 years of rule by one of these actors. See Franke, "The Italian City-State System," 432.

35. Ibid., 442-443; idem, "The Italian City-States," 85, 143-145.

36. Franke, "The Italian City-States, 84-86, 90.

So in none of the six crises were the essential rules successfully violated. However, the equilibrium that prevailed throughout the second phase was largely a product of two long-lasting alliances. The Florentine-Venetian League lasted about twenty-two years, and the Triple Alliance lasted for approximately the final sixteen years of the second phase, continuing into the third. These alliance relationships raise two questions. First, does either alliance contradict that portion of the sixth essential rule that states: "Treat all essential actors as acceptable role partners"? Second, does the long-term nature of either alliance preclude the classification of the system as a "balance of power" system? That is, should the system be classified as bipolar?

Franke argues that the Triple Alliance was an "atypical behavioral pattern" that resulted from "atypical, destabilizing parameters. . . ."[37] Franke considers the Triple Alliance to be atypical because it had long-term characteristics, whereas short-term, flexible alliances are more consistent with Kaplan's "balance of power" system. Because the characteristics of alliances are hypothesized on the basis of ideal conditions, and because the second phase departs from some of those conditions, Franke argues that there should be a departure from the theoretical action patterns. He views the Triple Alliance as such a departure from equilibrium.

The atypical parameters that he uses to account for this alliance were insufficient regulatory capacity inside the actor-systems (Milan and Naples), ancient feudal dynastic claims on the part of external actors (France and Spain), and inconstant personality inputs.[38] These various statements are theoretically reducible to the absence of institutionalized administrative structures in the actor-systems.[39] Another atypical parameter was the particular geographical configuration of Italy, which created logistical friction for actors attempting to assist Florence. The Triple Alliance was a means of preventing either a two-front war or an overwhelming combination of two essential actors from either hemisphere. (In effect, Florence was the linchpin in two three-actor systems.)[40]

Although the Triple Alliance was atypical, it was not a violation of the sixth rule, and it was not a bipolar type of alliance system. Nor was the Florentine-Venetian League. With respect to bipolarity, both alliances were long-lasting, but they were not based on long-term commitments. The alliances were bilateral,

---

37. Franke, "The Italian City-State System," 444.

38. Ibid., 444, 453-455.

39. The absence of administrative structures constitutes a regime characteristic that reduced international rationality. See Kaplan, *Towards Professionalism*, 86. Administrative structures would have provided the actors with internal regulatory capacity, trumped any external dynastic challenges, and controlled personality variations.

40. An analysis of three-actor systems is presented below in the section on Chinese warlords. The reason geographical considerations are atypical is that no actor is particularly vulnerable to geographic conditions in the basic theory. In fact, in the computer model, all the actors have only one front with every other actor. See Kaplan *Towards Professionalism*, 138.

instrumental, not ideologically motivated, and had no institutional apparatus.[41] Moreover, when the interests of the actors changed, the alliance was abandoned. Florence abandoned Venice and moved towards Sforza's Milan after 1447. In the third phase, Lorenzo de Medici abandoned the Triple Alliance when he (mistakenly) thought it prudent (1474-1480). And in 1482 during the war against Ferrara (a nonessential actor), Pope Sixtus IV switched his alignment from Venice (which was attacking Ferrara) to the Triple Alliance (which was defending it).[42]

Thus, the second phase was unambiguously in stable equilibrium and offers reasonable confirmation of the "balance of power" model. There were no successful rule violations during the phase. No essential actors—and increasingly fewer nonessential actors—were eliminated. The overall territorial distribution—a key component of capabilities—was preserved.[43] And the alliances were sufficiently flexible to regulate disequilibrial actions arising in the system.

The Third Phase (1474-1494). Most of the structural conditions of the second phase were maintained in the third phase. As would be expected, there were again no successful rule violations, though the system was becoming more active. There were now major inter-actor wars, in addition to another succession struggle in Milan. Therefore, greater regulatory skill was required. International rationality was, however, waning. This instability can be traced to the absence of institutionalized administrative structures inside the actors, which made the continuity of international rationality improbable. Unlike the second phase, where luck contributed to a diffusion of internationally skilled and moderate personality systems, during the third phase luck contributed to a diffusion of unskilled and immoderate personality systems. At the end of the phase, the combination proved fatal when France, a powerful external actor, was invited into the peninsular system.

Franke initiates the third phase in 1474, when the papacy adopted an expansionary policy aimed at Florence and Naples. Florence responded by abandoning Naples and forging a new triple alliance with Milan and Venice. Because it conforms to the focal presupposition, the Florentine change in alignment—which is a change in international political relationships—constitutes good grounds for phase demarcation.[44]

---

41. See Mattingly, *Renaissance Diplomacy*, 85-86. On the differences between bipolar and "balance-of-power" systems, see chap. 5, footnote 16, and the analyses below of the European state and loose bipolar systems.

42. Franke, "The Italian City-States," 114-115.

43. Ibid., 68.

44. Franke's demarcation of his third phase is thus consistent with his demarcation of the second, when Venice reoriented its policies to play an active role in peninsular balancing. Franke at times considered dividing the second phase into two phases, and he occasionally speaks of the second phase as comprised of two subphases. His point of demarcation would have been 1458, when Florence switched away from the Florentine-Venetian League to the Triple Alliance. This division, which would have resulted in the

As in the second phase, the correspondence of theoretical and empirical structures is fairly close. The same five essential actors participated in the regulation of the Italian system. The actors were in military contact with each other, and remained territorially independent and functionally undifferentiated (except again for the papacy in its spiritual role). Standing alliances in fact weakened. No actor had predominant capabilities. And information factors were in closer conformity with the model. Resident ambassadors were now widespread throughout the Italian system.

On the other hand, major instabilities were introduced through the regime characteristics of the system. In all the actors except Venice, the absence of institutionalized administrative structures was still a weakness in the international rationality of the actors. Decision-making in most actors remained personality-based.[45] This was not an acute problem during the second phase because leadership had changed infrequently in Milan, Naples, and Florence. Only the papacy was racked by frequent changes in leadership. As the second phase drew to a close, this situation was changing. All the actors except Naples manifested frequent personality changes, and most actors faced either extra-Italian or domestic instabilities that deflected their regulatory focus. This process resulted in a greater diffusion of internationally non-rational personalities throughout the system

Because the geographical position of Florence implied its role as balancer, Florentine rationality was particularly important for system stability.[46] The balancing role had made Cosimo de Medici the most important personality system throughout the second phase. Whereas Cosimo ruled for thirty years, his death in 1464 led to three leadership changes during the next thirty years. Piero I (1464-1469) lasted briefly, and ruled during a period of comparative peace. He was followed by Lorenzo (1469-1492). Lorenzo made his greatest mistake by abandoning the Triple Alliance in 1474. His age—about 21 when Piero died—and inexperience offer a likely explanation in a system that was so

---

addition of another phase, seems more consistent with Franke's second and third phase demarcations, as well as with more self-conscious use of the focal presupposition. It would also require adding additional phases after 1474: one in 1480 when Florence reforged the original Triple Alliance, and possibly one in 1482 when the papacy realigned its policies from Venice to the Triple Alliance in the war against Ferrara. Such a well-specified use of phase demarcations would in effect constitute an activity rate in "balance of power" systems. However, no such reconstruction of Franke's argument is undertaken in this chapter.

45. Only Venice had a political system that significantly controlled the personality system of its leader, the *doge*. Personal diplomacy and individual discretion were not compatible with the Venetian system. See Franke, "The Italian City-States," 150-151. Venice was a directive system, but it was far more system dominant than any of the other Italian actors. Cf. Scott Gordon, footnote 30.

46. Franke, "The Italian City-States," 110-111, 145-147; idem, "The Italian City-State System," 449-450.

personality-dependent. By the late 1480s, however, he demonstrated much greater skill in managing inter-actor relationships. In terms of the Italian system, Lorenzo's death in 1492 was a disaster. He was replaced by Piero II—dubbed "The Unfortunate" by historians—who was incompetent. It is improbable that this personality system would have improved, even with more time. His inclinations were towards athletics rather than politics. When the French invasion of Charles VIII was approaching Florence, Piero signed an agreement that the Florentines considered so disastrous that Piero was forced to flee the city.[47] In addition to these personality variations, there was also an economic parameter that undermined Florentine rationality. The Medici were primarily a textile and banking house. Their domestic political position depended largely on their wealth. Throughout the century they had become increasingly dependent on their foreign holdings.[48] They had substantial business interests in Paris and Lyons, for example, that made them vulnerable to decisions of the French crown. That factor alone would have increased their hesitancy to oppose French interests. As this phase drew to a close, for example, Florence did not direct diplomatic efforts at Spain or the Empire to deter France from further involvement in peninsular affairs.

Other actors were effected by exogenous parameters as well. Although the Venetian system controlled personality variations, their regulatory focus was nonetheless deflected. During this phase Venice and the Turks were again at war (1470s), and this reduced Venetian regulatory capacity in the Italian system. So even though Venice had a system that controlled personality inputs, its international rationality was divided between two different international systems—the Italian and the wider Mediterranean system.[49]

In Milan, succession problems interfered with international rationality. Shortly after Cosimo's death, Francesco Sforza died and was replaced by Galeazzo Sforza (1466-1476), an unreliable personality system. Galeazzo's reign was brief, interrupted by assassination. Gian Galeazzo II, Galeazzo's son, was too young to rule. This situation contributed to a succession struggle. The struggle was settled when Lodovico Sforza, the heir's uncle, seized the throne (1480). According to some historians, Lorenzo considered Lodovico "untrustworthy and difficult to handle." Moreover, the legitimate heir later married into the ruling family of Naples. So in addition to the unreliability of Lodovico, a war of succession, aided by Naples, became an increasing threat as this phase progressed.[50]

Naples had had a continuous and experienced leadership throughout most of this phase. Ferrante had been ruler since 1458. But his regime included large numbers of rebellious Neapolitan barons. These barons were periodically in

---

47. Franke, "The Italian City-States," 122-124.
48. Ibid., 102.
49. Ibid., 148.
50. Ibid., 120-121, 148-149; idem, "The Italian City-State System," 445-446.

open revolt during the phase, and were sometimes supported by the papacy.[51] And as Ferrante grew older, the probability increased of competition between Anjou and Aragon. This became increasingly dangerous as the heir to France (and now Anjou), Charles VIII, reached maturity. Charles had expansionist and integrationist objectives. When Ferrante died in 1494, the investiture of his son, Alfonso II, triggered the French invasion.

The most important personality variations were in the papacy. Although progress had been slow, Sixtus IV (1471-1484) benefited from the increasing reintegration and stability of the papal states under his control. Unlike his moderate predecessors, Pius and Paul, Sixtus was expansionist. In addition to consolidation of the papal regions, he also sought expansion into Florence and Naples. Throughout the first two phases, the substantial capabilities of the papacy had been dampened by its internal difficulties. Although Sixtus did not fully overcome rebellious elements, he was successful enough that he released some of the great latent capabilities of the papacy. Sixtus was succeeded by Innocent VIII (1484-1492). A Florentine diplomatic report indicated that Innocent's lack of experience would result in his dependence on others. He, in fact, turned to Cardinal Rovere, a nephew of Sixtus and the future Pope Julius II (1503-1513). Rovere was also expansionistic, and Innocent permitted him to control foreign policy. Finally, Innocent was replaced by Alexander VI (1492-1503), who was personally ambitious and in serious conflict with Cardinal Rovere.[52] Most of the crises during this phase were directly related to the immoderation of the papacy under Sixtus and Innocent.

According to Franke, in the third phase the accession of deviant rulers in several actor-systems led to changes in behavioral patterns.[53] As would be expected in a situation with a wider distribution of internationally irrational actors, there were a greater number of disequilibrial inputs during this phase. Equilibrium was nonetheless maintained. The fairly close correspondence of theoretical and actual international structural conditions, mentioned above, seems to account for this result.

Franke identified four major crises during this phase. In none of these crises were the essential rules successfully violated. But the increasing intensity and frequency of disequilibrial inputs required greater skill in regulating the system, skills that were in increasingly short supply.

The first disturbance of this phase resulted from Sixtus' efforts to invest his relatives in cities not fully under papal control. The first targets were Imola and Citta di Castello. Close to Florentine territory, both cities were in areas that Florence preferred to maintain as a cordon of disintegrated, petty border states. The papacy's consolidation of these cities would have helped build a solid

---

51. Franke, "The Italian City-States," 103-105, 115, 118.

52. Ibid., 98, 103-105, 118. The conflict between Alexander and Rovere was sufficiently intense that Rovere fled to France after Alexander conspired in an assassination attempt against him.

53. Franke, "The Italian City-State System," 446.

political entity surrounding Florence on three sides. In response, Lorenzo foolishly decided to abandon the Triple Alliance and form a new constellation of Florence, Milan, and Venice. This action entailed terrible consequences for Florence.

Florentine opposition led Sixtus to replace the Medici as papal bankers and (unsuccessfully) use his ecclesiastical authority to undermine Florence's domestic legitimacy. Most damaging, it drove Naples into alignment with the pope. Florence's new allies, Milan and Venice, were not in a position to assist Florence. Milan was involved in a succession struggle, and Venice was engaged in a lengthy war against the Turks. Florentine requests for French support also went unfulfilled. The situation then deteriorated. The pope conspired in a plot to overthrow the Medici. After an attempted assassination barely failed against Lorenzo, the Florentines executed the conspirators, including an archbishop. The result was war (1478-1480). The pope and his new ally, Naples, quickly reduced Florence to extreme danger.

The seizure of power in Milan by Lodovico Sforza, and the personal diplomacy of the now experienced Lorenzo, prevented the elimination of Florence. Sforza and Lorenzo convinced Ferrante that Naples should again join them in Triple Alliance (1480) in order to preserve Florence and check papal ambitions. Despite coming dangerously close due to Lorenzo's inexperience, no rules were successfully violated during this conflict.[54]

Immediately following the restoration of the Triple Alliance, Sixtus launched the second disturbance of this phase. He made overtures to Venice for the conquest of Ferrara, as well as the elimination of Ferrante from Naples. Venice was to receive Ferrara if Ferrante fell in Naples.

The Veneto-Papal war against Ferrara began in 1482. The Triple Alliance moved into action: Milan and Florence defended Ferrara, and Naples launched a campaign—supported by the papacy's traditional enemies—into the papal states. Nonetheless, Ferrara's position quickly verged toward collapse. But as the Veneto-papal forces were achieving victory over Ferrara, the pope realized that all benefits would go to Venice in the event that Ferrara fell. He had had no success against Naples, and threats of a new religious schism were developing. Sixtus therefore entered into negotiations with Naples and joined the Triple Alliance against Venice. By 1484 there had been no decisive campaigns and both sides had grown weary. A peace treaty was signed among the belligerents, except the recalcitrant Sixtus, who was excluded. Venice received some small territorial gains, but the overall status quo was restored. Papal and Venetian disequilibrial ambitions had been thwarted.

---

54. Ibid., 446-447; idem, "The Italian City-States," 106-108. N.B.: The Triple Alliance was formed in March, before the Turkish seizure of Otranto induced Naples to seek financial support from the Medici. At the later time Naples renounced further territorial acquisitions in Tuscany.

Sixtus died the night after the treaty was signed. His successor, Pope Innocent, then directed another disturbance at Naples, though again without successfully violating the essential rules. Innocent allowed Sixtus' nephew, Cardinal Rovere, to formulate a policy that demanded feudal tribute from Naples. When the tribute was not paid, Innocent declared war (1485) and encouraged revolt among the barons who opposed Ferrante. Despite both French and papal[55] diplomatic efforts, Lorenzo maintained his bond with Naples. He also played the role of mediator between the protagonists and launched a diplomatic campaign to keep Milan in the alliance and prevent Venice and some smaller states from joining the Pope. The policy succeeded and peace was made in 1486. Dispute erupted again in 1489 and was again settled by Lorenzo, just prior to his death in 1492. Innocent coincidentally died shortly thereafter.[56]

Compared to the second phase, the intensity and frequency of conflict was increasing, thus requiring greater regulatory skill on the part of the actors. But during this phase a series of regime instabilities became widely distributed across the system. Between 1492 and 1494 the diffusion of personality systems across the essential actors fell well short of the international rationality required to maintain the system. The new personality systems were either inexperienced or immoderate.

In the papacy, Innocent was replaced by the equally ambitious Alexander VI (1492). In Florence, Lorenzo was replaced by his incompetent son, Piero II (1492). In Naples, Ferrante was replaced by his son, Alfonso II (1494). A fourth actor, Milan, was threatened by a war of succession between Lodovico and his nephew, Gian Galeazzo, whose wife, Isabella, was Alfonso's daughter. In addition, Charles VIII had replaced the regency that had governed France since the death of his father, Louis IX, in 1483. Louis had no desire to involve France in peninsular affairs. Charles had plenty of desire, and in 1494 had all the experience and prudence of a twenty-four-year-old. When Ferrante's death rekindled the competing claims of Aragon and Anjou (which Charles had inherited), Charles claimed Naples as his own.

Coupled with this general poverty of experience were the extra-systemic motives of some of the personality systems that filled these roles. Piero, as previously mentioned, was incompetent. He preferred athletics to politics. Charles manufactured romantic dreams of a crusade against the infidel so that he could become the emperor of the East. He viewed Naples as a steppingstone to Constantinople. Ferrante and Alfonso desired to avenge Isabella's claim to the Milanese throne.

Legitimacy disputes in Milan and Naples were the immediate catalysts for the final crises. Lodovico had occupied Milan's throne for Gian Galeazzo, his

---

55. Lorenzo had better diplomatic relations with Innocent, who in 1489 named Giovanni, his 13-year-old son, a cardinal. Giovanni would later become Pope Leo X.
56. Franke, "The Italian City-States, 113-116, 118-121; idem, "The Italian City-State System," 447.

nephew and the legitimate heir. Gian Galeazzo sought his throne when he
reached maturity. Because he had married into Naples' ruling family, his wife
encouraged Naples to defend her husband's claim. A Neapolitan-Milanese war
was imminent. But rather than launching a diplomatic effort to repair this breach
in the Triple Alliance, or to mediate the conflict, Piero threw his support to
Naples. That drove Milan into reluctant alliance with France, where Charles VIII
had reached maturity and attained a crusading spirit.[57] Milan also formed a
league with the papacy and Venice. But the papacy and Naples soon reconciled,
and Venice retreated from further commitments. That left Milan dependent on
France. When Ferrante died in 1494, the pope recognized Ferrante's son,
Alfonso II. This apparent snub triggered the French invasion and plunged Italy
into a century of war, resulting in its absorption into the wider European
system.[58]

Thus, the wide distribution of unskilled and internationally immoderate
personality systems resulted in extensive rule violations and the subsequent
destruction of the Italian city-state system. The first essential rule was violated
in that Milan and Naples were unwilling to negotiate. Relations between the two
actors were governed by personal and familial ties rather than international power
considerations. Piero's incompetence in handling the dispute led Milan to seek
stronger bonds with France. France was an extremely powerful actor compared
to the Italian actors. The failure of the Italian actors to oppose France, which
had hegemonial ambitions, may be treated as a violation of rules four and five.
France then initiated a process that reduced the Italian system to nonessential
status in the wider European international system. This process included the
wholesale violations of the third and sixth rules, which prescribe the maintenance
of essential actors.

The First Phase (1300-1425). The second and third phases indicate how the
"balance of power" model applies when there is close correspondence between
theoretical and actual initial conditions, particularly structural conditions. Of the
three, the first phase had the least correspondence with the conditions for a
"balance of power" system, both in terms of structure and regime characteristics.
As would be expected under such conditions, this phase also manifests the
greatest disequilibrial tendencies. There are more rule violations in the first
phase than in any other phase.

The structure of the system did not closely approximate model conditions.
There are departures from the optimal number of actors, their capabilities, and
the informational transparency of the system. The first phase does meet the
minimum requirement for numbers of essential actors. Franke identifies seven
core areas out of which seven essential actors would arise (an eighth, Pisa, was
reduced in 1284). In addition to the five previously mentioned actors, essential

57. Charles had settled his problems in Europe by this time. Franke, "The Italian City-
States," 105n.
58. Ibid., 121-124; idem, "The Italian City-State System," 447-448.

actors in this phase also included Genoa and Verona. But large numbers of nonessential actors posed difficulties for the emerging essential actors in their respective regions.   In 1300 there were at least 80 and possibly over 100 independent (communal) actors in northern and central Italy alone. Although most of these actors had no chance of becoming essential actors, the large number of them increased information and regulatory costs dramatically. Moreover, this phase also occurs prior to the establishment of a peninsular-wide diplomatic system of resident ambassadors.   Informational transparency was therefore more limited in this phase.[59] Because of these structural problems, most of the emerging essential actors could aspire only to regional hegemony in what was mostly a phase of regional consolidation.

Florence had been a prosperous commercial center since the third century. During the twelfth and thirteenth centuries, the economic and political power of the city grew. At the outset of this phase, Florence had a population of about 100,000. The woolen industry and banking were dominant, and provided capital. This provided a basis for hiring mercenaries, a form of military organization that appeared in Italy during the 1330s. But Florentine capacity was diminished severely in 1348, when the Black Death cut the population in half. A depressed economic situation throughout the rest of the century reduced expansionary options.[60]   In addition, Florence was surrounded by mountains and wedged between neighboring essential actors.   Therefore, it would have been very expensive to develop capabilities or a foreign policy orientation that could be used beyond Tuscany. Such a policy was incompatible with the commercial objectives of the Florentine system, especially in light of the troubled economy throughout the latter part of the fourteenth century.

Milan had famous metal and textile industries, and was rich in agricultural and mineral resources. It also had a substantial armaments industry. Its population in 1300 was substantially in excess of 50,000, and some estimates place it in a range approximating that of Venice and Florence. The control of the city by the Visconti, beginning in 1287, was correlated with continuing expansion of the industrial and mercantile economy. Because the Italian wars were largely fought with mercenary forces, the possession of substantial economic capacity was tantamount to an essential role in the system. And the tight-fisted control of the Visconti provided substantial tax revenues. Towards the end of the phase, Milan also established the first secular, institutionalized foreign office. Thus, the state directly commanded great information resources. Milan almost certainly had the capabilities to achieve northern hegemony. But luck (see below) prevented this outcome.

---

59. Franke, "The Italian City-State System," 428-432; idem, "The Italian City-States," 30-31.

60. Franke, "The Italian City-States," 59. The conquest of Pisa in 1406 was one of the few expansionary moves in the latter part of this phase, and made Florence a maritime power.

Venice was primarily a naval power, with colonial interests accessible via the Mediterranean Sea. Its population exceeded 100,000 at the outset of this phase, and its colonial tax base was about 1.5 million. Venice was just as capable as Milan and Florence in terms of manpower, economic capacity, and overall capabilities, but it lacked territory. Venice was a trading power with wide interests throughout the Mediterranean and territory was less necessary. But as Turkish power advanced in the East, Venice became involved in frequent wars off the peninsula during most of this phase.[61] It also had to acquire territory on the peninsula in order to compensate its colonial losses. Its peninsular capabilities were therefore highly limited at this time. Venice had no expansionary capabilities beyond its immediate region. It had to acquire territory before it could become an effective Italian player.

Genoa, too, was a naval power with a fine harbor (the value of which made it a lightning rod for French and Aragonese intervention). In 1300, its population was about the size of Milan. Genoa also was a Mediterranean trading power, and competed with Venice. Genoese-Venetian competition was highly antagonistic throughout most of this phase. Throughout the fourteenth century, their capabilities were largely earmarked against each other. That force posture was another reason both actors had insufficient capabilities for peninsular expansion.

Verona had a capable duke, controlled the most important Alpine passes to Germany, and had military and economic capabilities on par with Milan.[62] It had been one of the four most important Austrian cities in northern Italy, part of the Quadrilateral. Verona used its capabilities for substantial regional expansion, to the point of posing a serious threat to Venice, Milan, and Florence.

In addition to these structural departures from initial conditions, international rationality was a particularly acute problem during this phase. The papacy and Naples also had substantial capabilities, but these capabilities were mitigated by regime problems and dynastic challenges from external actors. As mentioned previously, the papacy was racked by exile and schism, and the papal states resisted control. These internal problems rendered papal capabilities impotent during most of this phase. In Naples, capabilities were absorbed by the conflict between Anjou and Aragon, as well as dynastic disputes within the Angevin House.

Rationality was undermined by other factors as well. The Italian system rose following imperial and papal competition for control of the peninsula. Guelph (papal) and Ghibelline (imperial) factions existed throughout much of Italy. This rivalry entailed an ideological motive for conflict that undermined internationally rational policies. This problem diminished during the course of the fourteenth century, but remained significant in many places. For example, after Genoa's

---

61. Franke, "The Italian City-States," 44-45.
62. Franke, "The Italian City-State System," 430.

naval defeat by Venice (1380), this rivalry helped plunge Genoa into a long series of revolutions and foreign rule.[63]

Guelph and Ghibelline factions also competed for control of Milan during the early part of this phase. Milanese expansion was not possible while control was in dispute. The Visconti (Ghibelline) crushed their chief opponent, the Della Torre family, in 1310, but conflict continued with the papacy for another two decades. Moreover there were frequent personality changes in the Visconti leadership. Although Milan expanded under competent dukes, incompetent dukes or divided lordship usually followed.[64]

These departures from the initial conditions of the model are correlated with significant departures from the hypothesized action patterns. The lack of peninsular-wide capabilities, the large number of nonessential actors in each region, and dysfunctional regime characteristics forestalled further integration of the system. This led to more successful rule violations than in any other phase.[65]

The elimination of both Verona (1339) and Genoa (1380) as essential actors are the most significant rule violations of this phase. In both cases, fighting did not stop prior to the elimination of these actors as essential players, and neither actor regained its essential actor status. Thus, the third and sixth rules were successfully violated.

In both cases, the eliminated actors had themselves been rule violators. Verona had launched its own expansionary drive. It had practically surrounded

---

63. Ibid., 429. See footnote 34.

64. Matteo Visconti was captain general during most of the first twenty-two years of the fourteenth century. He was replaced by Galeazzo I (1322-28). This was an intense period of Guelph-Ghibelline rivalry, which ended during the reign of Azzo (1328-39). Azzo left no heirs. He was replaced by two uncles. Luchino and Giovanni, who ruled jointly (1339-1349) until Luchino's death (1349). This was a period of expansion in which territory previously lost to the pope was regained. Giovanni then acquired hereditary rights to the lordship. At his death in 1354, the Visconti dominions were shared among his three nephews. Matteo II died the following year, and Bernabo and Galeazzo II divided rule into eastern and western areas. This was not a period of significant expansion. Galeazzo died in 1378. He was replaced by his son, Gian Galeazzo. When Bernabo concluded an alliance with France in 1385, Gian Galeazzo captured Bernabo, probably fearing the power of the new alliance. Bernabo died a few months later in prison, possibly by poisoning. It was then that the expansion was resumed. Milan was driving for at least northern hegemony when Gian Galeazzo succumbed to plague in 1402. He was replaced by the incompetent reign of Giovanni Maria (1402-12), who lost most of his father's state. His assassination led to the rule of Filippo Maria (1412-47), his brother, who resuscitated the Milanese expansion during the final years of the first phase, and maintained his gains throughout the first half of the second.

65. In addition, there were more nonessential actors eliminated during the first phase than any of the others. This indicates instability of the regional equilibria, as the emerging essential actors achieved regional predominance.

Venice and had taken Lucca, Florence's most coveted Tuscan city. The Veronese expansion also threatened Milan's interests. Verona refused to negotiate with Venice, thus violating the first rule and casting the specter of a violation of rules three and six.

Genoa also manifested a deviant operational code. Genoa had organized a league to defeat Venice, its long-standing rival. The league included Naples, Padua, Hungary and Austria. Genoa did not seek to negotiate in its drive to eliminate Venice. Had Venice not succeeded in eliminating Genoa, the league would have undoubtedly eliminated it. Genoa's campaign was a near successful violation of the third and sixth rules.

In three other cases, successful violations were forestalled only by unexpected death. The elimination of Verona as an essential actor created a vacuum that Milan tried to fill. This expansion was particularly menacing between 1339-1354, and 1378-1402.[66] In the first case, Giovanni Visconti's expansion was interrupted when he died, only to be replaced by the division of Milanese rule into eastern and western halves. These halves were not reintegrated until Gian Galeazzo captured his uncle, Bernabo, in 1385. Gian probably feared Bernabo's newly-forged alliance with France. In the second case, Milan was on the verge of at least northern domination, which was a violation of rule three and potentially rules four through six, when the plague ended the life of Gian Galeazzo, Milan's highly skilled duke. Florence, aided by smaller cities, was the only essential actor to oppose Milan. The lack of regulation by the other essential actors was a violation—or a violation in the making—of the fourth and fifth rules.

In the third case, Naples attempted to achieve hegemony in a northern drive through the papal states that began in 1408. Naples was stopped in Tuscany by a Florentine-led league. As a result, Naples signed a separate peace with Florence and then began a second, massive campaign against the papacy. The successful violations of rules three through six were prevented only by the sudden death of Naples' ruler, Ladislas, in 1414.

The last successful rule violation also occurred in Milan. Following the death of Gian Galeazzo (1402), his incompetent son, Giovanni Maria, lost most of his father's state. His incompetent rule ended with his assassination in 1412. His younger brother, Filippo Maria, reconstructed his father's state in ten years, and then began pressing outside of Lombardy. The failure of Venice to assist Florence in constraining Milan violated the fourth rule, and potentially the fifth. Only the reorientation of Venetian policy (see second phase) reversed this situation.[67]

---

66. See footnote 64 for a brief survey of the Visconti succession.

67. Franke mentions three other cases, but none constitute clearly successful violations of the essential rules. Pope Boniface did not have loyalty from any of the factions he supported in Florence. The Veneto-papal competition over Ferrara concerned a nonessential actor. Naples overextended itself and did not succeed in consolidating its position in either Florence or Genoa. See "The Italian City-State System," 436-437.

A number of factors prevented the system from destroying itself during this disequilibrial phase. The war-fighting system was based on mercenary forces. Mercenaries had no incentive to eliminate their employers or deplete their manpower, which constituted their political and military capital. And it would have been necessary to expend a great many troops to seize control of Italy. It was extremely expensive to seize cities, which were fortified. Thus, the defense had the advantage. The terrain of Italy also made rapid movement of troops difficult. These factors increased the stability of the system—much as nuclear weapons did in the post-1945 bipolar system. Luck was also a factor. As with the second and third phases, the system was personality-based. In such systems the distribution of international rationality is largely a random process. The system was preserved in the first phase partly because the internationally immoderate personality systems had a tendency to die before achieving their hegemonial ambitions. Finally, the general absence of ideological loyalty among subject cities facilitated easy territorial transfer. This factor provided a medium of exchange for conflict resolution.[68]

Thus the "balance of power" model partly explains the Italian case, particularly the second and third phases. But it also indicates the importance of regime characteristics. Although international structural factors were at equilibrial values during the second and third phases, the absence of stable administrative structures undermined the international rationality of the actors. On the other hand, the following study of the Chinese warlord system underlines the importance of structural factors in macrosystem analysis. In particular, this study illuminates the role that numbers of actors play in the stability of an international system. The small number of essential actors seems to be a major reason for this system's short and disequilibrial life.

Chinese Warlord System

Hsi-sheng Ch'i analyzed warlord politics in China as a "balance of power" system. I present Ch'i's results only briefly. There are three reasons for this brevity. First, Ch'i clearly presented his argument in book form. So it is accessible to scholars in the field.[69] Second, the Italian case study presented above provides the reader with analytical background that does not have to be revisited. Third, the system was unstable, leading it to terminate quickly. Therefore, there is comparatively less historical scope to warlord politics in China.

---

68. Franke, "The Italian City-States," 69-72; idem, "The Italian City-State System," 441-442.

69. Hsi-sheng Ch'i, *Warlord Politics in China, 1916-1928* (Stanford: Stanford University Press, 1976), especially chap. 9. Also see idem, "The Chinese Warlord System as an International System," in Morton A. Kaplan, ed., *New Approaches to International Relations* (New York: St. Martin's Press, 1968), 405-425; and idem, "The Chinese Warlord System," (Ph.D. Dissertation, The University of Chicago, 1969).

The warlord system (1916-1928) was also divided into three phases. The first (1916-1920) was a period of regional consolidation, in which there was an absence of systemwide interaction. In the second (1920-1924), major interactions occurred among three essential actors. Much of their behavior resembles "balance of power" action. However, rule violations do occur during the phase. During the third phase (1924-1928), the system became unstable and terminal.[70] Thus, warlord politics was an unstable system that briefly exhibited some equilibrial action.

The most important theoretical lesson about the Chinese case study is the relationship between numbers of essential actors and stability. The Chinese system produced only three essential actors. Kaplan's "balance of power" model states that five actors are probably a minimum number necessary for stability. The basic argument against three as a lower boundary for stability is relatively simple. In a three-actor system, the second- and third-ranked actors must oppose the strongest actor's efforts to increase its capabilities.[71]

So, if in a three-actor system one of the weaker actors miscalculates, there is a high probability that a preponderant alliance will form against the odd actor. Such an alliance is likely to eliminate the odd actor. There is always in principle a reasonable probability that any given actor will miscalculate on any particular move. This danger is particularly high in personality-dominant actors such as the warlords or the Italian city-states. But even if all actors possess a highly rational foreign policy apparatus—a state bureaucracy—there is always some probability that an actor will miscalculate. The difference between the three- and five-actor system is that in the five-actor system there are other actors to correct any miscalculations. In the three-actor system, once a weak actor allies with the strongest, there are no actors available to assist the excluded weakling. Therefore, the probability increases that a three-actor system will be short-lived.

In the Italian system the peculiar geography of Italy produced a situation that somewhat fits the three-actor logic. Because Florence was centrally located, it was to some extent a member of two different three-actor systems: one in the northern hemisphere and one in the southern. That was the reason that Cosimo's Triple Alliance was necessary. Florence had to ally with the two actors who posed the least danger (Milan and Naples) in each hemisphere. And that is why Lorenzo's reorientation to a northern-focused triple alliance was imprudent. It left him open to an overwhelming combination from the southern hemisphere, partly because geographical factors and threats by exogenous actors strongly impeded the ability of Milan and Venice to regulate disturbances arising in the south.[72] But the instability of three-actor systems is most clearly indicated in the Chinese warlord system.

---

70. Ch'i considers the period after 1928 to be significantly different from the conditions of a "balance of power" system. For his reasons, see *Warlord Politics*, 237ff.

71. Kaplan, *Towards Professionalism*, 137; Ch'i, *Warlord Politics*, 234.

72. cf. Franke, "The Italian City-State System," 449.

As with the Italian system, regional consolidation characterizes the first phase of the warlord system. There were a large number of independent or semi-independent warlords. The large number of actors greatly increased information and regulatory costs. Given their limited capabilities, this precluded any warlord from becoming a systemwide actor. Military units were generally small in size, poorly equipped, and logistically inefficient. As a result, all wars were localized and casualties were few. Wars, however, were frequent, and the phase was characterized by much grouping, splitting up, and regrouping. This phase may be seen as one of extensive intra-regional activity aimed at consolidation. There was an absence of systemwide interaction. Anhwei was the most powerful actor by the end of the first phase (1918-1920), to a large extent because it controlled Peking. As a result, it launched a policy to reunify the nation by force. Anhwei attacked Hunan, and this led warlords to form larger groups. These processes finally crystallized around 1918-1919 in the emergence of three strong warlords who participated in the balancing process.[73]

The three essential actors during the second phase were Fengtien, Chihli, and Anhwei. There were also four nonessential warlord-actors.[74] This phase most closely corresponds to the theoretical action patterns of the "balance of power" system. Most of the essential rules were followed.

The frequency of wars during this phase—three in less than five years—indicates the sensitivity of the actors to imbalance. In the first and third wars, the weaker two actors banded together to frustrate the hegemonial ambitions of the stronger actor. As a result the stronger actor had to act alone against at least two others. As stated above, that pattern is consistent with the requirements of a "balance of power" system.

In the war of 1920, Anhwei was the most powerful actor. Opposed by Chihli and Fengtien, Anhwei was defeated and its capabilities were significantly reduced. After its defeat both victors cooperated in the installation of a new government, but by 1922 cooperation had broken down.

In the second war (1922), the victors fought. This war was characterized by a greatly increased number of combatants. Chihli had gained power after its troops underwent a period of intensive training. Because of alliance promises Fengtien had received, Chihli's increasing relative power may have seemed inconsequential. Fengtien, however, did not receive the promised support of either Kuomintang (KMT)—which was divided internally—or the remnants of Anhwei. The unavailability of actors to support Fengtien violated the rule to oppose actors attempting to achieve predominance.

---

73. Ch'i, "Warlord System," 414, 409-411.

74. Essential actors included Fengtien, Chihli, Anhwei (before 1924), Kuominchun (after 1924), and Kuomintang (after 1924). In addition to the Kuomintang, nonessential actors in the first two phases included Shansi, Szechwan, and Hunan. All actors were highly subsystem dominant and directive. Ch'i, "Warlord System," 409.

After a week, Chihli defeated Fengtien. Chihli thereby became the most powerful actor in the system, and its expectations rose. It gained control of the cabinet, and then bribed its way into the presidency. It then further expanded into Anhwei-controlled areas. The following year, it demanded further concessions from the seriously weakened Anhwei. This led to the third war (1924), in which Fengtien and Anhwei both opposed Chihli. Although this combination is consistent with the requirements of a "balance of power" system, it was unsuccessful. The war completed the elimination of Anhwei as an essential actor. But during intense conflict between the remaining two actors, one of Chihli's generals returned from the front, occupied the capital, and took over the central government. This shattered the morale of the remaining Chihli forces. Within days, their front was broken and their forces retreated to the south.

Despite rough resemblance to "balance of power" rules, there were still significant violations during this phase. During the second war, the failure of any actors to join Fengtien against Chihli violated the fourth rule: act to oppose actors that assume a position of predominance. The progressive elimination of Anhwei violated the third rule: stop fighting before eliminating an essential actor. There is no evidence that the victors wanted either Anhwei to remain in the system, or any other essential actor to replace it. This violated the sixth rule as well.[75] It is even arguable that the first war was a violation of the third rule. After all, Anhwei was very severely reduced (from approximately ten to approximately two provinces).

According to Ch'i, this high level of disequilibrial action resulted from a number of factors. These factors included improved weaponry and an expansion in the size of armies. That led to an expansion in the scale of war and mounting casualties. The increasing use of offensive artillery meant the end of siege warfare against city walls. Lines of communication became important as warfare moved into the field. Subsequent wars tended to be fought along main lines of communication, particularly railways. Artillery easily permitted victors to march into the territory of the loser and occupy it. Each of these factors undermined the stability of the system. (This was unlike geographical factors in the Italian case, for example, which amplified the stability of the system). And the small number of actors had insufficient capacity to regulate this disequilibrial behavior.

At the outset of the third phase (1924-1928), the warlord system departed further from the theoretically specified action patterns. As mentioned above, in the war of 1924 Anhwei was eliminated as an essential actor. Furthermore, Chihli's predominance was reversed by its split-away faction and Fengtien. The

---

75. The nonessential actors manifested a different pattern. Except for Hunan, they avoided entanglements. That kind of self-preservation formula could only work if the three essential actors were capable of regulating hegemonial attempts. And during the second phase they were only somewhat successful. See Ch'i, "Warlord System," 411-412.

split-away faction formed a new essential actor, the Kuominchun (KMC). The emergence of KMC maintained the number of actors at three, despite Anhwei's elimination. Its emergence also led the weakened Chihli to retreat.

Fengtien was now the strongest actor in the system. However, the Fengtien-KMC alliance immediately fought over division of spoils. (Fengtien successfully replaced the pro-KMC governor of Tientsin). But two factors temporarily dampened the conflict. One was the need of both actors for internal consolidation and military growth. Second, during 1925 Fengtien preferred to expand against Chihli-controlled territory. During this thrust, by Fengtien the KMC did not participate in regulating the system. It was busy consolidating its internal position. But about a year later the KMC moved against Fengtien. That action was consistent with optimal behavior. The two weaker actors—KMC and Chihli—opposed the strongest. Although Fengtien-KMC diplomatic negotiations quieted their relations briefly, as soon as a powerful Fengtien general defected and attacked Fengtien's home base, with the knowledge of the KMC, the KMC opened a second front. Fengtien, however, held its ground. It defeated its former general, and the KMC backed off. Chihli then made its next move. But instead of joining forces with the KMC, which was weaker, it joined Fengtien. That move constituted the system's first aggressive alliance. In terms of the theory, it was a major miscalculation, for it made the second-ranked KMC the odd actor.

The reason for this miscalculation was the result of an ideological parameter that undermined international rationality. Because the KMC had split off from Chihli in 1924, Chihli resented its disloyalty and would not consider it as a potential alliance partner. Thus, the Chihli-Fengtien alignment violated the rules to oppose hegemonial coalitions (fourth rule) and to treat all actors as acceptable alliance partners (sixth rule).

Henceforth, the KMC was continually at war with either Fengtien, or Chihli, or both. Faced with this combination, the probability of KMC elimination greatly increased. But amidst this northern conflict, the KMT emerged from the south as a now-powerful essential actor. Prior to this, KMT internal divisions and opposition by regional warlords precluded its systemwide role. But it underwent reorganization in 1923-1924 that transformed it into an essential actor with a nationalist (immoderate) ideology. In June 1926, it launched a northern expedition that by 1928 had destroyed the warlord system as a "balance of power" system.[76]

The KMT began by attacking Chihli from the south, while Chihli was preoccupied with the KMC in the north. The KMT penetrated deeply into Chihli territory and also forged an alliance with the KMC in September 1926. Although battlefield and internal problems delayed KMT's victory over Chihli, victory was achieved in August 1927. Meanwhile, the KMC also continued fighting Fengtien. They were slowly pushing Fengtien back when they were

76. See footnote 70.

joined first by Shansi, a nonessential actor, and then by the KMT (after it had finished off Chihli). By spring 1928, Fengtien's defense perimeter began to crumble. By June, the war was over. In December, Fengtien relinquished its autonomous status and returned all administrative and military authority to the nationalist government.

The third phase violated numerous essential rules. Negotiations as a means of conflict resolution declined as a result of the KMT. Its nationalist ideology did not permit negotiations beyond a choice of "collaborate or surrender." They also exhibited very little tolerance for the continued existence of other essential actors. The rule to oppose actors who aspire to a position of predominance was violated in 1925; no actors assisted Chihli when Fengtien attempted to expand. It was also violated by Chihli, when it joined Fengtien against the KMC. The latter move also violated the rules to treat all actors as acceptable alliance partners, and to negotiate rather than fight (the KMC had attempted to negotiate with Chihli, but Chihli rejected the offer). As a result, the KMC was almost eliminated. But it was able to form an alliance with the newly emerged KMT. In doing so, the KMC was transformed into an ideologically rigid actor. The KMT trained the KMC in its supranational (suprafactional) ideology. The system thereby entered into a highly unstable bipolar phase. All nonessential actors were absorbed into the conflict. Both alliances—the KMT-KMC and Chihli-Fengtien—now exhibited complete hostility. Neither camp considered actors in the other camp as acceptable role partners. This was particularly true of the KMT, which achieved predominance.[77]

In addition to the suboptimal number of actors, other factors amplified the disequilibrial tendencies and instability of the system. First, Peking was a center of legitimacy for all of China. All actors expected China to be unified at some point in the future. Peking was, therefore, a symbol of national unity that served as a lightning-rod for conflict. In game-theoretic terms, the actors very highly discounted the future. They did not expect to play "balance of power" politics indefinitely, a belief that increased insecurity and meant that capability advantages would be exploited to achieve hegemony. This insecurity was amplified by the fact that defeated actors could not really be preserved because they had no basis for control other than military power. Defeat in battle implied a power vacuum that had to be filled by the victor before someone else filled it.[78] These beliefs reduced international rationality. There was no reason for moderation in a system in which the other actors were likely to be immoderate at the first opportunity. A further indication of this problem was that the actors were economic mismanagers. Rational economic development was, of course, unlikely when the actors were rootless occupiers who could not reasonably calculate their longevity.

---

77. Ch'i, *Warlord Politics*, 226-232; idem, "Warlord System," 412-413.
78. Ch'i, "Warlord System," 413-414, 415-420; idem, *Warlord Politics*, 232ff.

In a strict sense of "explain," the "balance of power" model explains very little of the Chinese Warlord System. When the initial conditions of the model bore some resemblance to the empirical situation, the warlord system manifested the closest resemblance to the expected action patterns. This situation occurred during the second phase, when the two weaker actors banded together to oppose the strongest, though even then this pattern was violated. But in a wider sense, the theory does explain the disequilibrial actions and instability of the system. The number of actors—three—falls below the minimum threshold of five. As predicted by the theory, the balancing process is likely to be unsustainable under this condition. Moreover, part of the basic theory of bipolarity is confirmed in this case.[79] During the third phase, the system resembled a tight bipolar system. All actors were gobbled up into two rigidly opposed camps, one of which was based on a suprafactional ideology and training program. This camp also had superior capabilities—though by no means overwhelmingly superior capabilities. This bipolarity destroyed the "balance of power" characteristics of the system. And it was highly unstable, a result that is consistent with the basic theory of bipolarity.

European State System

The Italian and Chinese cases demonstrate the applicability of the "balance of power" model under both equilibrial and nonequilibrial conditions. However, the model was originally designed with the European state system in mind. In this section, I discuss the model's applicability to the pre-World War I period of this system.

Because the behavior of the actors—particularly after France and Germany became implacable opponents in 1871—violates a number of essential rules and properties of a theoretical "balance of power" system, it raises the question of whether another model better fits the historical data. Some writers have treated the post-1890 period of this system as a bipolar system. And Kaplan has raised—and rebutted—the idea that this period should be treated as a rigid balance of power system. (Still others consider the period as a multipolar system. However, the inapplicability of the bipolar-multipolar dichotomy has been treated in chapter 5 and will not be revisited here.)

The problem of model-fitting to this period entails a two-step process. The first question is to determine whether the pre-World War I period should be classified as a "balance of power" or bipolar system. I argue that the "balance of power" classification provides a much better fit across cases.

A respectable argument consistent with the focal presupposition classifies the period after 1890, and particularly after 1907, as a "bipolar" system. The argument is based on the existence of two rigid alliances, the Triple Alliance (Germany, Austria-Hungary, and Italy) and the Triple Entente (France, Russia,

---

79. See below.

and Great Britain). Furthermore, this argument characterizes World War I as a result of this bipolarity: "It is enough to say that in the simplest terms, the First World War resulted from the inflexibility of the alliances and the lack of control by the senior members over the most irresponsible of their partners."[80] The statement that the inflexibility of the system was a major precipitant of World War I is unobjectionable. And as argued below, this rigidity also partially accounts for the severity of that war. But the inflexibility occurs primarily in Franco-German relations,[81] making the bipolar classification a poor fit. If it were to apply here, it cannot be applied to the post-1945 Western-Warsaw system without either doing violence to consistency or making the concept so superficial that it loses its theoretical significance. The two systems even present different symptoms. Blocs in the post-1945 system had ideological bases, institutional apparatuses, were based in part on a "three musketeer" principle—all for one and one for all—and were multilateral. On the other hand, the argument that was applied to the Italian triple alliance during the 1400s is again applicable in the pre-World War I European system. Although the European Triple Alliance and Triple Entente were somewhat long-lasting, they were not based on long-term commitments. The alliances were bilateral, instrumental, were not ideologically motivated, and had no institutional apparatus. Moreover, the bilateral arrangements resulted in clauses that applied differentially among the actors.[82]

Although Franco-German relations were rigid, the argument that the alliances were rigid is also shaky. Italy and France, for example, agreed in 1902 to remain neutral if the other was attacked. This diluted Italy's pledges to the other members of the Triple Alliance. In fact, in 1914 Italy chose neutrality when Austria attacked Serbia, and in 1915 declared war on Austria. The following year, Italy declared war on Germany. And although Great Britain drifted closer to France and Russia, neither the Entente Cordiale nor the Anglo-Russian agreement of 1907 were alliances. It is quite plausible that without the German naval program, Britain would have shown greater indifference toward Germany,

---

80. Gordon A. Craig and Alexander L. George, *Force and Statecraft* (New York: Oxford University Press, 1988), 40ff. Cf. Richard N. Rosecrance, *Action and Reaction in World Politics: International Systems in Perspective* (Boston: Little, Brown and Co., 1963), 254, 257.

81. Although Austrian-Russian relations were in conflict over the Balkans, there was nothing in principle that prevented a resolution of their differing interests, whereas Franco-German relations became nationalistically rigid following the annexation of Alsace-Lorraine. As a result, public opinion made any Franco-German alignment highly implausible.

82. In the Triple Alliance, Italy promised assistance if either of its allies were attacked by two or more great powers, assistance to Germany if it were attacked by France, but only neutrality in the event of war between Austria-Hungary and Russia. Both Austria-Hungary and Germany were to assist Italy if it was attacked by France. At Italy's request, in no case would the treaty operate against Great Britain.

whereas in the post-1945 bipolar system British commitments to NATO were not based on specific Soviet armaments policies. Therefore, it seems far more consistent to treat the actors as part of a "balance of power" system, since their relationships are in closer conformity with the initial conditions of that model.

All the essential actors were territorially independent, functionally undifferentiated, and constituted separate centers of legitimacy. In other words, there were no collective actors in Europe at this time. Alone, however, this closer fit does not constitute an explanation. Despite the closer fit, the behavioral pattern of the actual historical system departs from the theoretical action pattern. In the theory, alignments are supposed to be flexible and short-term, and wars are supposed to be limited. Although alliance relations were not bipolar, they were clearly much less flexible than the theory suggests. And World War I was not limited. These discrepancies raise the second question of whether the underlying theory of the "balance of power" model can be used to explain the behavioral pattern of this period, or whether an alternative, such as a rigid balance of power theory, must be formulated.

There are two good reasons to reject the formulation of an alternative theory to replace the "balance of power" model in the pre-World War I period. The first is scope. Of two theories, that both explain a particular phenomenon, the one that also explains other phenomena is preferable. This guards against the multiplication of theories. It is in this sense that the "balance of power" model is preferred over a rigid balance of power model. The "balance of power" model successfully explains large parts of the European state system and the Italian city-state system. Departures from the initial conditions of the model are correlated with departures from equilibrium in the Chinese warlord system and some phases of the Italian system. These results indicate that the model has wide and substantial applicability. If departures from equilibrium in the European state system are also correlated with departures in the initial conditions of the model, such that we can understand the disequilibrial behavior (rule violations) on the basis of the divergence of empirical conditions from the theoretical specifications, then the "balance of power" model is to be preferred to alternatives that lack this breadth.

As mentioned above, after 1871 the European system violated a number of essential rules of a "balance of power" system. In particular, the unlimited nature of World War I was a violation of the third (war limitation) rule, the unwillingness of France to consider Germany as an alliance partner violated the sixth rule, (treat all essential actors as acceptable alliance partners), and the unwillingness to negotiate over Alsace-Lorraine violated the first rule.

These violations, in fact, are correlated with departures from the initial conditions of the model. In particular, the model is premised upon the international rationality of the actors. As stated above, this means that the values of the actors are focused on optimizing security, and no intra-actor factors interfere with this objective. However, Bismarck's war with France in 1871 was to some extent based on the danger of losing the momentum, particularly among the south German states, towards German national integration.[83] Thus, the war, and the subsequent annexation of Alsace-Lorraine, were not fully motivated by international calculations. There is evidence that Bismarck recognized that the annexation would cause long-term problems in the functioning of the system.[84]

The annexation of Alsace-Lorraine may be compared with the first phase of the Italian city-state system. One of the factors that prevented the destabilization of the Italian system during the first phase was the ease of territorial transfer. The smaller cities had no ideological attachments to the essential actors. Therefore, the transfer of the smaller territories among the essential actors facilitated conflict resolution. But the annexation of Alsace-Lorraine occurred during a period of nationalism. Bismarck, in fact, encouraged these sentiments in order to annex the territories, and the annexation in turn fanned the flames of French nationalism. After this time, Franco-German relations could not be calculated on the basis of internationally rational considerations. Nationalistic sentiments interfered with security calculations. A Franco-German alignment became implausible, which is a violation of the sixth rule.

One of the main reasons for the war-limitation (third) rule, is the need to preserve future alliance partners. The violation of the sixth rule thereby destroyed the reason for war limitation. There is ample evidence that Poincare (a Lorrainer), Clemenceau, Joffre, and Foch wanted a complete victory over Germany that would guarantee the restoration of the lost provinces.[85] Thus, the unlimited nature of World War I follows (at least partially) from the deviations of actual from theoretical conditions. In the context of the model's other successes, the corroboration of the model in this phase of the European system further erodes the prudence of formulating an alternative balance of power model.

LOOSE BIPOLAR SYSTEM

The loose bipolar system is not a variant of the "balance of power" system. The initial structural and regime characteristics, and the optimal equilibrial action pattern are of a different type. It was this fundamental insight, shared roughly at the same time by Kaplan and Arthur Lee Burns, that launched the variegated efforts to understand how different types of international systems function. The post-1945 international system of Western-Warsaw competition was the concrete system that these social scientists attempted to model theoretically. In Kaplan's case, the general idea behind the argument is that different alliance relations among actors imply different optimal action patterns.

---

83. Otto von Bismarck, *Bismarck: The Man and the Statesman*, 2 vols. (New York: Harper and Brothers, 1898), II: 98-100, 121-22.

84. Ibid., 251-252.

85. See, for example, David S. Newhall, *Clemenceau* (Lewiston, NY: The Edwin Mellen Press, 1991), 64-65, 114, 135, 278; and Edgar Holt, *The Tiger: The Life of George Clemenceau, 1841-1929* (London: Hamilton, 1976), 24-25, 47, 99, 120, 159-160.

The basic bipolar action pattern is one of long-term, intrinsically motivated competition between two blocs of actors in pursuit of rival conceptions of international order. The basic theoretical problem of this pattern is: How is a stable order possible in the face of this rigid opposition? And the basic answer is that the blocs must maintain their solidarity, membership, and defensive capabilities. Thus, in a bipolar system the substantive focus shifts from the analysis of autonomous entities in pursuit of self-aggrandizement to the analysis of collectivities in pursuit of consolidated security. As a result, most of the initial conditions and their interrelationships are starkly different than in the "balance of power" system.

Initial Conditions

The initial conditions of Kaplan's loose bipolar system are divided into the same formal sets of variables—international structure, regime characteristics, and action patterns—as the "balance of power" model. However, the content of these variables differs.

International Structure. The essential actors in Kaplan's loose bipolar system are two blocs, each with leading and nonleading members, a universal actor, and a group of uncommitted (nonbloc) actors. The blocs constitute long-term, "permanent" alliance relationships based on intrinsic interests. A bloc approaches the form of an institutionalized collectivity. In contrast, the uncommitted actors are similar to a latent group: they have a common interests, but lack organizational order and stability outside of what they gain from membership in the universal actor.

There is also role differentiation in this system. Bloc leaders and bloc members, the universal actor, and the uncommitted actors each have different role functions. For example, military intervention on the part of a bloc member violates the norms of the system unless it is accepted by the member's bloc leader. Thus, national actors that are bloc members cannot exclusively follow their own narrowly construed self-interest, but must partly integrate their individual and group identities. Uncommitted and universal actors also play different roles—in particular a mediatory role. The different role functions imply different optimal behavior for each kind of actor-system. (These rules are specified below in the section on action patterns.)

Compared to one another, the blocs are within a similar capability range. The weaponry in the loose bipolar system—at least in the twentieth century—is nuclear. To the extent that the bipolar system has stability, stable nuclear systems are a major component in the explanation. In the absence of stable nuclear systems, advanced logistic and operational capabilities would increase the probability of one bloc overwhelming the other.

Compared to the other actors, the blocs have operationally predominant capabilities that render them relatively immune from national security threats arising from nonbloc international actors. But the universal and uncommitted actors have sufficient capabilities to influence a contest between the blocs.

As with the "balance of power" system, there must be sufficient informational transparency for the actors to act rationally. But in bipolar systems, informational transparency is likely to fall below an optimal level, since high levels of dysfunctional tension and ideological solidarity are not conducive to communication across the interbloc boundary. (In the post-1945 international system, this factor was mitigated by technological developments in satellites and optics.)

Regime Characteristics.   Regime characteristics are a place-holder for international rationality. In the model the actors are rational; in the real world the actors have regime characteristics. The internationally rational actor, it will be recalled, prefers a high probability of survival to a moderate probability of hegemony at the risk of elimination. As with "balance of power" systems, regime characteristics refer to intra-actor organizational characteristics. But because the focus has shifted away from autonomous actors to blocs, regime characteristics in a bipolar system refer to intrabloc organizational characteristics.[86] In this type of system, security is likely to be optimal if blocs are neither too directive and hierarchical nor too nondirective and nonhierarchical.[87]

In Kaplan's lexicon, a bloc can be hierarchical, mixed-hierarchical, or nonhierarchical. The relative independence of the member's national political functions—especially their foreign offices—is an important touchstone of bloc hierarchy. A bloc in which these functions have been replaced by a single foreign office and integrated national functions is a hierarchical bloc. A bloc in which these functions are decentralized among the members and in which the bloc makes decisions through bargaining and consensual procedures is a nonhierarchical bloc. A bloc in which these functions exist, but are largely subordinate to the bloc leader's direction is a mixed-hierarchical bloc. In the post-1945 international system, the Western bloc was a nonhierarchical system and the Soviet bloc was a mixed-hierarchical system. Moreover, in comparison the Western bloc was nondirective (democratic) and the Soviet bloc was directive (dictatorial).

The mixed-hierarchical bloc is likely to be more internationally rational than the nonhierarchical bloc. Because the bloc has significant hierarchical features, the bloc leader is relatively insulated from the opinions of bloc members. Therefore, mixed-hierarchical blocs are likely to maintain a more consistent

---

86. The situation is actually more complex than this statement implies. The relative system or subsystem dominance, and the directive or nondirective characteristics of the national actors will be parameters that interact with bloc regime characteristics in a manner that further modifies the rationality of the actors. That level of complexity is beyond the scope of this text, and would best be treated in a computer model. Kaplan specifies some general relationships in *System and Process*, chaps. 3, 5, and 6.

87. In somewhat oversimplified terms, the more hierarchical a system, the more it is directive (dictatorial). Military chain-of-command systems, for example, tend towards this form. The less hierarchical a system, the more it is nondirective. Committee structures tend towards this form. See Kaplan, *System and Process*, 18.

international focus.   Nonhierarchial blocs are more likely to suffer from collective action problems.

Thus, more than the mere presence of blocs, or their number, is involved in Kaplan's basic theory.   The functioning of the loose bipolar system depends on the organizational characteristics of the blocs.   Consider two permutations.   If both blocs are nonhierarchical, the system will tend to resemble a "balance of power" system.   However, if one bloc tends towards mixed-hierarchy and the other towards nonhierarchy—as in the post-1945 system—the system will have more diverse characteristics.   The mixed-hierarchical bloc will tend to retain its membership, regardless of member preferences.   This involuntary retention will pose a threat to all other actors.   The nonhierarchical bloc will tend to have a looser hold over its members but will maintain those relationships in part because of the threat posed by the hierarchical bloc.[88]

In any empirical bipolar system, ideological signals may be present in at least one of the blocs.   If those signals are internalized they will probably further reduce the international rationality in the system.   The origin of bipolar systems—as opposed to their functioning—may be in part a product of such signals.   That was certainly the case in the post-1945 international system, and is evident during the semi-bipolar aspects of the Chinese warlord system (KMT-KMC vs. Fengtien and Chihli) as well as those aspects of the ancient Greek system that resemble bipolarity.[89]

However, the origin of the system was not primarily ideological.   The Soviet Union imposed a mixed-hierarchical bloc on the Eastern European states.   The West had to defend itself.   The Western response would have occurred even if the Soviet Union was capitalistic but still mixed-hierarchical.   The ideological factors are symptomatic.   And there were clearly asymmetric differences in the two blocs.   Whereas all the Western bloc members would tend to welcome the disintegration of the Soviet bloc, Soviet bloc members could not afford the victory of the Soviet Union.   These factors, unlike ideology, are concrete system parameters responsible for the origin of the loose bipolar system.

---

88. Kaplan, *System and Process*, 37-38.   I here ignore the possibility of two hierarchical blocs, as Kaplan uses that term.   In my judgment, Kaplan's hierarchical bloc is so close to a hierarchical actor—a state—that the concept of bloc may no longer apply, except perhaps in the embryonic or terminal phases of the actor's development.   Two hierarchical blocs would tend to resemble a dyarchic state system (if the blocs were directive and all the other actors had been incorporated or were too weak to influence interbloc competition), or a "balance of power" system (if the other actors were sufficiently strong to contribute to their own protection).   See also ibid., 40-41, 75ff.

89. It is not clear how to classify the ancient Greek system during the fifth century B.C.   The leagues led by Athens and Sparta bear some resemblance to blocs, had institutional apparatus in the case of the Delian League, had strong ideological characteristics, and were in many ways based on long-term mind-sets.   However, there were essential actors—Boeotia, Corinth, Argos—whose flexible and shifting alliance behavior more closely resembles a "balance of power" system.

In the earliest formulation of the loose bipolar system, Kaplan included a number of regime parameters in the specification of the basic theory. The original essential rules, for example, differentiated between mixed-hierarchical and nonhierarchical blocs. In later formulations, Kaplan formulated the rules in undifferentiated form. The latter approach is more consistent with the formulation and methods of the "balance of power" system. The earlier formulation indicated a greater reliance on the characteristics of the historically concrete bipolar system that inspired the model. In the following specification of essential rules, I present the later formulation—which ignores organizational departures from rationality. In the next section, I discuss the prudence of further modifications of the essential rules. In particular, I scrutinize the relevance of universal and uncommitted actors in the basic theory. I also discuss the relevance of including nuclear weapons technology in the theory.

Action Patterns. As a result of its different international structure, the essential rules that can be expected in a bipolar system bear only scant resemblance to those in the "balance of power" system. If the initial conditions stated above are at specified values, the hypothesized essential rules of Kaplan's loose bipolar system are as follows.[90]

1. Blocs strive to increase their relative capabilities.

2. Blocs tend to be willing to run at least some risks to eliminate rival blocs.

3. Blocs tend to engage in major war rather than to permit rival blocs to attain predominance.

4. Blocs tend to subordinate objectives of the universal actor to objectives of the bloc but subordinate objectives of rival blocs to the universal actor.

5. Nonbloc actors tend to support the universal actor generally and specifically against contrary objectives of blocs.

6. Nonbloc and universal actors tend to act to reduce the danger of war between blocs.

7. Nonbloc actors tend to be neutral between blocs except where important objectives of the universal actor are involved.

8. Blocs tend to extend membership but tend to tolerate the status of nonbloc actors.

---

90. Morton A. Kaplan, ed., *New Approaches*, 393, reprinted in Kaplan, *Towards Professionalism*, 141.

Bipolar Theory: Basics and Boundaries

The empirical application of bipolar conceptions is beyond the scope of this book. Elsewhere I present and apply an extended theory of bipolarity. Here I simply mention some difficulties in Kaplan's basic theory. Each of these difficulties is part of the general question of whether Kaplan's particular model is too boundary-laden, that is, too dependent on the concrete structure of the post-1945 system.

An historical clue to these difficulties has been aforementioned. Kaplan had an earlier and later formulation of the rules for a loose bipolar system. The later formulation, more simplified and less dependent on the historically concrete post-1945 system, was presented above. That formulation abstracts from the regime characteristics of the blocs and presents rules for undifferentiated bloc actors. However, this does not seem to go far enough. The presence of nonbloc actors, universal actors, ideology, and nuclear weapons in the basic theory—as opposed to the real world—warrants additional scrutiny. Whereas there is no doubt whatsoever that these factors are relevant and necessary in the explanation of the historically concrete post-1945 system, there is reasonable doubt that the basic theory of bipolar systems should include these factors.

The general theoretical reason to remove these factors is that it may increase the power of the theory and make it applicable to a wider range of phenomena. Clearly, a theory that attempts to remove too many factors will become so abstract that it will constitute a generality rather than a generalization. And a theory that avoids abstraction will travel a road of descriptive detail to a pointless conclusion. Kaplan's loose bipolar system is very good middle ground between these two extremes. But the particular trade-off between the theoretical and empirical poles of analysis may not be optimal. Some careful tweaking may improve the theory's consistency with other aspects of the theory of international politics, increase its empirical extension, and facilitate research.

Actors. The types of actors specified in Kaplan's loose bipolar system are blocs (with both leading and nonleading members), nonbloc (uncommitted) national actors, and a universal actor (somewhat analogous to the United Nations). As the essential rules indicate, these types of actors all have specialized role functions in the model. In particular, uncommitted and universal actors mediate the dysfunctional tension inherent in a bipolar international system. In order to do so, these actors must have sufficient capabilities "to influence a contest between the blocs." Kaplan believes that failures of these actors to fulfill this mediatory function—failures in essential rules five through seven—increase the instability of the loose bipolar system.[91]

However, it is by no means unambiguous why universal and uncommitted actors are necessary in a model of bipolarity. There are two reasons to question the inclusion of these actors. First, the grounds for their classification as essential actors is not strong.

---

91. Kaplan, *System and Process*, 39-40.

The inclusion of actors in the class, essential actors, seems to beg for a stronger standard than "influence." One standard might be: an actor that is capable of threatening the survival of another essential actor if it becomes deviant. Nonbloc actors in the post-1945 system did not generally meet this standard. Though a great power, even China is an unlikely candidate. And to the extent that they are treated as a group, the uncommitted actors are a latent group unlikely to act together with respect to role function. With respect to the United Nations, even as the repository of the uncommitted it lacked sufficient capacity to meet this standard. If the universal and nonbloc actors had such power it is unclear that the system would be bipolar. Kaplan himself states: "If a universal actor is completely successful in carrying out its role functions, it may destroy the bipolar system and produce a universal international system."[92] He also recognizes the limited weight of these actors: "The loose bipolar system has a considerable degree of inherent instability since the action of non-member actors or universal actors is rarely of decisive importance in determining policies pursued by the bloc actors."[93]

In addition to strengthening the foundation for the classification of essential actors, the elimination of these actors from the basic theoretical model has a corollary benefit. It makes the basic model more consistent with the basic model used in the "balance of power" system. The presence of nonessential actors also affects historical "balance of power" systems. In the Italian system, for example, large numbers of nonideological, nonessential actors contributed to stability during the first phase. Despite the disequilibrial tendencies of the essential actors, the existence of large numbers of other actors facilitated territorial transfers that served as a mechanism of conflict resolution. But such actors are not included in the model of that system. On similar grounds, the presence—rather than the behavior—of uncommitted and universal actors may be sufficient to reduce the dysfunctional tension between the blocs.

The second reason to drop these actors is that their hypothesized optimal behavior—specified in rules five through seven—is unnecessary if the blocs follow the other rules. If it could be shown that their behavior is a major international factor that will lead the blocs to follow their proper role function, then grounds would exist for their retention. But that would be a difficult argument to maintain, since those rules were often followed only weakly in the post-1945 system, and the system nonetheless persisted for a considerable period of time. Thus, the theoretical problem is that these actors do not seem systematically relevant to a bipolar model.

Although in the actual post-1945 system these actor-systems cannot be dismissed without abandoning many major postwar events, they seem to have too much analytical weight in the theoretical model to permit the development of a theory as powerful as the "balance of power" theory. Therefore, it seems

---

92. Ibid., 42.
93. Ibid.

plausible to drop Kaplan's simplified fifth, sixth, and seventh rules about nonbloc and universal actors.

Ideology. As mentioned above, the earliest formulation of the loose bipolar system included bloc regime characteristics in the basic theory. Also included were statements specifying that the origins of the system were partly the result of the ideological characteristics of the Soviet bloc. Earlier portions of this book have continued this argument, using ideological characteristics of blocs as one of the distinguishing features between "balance of power" and bipolar systems. Both types of factors are almost certain to be present in any empirical bipolar system—much as fever is likely to be present in many diseases. However, both factors should be removed from the basic theory of bipolarity.

The basic theory of bipolarity should focus on the equilibrial functioning of the blocs. In the early formulation of the loose bipolar system Kaplan states that the functioning of the system depends on the organizational characteristics of the supranational blocs.[94] But Kaplan's term "loose" is irrelevant, because the argument which follows indicates that it is the very looseness of any bipolar system that will be effected by the organizational characteristics of the blocs.

However, if this factor has such weight, then Kaplan's original essential rules could not be consistent with all three starting states. Thus, it was necessary to formulate a set of rules that apply to blocs generally. In fact, the simplification of the essential rules along these lines is consistent with Kaplan's later formulation. All the later rules referring to bloc actors eliminate the formulations that differentiated blocs in terms of their intra-organizational structure.[95] Then bloc organizational structure and ideological characteristics can be engineered as "actor regime" parameters in specific concrete cases. Whether both blocs are hierarchical, nonhierarchical, or include one of each type is a parameter—initial condition—for the empirical application of an extended bipolar model. The same rationale entails the suppression of ideological factors as part of the basic theory, factors which are necessary for determining the directivity of the bloc. Although ideological factors may be too ephemeral to receive systematic theoretical treatment, bloc organizational characteristics are systematized in my extended theory of bipolarity.[96]

Weapons Technology. Did nuclear weapons transform international politics and amplify the equilibrium and stability of the postwar bipolar system? The answer must almost certainly be yes. The reason that nuclear weapons seem relevant is that they increase the absolute costs of war and the velocity of destruction. Thus, they make essential actor wars far more risky and irreversible than wars in the "balance of power" system. Balancing behavior tends to become highly dysfunctional. But does that constitute a rationale for the

---

94. Ibid., 37-38, 74-83.
95. See footnote 90.
96. Dunne, *The Life and Death of Bipolar Systems* (manuscript).

inclusion of technology in the basic theory of bipolarity? Here the answer is more ambiguous.

If nuclear weapons—or transformations in the cost-of-war parameter which they represent—are included in the basic theory of bipolarity, then the basic theory becomes very difficult to apply to cases prior to 1945. If a clear-cut case of bipolarity existed prior to the nuclear revolution—and that is by no means clear—it would be far more difficult to sort out the explanation, particularly in the case that the system was unstable.

Although this is a rather weak criticism of Kaplan's model, I include it merely to emphasize the importance of separating basic from parametric aspects of the theory. However, one system in which nuclear weapons are basic to the theoretical formulation—since the system is inconceivable in their absence—is the unit-veto system. The step-functional effect of nuclear weapons on international politics is best examined in the following brief discussion of this system.

THE UNIT-VETO SYSTEM

The unit-veto system has no historical counterpart. It was developed largely as a mind-stretching exercise in order to consider some implications of nuclear weapons on the international system. The basic idea of the system is one in which nuclear weapons have proliferated to a large number of states that tend to recoil from alignments and rely on a self-sufficient conception of security. Thus, the unit-veto system is a highly nonintegrated system.

As with the bipolar system, Kaplan's specification of this system evolved over time. The early version was somewhat darker and more pessimistic than the later. In fact, because the early formulation was characterized as highly unstable, its status as an equilibrium model may be questioned. But the early formulation was based on an assured destruction conception of nuclear strategy, whereas the later version is consistent with more developed nuclear strategic conceptions. The following brief presentation is based largely on the later formulation.[97]

The structure of the system includes perhaps twenty-odd nuclear-capable actors. These actors possess a not incredible first-strike capability. This means that actors will not have an unambiguous capability to destroy an opponent in a first strike, but may have sufficient capability to greatly reduce an opponent's forces. Starting a war might therefore be contemplated. Alignments will not be highly valued in this system, and essential actors will tend to be national actors. Any role differentiation that occurs will be based on the capabilities of the actors. Great nuclear powers with credible second-strike capabilities would probably exist as a subset of nuclear capable actors. For at least a significant number of nuclear-capable actors there must be adequate command and control resources to ensure uninterrupted information during war. In any empirical

---

97. Compare *System and Process*, 50-52, with *Towards Professionalism*, 145-147.

system likely to evolve into this form, non-nuclear actors will probably exist, and possibly a universal actor. But the importance of such actors would be even more limited than it was during the post-1945 bipolar system.

The action patterns of this system would be unique. Any first strike that succeeded against a nuclear-capable actor would leave the sender vulnerable to complete destruction—because of the depleted arsenal—by other nuclear actors. Therefore, no nuclear capable actor should launch a first strike except under extreme provocation. Limited non-nuclear wars would be preferable to limited retaliatory wars or warning shots, and these action patterns would be preferable to countervalue or counterforce wars. To the extent that coalitions—though not highly valued—form, they must be nonideological and committed to retaliation against aggressors. Actors not directly involved in a dispute should attempt to mediate the dispute, though their success is likely to be weak. Self-sufficiency would tend to be the most powerful norm in conflict resolution. Interventionary activities might trigger conflicts, but the danger of nuclear escalation would tend to limit the number of interventionary actions. On the other hand, the danger would probably increase the tolerance for the scale of intervention (when compared to the bipolar system.) Finally, the great nuclear powers would tend to become isolationist, because the system, based on self-sufficiency, would not single out any particular actor for a leadership role. (A somewhat analogous situation occurred in the Balkan conflict during the 1990s).

With respect to regime characteristics, directive, subsystem dominant actors will be most internationally rational. In fact one could argue that the system would encourage actors that were nondirective and system dominant to mutate towards this form, at least with respect to security functions. This possibility is not without precedent. The rise of the national security state in the United States after 1947 certainly mitigated some of the democratic procedures that had previously existed in the federal government. The unit-veto system would be a far more dangerous and paranoia-generating system that would amplify the tendencies for these kinds of mutations.

Although under these conditions a unit-veto system might be stable, the reader will note the narrow range of its stability. The aloofness of great nuclear powers would tend to encourage sub-limited and limited wars among minor actors. The great might also annex smaller powers or otherwise threaten them. If the number of actors were reduced, or if limited acquisitions reduced the buffer areas between some states, the potential for hostility would rise. Moreover, the system is predicated on the existence of a large number of nuclear powers above the threshold of a not incredible first-strike capability but below the threshold of a credible or splendid first-strike capability. This range would seem unlikely to be stable across time. Of course, regardless of this system's stability, its peculiarity is theoretically interesting, even though it is empirically undesirable.

8

Basic Analytical Macrotheory

The previous chapter explored the distinctions between the initial conditions of basic theories of international politics and the applicability of those theories to concrete historical systems. This chapter analyzes some of the analytical characteristics of international macrotheory. The analysis covers the meaning and boundaries of basic theoretical concepts, their logical interrelationships, and the use of computers in theoretical analysis.

PARTIAL EQUILIBRIA

Kaplan's theoretical approach employs partial equilibrium models. Kaplan has consistently, and perhaps convincingly, maintained that general models of international systems are inappropriate to pursue. During the 1950s and 1960s, many social scientists attempted to construct general systems theory. Some were Kaplan's colleagues at The University of Chicago, such as David Easton. Arthur Lee Burns considered this possibility, and Chalmers Johnson and Ludwig Bertalanfy were prestigious proponents of general systems theory. It may be surmised that many of Kaplan's critics who accused him of constructing general systems models were drawing their inferences more by the associations of words and institutional affiliations than by any analysis of concepts. For example, Donald Puchala states: "Morton Kaplan contended that he was working deductively from the tenets of general systems theory . . ." It is difficult to comprehend such criticism. Neither the 1975 reprinted edition nor the 1957 edition supports this interpretation. *System and Process* cited none of the general system theorists. Kaplan cited only W. Ross Ashby, and the book presented six distinct international system models rather than a monotypical model. In fact, there is only scanty reference to what might be construed as a proposal for a general model of the international system.[1]

Puchala, however, seems to be reading a different book. His citation of *System and Process* is from a 1957 edition published by Columbia University Press.[2] I have been unable to find this edition. But perhaps Puchala's discovery will provide opportunities that scholars in philosophy have had when they've compared various editions of Locke's *Two Treatises of Government*, or the first and second edition of Kant's *Critique of Pure Reason*. But until the comparison of the original and the "hidden" text of the critics is published, the author has had to operate under the constraint of using the original text and Kaplan's other published works. And on those grounds, Kaplan cannot be said to have adopted general systems theory.[3]

The previous chapter provides substantive evidence for the part-systems quality of Kaplan's models. The particular types of political relationship in the initial structural conditions imply different optimal action patterns. When the theory is extended to include regime characteristics, geographical factors, weaponry, or other boundary conditions, further refinements in the equilibrial pattern are mandated. Cosimo de Medici's Triple Alliance was one such refinement. Thus, changes at the boundary partially determine the equilibrial pattern in any particular case.

Kaplan's basic framework, including the use of variables and parameters, attempts to construct an object language, not a general theory. This object

---

1. Kaplan left open the question of whether the six models of the international system were distinct systems or distinct equilibria within one ultrastable international system. *System and Process in International Politics* (New York: John Wiley, 1957), 21. Kaplan's most mature statement basing knowledge on the analysis of part-systems is in *Science, Language, and the Human Condition* (New York: Paragon House, 1984). Cf., W. Ross Ashby, *Design for a Brain* (New York: John Wiley, 1952), cited in *System and Process*, 7.

2. Donald J. Puchala, "Woe to the Orphans of the Scientific Revolution," in Robert L. Rothstein, ed., *The Evolution of Theory in International Relations: Essays in Honor of William T. R. Fox* (Columbia: University of South Carolina Press, 1991), 39-60, especially 53, 56. The article is generally a poor guide. For example, it equates positivism and science, which is unnecessary and confuses central ideas in the philosophy of science. In fact, Hoffmann, who Puchala likes, claimed to be committed to empirical theory, and represents a quite primitive positivism, one which lacks the coding criteria of twentieth century positivists such as Carnap. It is probably this confusion which leads Puchala to believe that Kaplan's greatest theoretical contributions were made when he was "thinking as a metaphysician," a position explicitly denied by Kaplan. Ibid., 40. And although on p. 48 Puchala cites Cassirer to bolster his attack on science, Cassirer held science in very high esteem. See, for example, Ernst Cassirer, *An Essay on Man: An Introduction to a Philosophy of Human Culture* (New Haven: Yale University Press, 1944), 207.

3. See also Kaplan, *Macropolitics: Essays on the Philosophy and Science of Politics* (New York: Free Press, 1969), 57.

language is a loose dictionary designed to avoid evocative and polemical discourse. The language and categories of analysis are for the most part generalized. Later in the chapter it will be shown that there are certain problems in this object language that made it difficult to manipulate analytically and apply empirically. But it is first necessary to consider the basic parts of this language.

In Kaplan's terminology there are three foci of equilibrium: within the set of essential rules, between the essential rules and the other variables, and between the essential rules and the environment. A stable equilibrium results from the compatibility of these three foci. Furthermore, departures from this tripartite consistency are the key to change.[4]

Although there are no substantive problems in this conception, the designation of all three foci under the label of "equilibrium" obscures some of the dynamic qualities of Kaplan's formulation. In order to provide the reader with brighter navigational flags, these three foci are redesignated as equilibrium analysis, stability analysis, and transformation analysis. Formal protocols governing the use of these concepts will be provided below in the section titled "Set Theory." Those protocols employ the three sets of initial conditions specified in chapter one and applied in the previous chapter. They state explicitly how the logical relationships among action patterns (essential rules), international structure (the other variables), and regime characteristics (the environment) vary depending on which kind of analysis is under investigation.

Because transformation analysis is dependent on either disequilibrial actions or unstable structures, it is useful, if not necessary, to first examine equilibrium analysis and stability analysis.

Equilibrium and Stability

Although not absolutely distinct, the concepts of stability and equilibrium have separate analytical centers. The meaning of equilibrium analysis centers upon a system's action patterns, whereas stability analysis centers upon the structure of international relationships. It is impossible to precisely discuss either concept alone, but the terms do refer to different aspects of a system.

Take alcohol consumption as an illustration. The action pattern of the moderate drinker does not generally damage the physiological structure of the human organism. Thus the action pattern is equilibrial and the structure in which it is embedded remains, other things being equal, stable.

The action pattern of the alcoholic, however, is one of increasing and indiscriminate consumption of alcohol. Continual alcohol consumption creates a need for further alcohol consumption. Thus, the action pattern produces

---

4. Kaplan, *Towards Professionalism in International Theory: Macrosystem Analysis* (New York: The Free Press, 1979), 57-58, 67; idem, *System and Process*, 25-26; idem, *New Approaches to International Relations* (New York: St. Martin's Press, 1968), 388.

changes in physiological structure that amplify the action pattern.[5] In this case the action pattern is disequilibrial, and structural stability is undermined by the disequilibrial behavior.

What may allow an alcoholic pattern to continue—to be stable at least in the short-term—is related to the human physiological system. There are no human arsenic junkies, and necessarily so, because human physiological systems lack the capacity to process arsenic. The alcohol pattern can be supported within a fairly wide toxilogical range, especially if rules for purity, rate of consumption per unit of time, and periodic abstinence are not regularly violated. The more unregulated—that is, disequilibrial—the action pattern, the more likely that it will destroy essential components of the physiological system. If severe enough, the system will terminate as a human system; or it may transform into a teetotaler system, if, for example, a medical problem develops. But it is the action pattern that is at the center of equilibrium analysis. The theoretical objective in formulating optimal action patterns is to make them consistent with the structure and regime characteristics of a system.

Even if the specific set of rules are consistent with a particular system, the structure itself may be unstable. In customary English usage, stability generally refers to that which supports something else. Thus, the stability of a house rests on its foundation, the stability of one's finances rests on one's assets, and the stability of a nation's security rests on its military forces. Kaplan does to some extent employ this structural concept of stability.

Consider the French political system in the late eighteenth . . . and early nineteenth century. If one examined it . . . paying particular attention to the form of government, it would have seemed highly unstable. If one examined it again in 1815, with the restoration of the Bourbon monarchy, it might have seemed stable. . . .[But] If it had been possible to examine other political, social, and economic aspects of the French political system . . . it would have been discovered that cumulative and probably irreversible *shifts in structure* were occurring. The system would have been . . . approaching a boundary beyond which it would no longer return to . . . Bourbon monarchy.[6]

Thus, it is the structure that is specified as making the equilibrial political action—monarchical decision-making—a result. And as shown in the previous chapter, it is the role functions, number, capabilities, and information of the

---

5. There is no evidence that Kaplan takes the position that equilibrium and stability are necessarily good qualities. To state that a system is in stable equilibrium does not make it a good system. Kaplan does take the position that an existing system creates a system of secondary needs that is valued, but not necessarily valuable from a more knowledge-able perspective. Thus, alcohol becomes increasingly valuable for such a system, but comparative analysis provides a basis for the hypothesis that alcohol, at least in large and indiscriminate doses, is not good and not valuable for the health of the physiological system.

6. Kaplan, *System and Process*, 7-8. Emphasis supplied.

actors making up the international system—the structure—that implies some optimal equilibrial pattern.

So what must be distinguished analytically is the question under investigation. The question in equilibrium analysis is: What structural conditions imply what equilibrial actions? Answers to this question are within the scope of Kaplan's first foci, the equilibrium within the set of rules. The question in stability analysis is: What effects do varying patterns of international action have on international structure? The answers to this question are within the scope of Kaplan's second foci, the relationship between the essential rules and the other variables. The alcoholic who breaks the equilibrial action pattern has a disequilibrial pattern that will greatly increase the probability of destabilizing his physical and psychological structures. Clearly these two questions are intimately related in the analysis of an international system.

AN EXPERIMENTAL INTERNATIONAL SYSTEM

With respect to international politics, the clearest use of Kaplan's first and second foci occur in the computer project developed by Donald Reinken in collaboration with Kaplan. The rationale for the computer project was not to retrodict or predict historical events. It was a tool to analyze the logical implications of Kaplan's "balance of power" model within explicitly stated boundary conditions, and to conduct parameter sensitivity studies: "Such a model is theoretical insofar as its propositions . . . admit of a test on the level of formal logical consistency and implication, apart from any factual embodiment, i.e., prior to application of the theory."[7] In this conception the computer serves as an equivalent of a controlled scientific experiment, and Reinken made it quite clear that he did not believe that the computer project could simulate reality.[8] Instead the project was presented as an effort to explore the idea of the balance of power, an idea that he dated to at least 1700.

The basic balance of power action pattern is one of short-term, instrumentally motivated, shifting alignments among autonomous actors in pursuit of self-aggrandizement. One of the major problems confronting pioneer social scientists was the difficulty of giving precise meaning to the concept of balancing.

I used to be puzzled, as a schoolboy, by historians of eighteenth-century wars who would end their accounts of peace treaties, ". . . and thus the balance of power was restored." What mysterious scales tilted level, what transcendent chandelier burned down to an

---

7. Donald L. Reinken, "Computer Explorations of the 'Balance of Power': A Project Report," in Morton A. Kaplan, ed., *New Approaches to International Relations* (New York: St. Martin's Press, 1968), 459; cf., idem, "Computable Models for Exploring the Idea of the 'Balance of Power'" (Ph.D. dissertation, The University of Chicago, 1969), 1.

   8. Reinken, "Computer Explorations," 463.

equipoise? What observations could possibly check the truth of these portentous opinions?

To attempt serious answers to the latter question is to undertake the theory of international politics.[9]

Indeed, if the mysterious expression could be objectified, it would, according to some, increase the possibility of using those objectifications to maintain peace. Lasswell, for example, summarized the problem:

> If certain conditions are fulfilled, the balancing of power process can maintain peace despite the expectation of violence. . . . The conditions will be formulated as follows:
>
> a. If variations in power (fighting effectiveness) can be accurately measured;
>
> b. If variations in fighting effectiveness are convertible and distributable among participants in the balancing process;
>
> c. If variations in power are visible in the early stages of their development;
>
> d. If the estimating process can be sentimentalized.[10]

Lasswell then argues how difficult these conditions are to fulfill. It is extremely difficult to empirically estimate fighting effectiveness. Technological innovation, for instance, imposes a continually potential source of error. A convertible and distributable medium of exchange is also an extremely difficult condition to fulfill, as anyone who has studied Soviet-American arms control knows. It generally takes years to negotiate the counting rules that have been developed to determine operational equivalents for army divisions, nuclear missiles, bombers, warheads, and so forth. The ability to accomplish these tasks in the eighteenth and nineteenth centuries—prior to satellites and computers—was obviously not present. Thus, the requirement for visibility was onerous. Finally, Lasswell's notion of "sentimentibility" was meant as a psychological substitute for the glorification of war that sometimes occurs in strategic circles; actors would instead have to develop a sort of romantic attachment to "counting" as such.

The last point is not terribly relevant for understanding the Reinken-Kaplan computer project, for even if researchers achieved such romantic attachments, the computer certainly did not. Moreover, the historical and technical problems of counting and otherwise measuring effectiveness is not of great importance. It

---

9. Arthur Lee Burns, *Of Powers and Their Politics: A Critique of Theoretical Approaches* (Englewood Cliffs, NJ: Prentice Hall, 1968), 4-5.

10. Harold D. Lasswell, *World Politics and Personal Insecurity* (New York: Whittlesey House, 1935), 57.

has already been stated that the project was designed to test the logic of Kaplan's "balance of power" system, rather than predict events in the world. Given this, two problems are immediately resolvable: the actors' capabilities (SIZEs) can be specified, and "visibility" can be made perfect; that is, the system can be treated as one of perfect information.

The problem of making the medium of exchange convertible and distributable, however, was a difficult theoretical hurdle. Historically, international actors in "balance of power" systems did make rough calculations as to the military capabilities of their potential opponents and allies, and a major mechanism by which those systems were maintained was to form alliances that would balance those capabilities. A limited war might then be fought, and the victorious coalition would be compensated in some way, usually with territory. The theoretical problem is that the balancing mechanism, the shifting alliances, entails ninety distinct combinations in the five-actor system—ninety-one if systemwide neutrality is included. And to this complexity must be added time, cost-benefit, and motivational uncertainties.

First consider the time factor. If two actors—A and C, for example—declare war on each other, that greatly reduces the remaining alliance combinations, as does each subsequent choice by the remaining actors. But how could A and C make such a choice not knowing what B, D, and E would do?

Uncertainty does not end with the number of alliance possibilities. The cost-benefit relationship of a particular war must also enter the calculations. There would be no value to a victory if there was little profit to be had. In addition, motivational factors further complicate decision-making. What modifications in the system's pattern of action are necessary if the number of deviants (Napoleons or Hitlers) increase?

Obviously, the number of system permutations and mixtures entailed by such complexity is daunting.[11] The computer is perhaps the only way to analyze the interrelationships in such a complex system, as contemporary physicists working with complex phenomena now understand. Indeed, contemporary meteorological

---

11. These complexities are perhaps what led previous researchers to turn balance of power into an ideological principle—a something that just occurs, a universal principle. From the perspective of human intellectual weakness, this approach is natural. Anthropologists have found two features that lead humans into mythical forms of consciousness. Myths are transduced in situations characterized by a knowledge gap and high fear. On this point see Ernst Cassirer, *An Essay on Man*, chap. VII, especially 92, where he states: "But a highly developed magic and, connected with it, a mythology always occur if a pursuit is dangerous and its issues uncertain." The knowledge gap in the possible alliance combinations has just been demonstrated, whereas the fear that attaches to war is obvious. Thus, it is perfectly understandable that the balance of power idea became as expansive as it did. On the other hand, Kaplan presented his theory sketches as plausible, and he did not imply that his systems were logically rigorous. See, for example, the first page of the original preface to *System and Process* as well as the 1964 preface to the paperback edition.

analysis is highly dependent on deterministic computer models, and despite popular notions that weathermen know little, modern meteorological science saves countless resources for the economy and countless lives every year.

Reinken's Realization Models

In fact, the particular models that were constructed were named "realization-models" which, Reinken claimed:

are incomplete representations of the "balance of power" idea, [which] do not supplant verbal theory. For the foreseeable future they only give advice on how theory . . . might be put together.[12]

By realization-model I mean a partial representation, where less useful details are suppressed if possible. The minimum is a concrete system of $\underline{n}$ actors capable of inflicting damage on each other's relative capabilities and behaving in patterns not clearly irrelevant to the "balance of power" idea.[13]

The War Game. Reinken's realization model was based on a two-sided war game under the Lanchester equations. Booty and loss factors for the winning and losing coalition are parameters in the equations, the ratio of which is equivalent to the cost of war. Individual members (actors) of a victorious coalition receive a proportional share of fortune based on their relative SIZE in the coalition: "The following are practically the simplest reasonable rules for military exchange between two coalitions (sides) which take account of the members' several military-economic SIZEs. In a war between two sides, each side simultaneously inflicts upon the other side a fraction of the inflicter's total SIZE. Of these inflicted losses a fraction is gained by the [victorious] inflicter as booty."[14]

The actors are initially all of identical SIZE, thus the system is in perfect balance. One proposition of Kaplan's theory sketch, however, was that actors in such a system have a preference to maintain a margin of security (hence, rule 1). This preference is prudent in such a system even if the actor is not hegemonial: "[O]ne may assume, with Kaplan, that they all desire a margin of superiority if only to ensure their safety against chance redistribution of power. Technological breakthroughs and bad harvests are examples of such chances."[15]

To achieve such a margin in the realization model requires victory in war. A margin of superiority can be gained for some actors in some of the possible

---

12. Reinken, "Computable Models," 2n.

13. Ibid., 4.

14. Ibid., 8-9. Since the time of Reinken's research, Lanchester equations have been called into serious doubt by Joshua Epstein. Epstein's doubts, however, do not affect the results of this computer project. On this point see Appendix A.

15. Ibid., 20.

ninety-one wars, and for other actors in other possible wars. Because the computer can calculate the postwar result that each of the ninety-one possible coalitions will have on the postwar system of SIZES, the perfectly balanced system can be compared with every possible unbalanced system.

It would have been very easy at this point in the design to program the computer to select wars that were most balanced, 3-2 for example, and then assert why rational actors would have that preference. The computer project, however, did not succumb to this fallacy, which in logic is known as the fallacy of affirming the consequent: "[T]he pilot model . . . controvert[s] a bland assumption virtually written into its own design. This assumption that balanced systems tend to have "balanced" wars has been made by established writers in the field. '(S)elf interest . . . produce(s) very nearly evenly matched coalitions.'"[16]

Alliance Formation. Instead, the entire set of possible postwar results could be used as inputs that the actors would use in a diplomatic pre-war period, in what can be called an alliance formation cycle. Thus individual computer actors would compare information about the next international system with their current international system. Many researchers might have made this comparison and formed the alliances based on their own preferences and values, or so-called plausible assumptions. Kaplan and Reinken, however, wanted to base the comparison on the preferences and values of the actors, which required variables for actors' styles. In effect, the actors were given an operational code, a sort of personality. This parameter was called "satisfaction."

The [alliance formation] cycle begins . . . [by] using parameters describing the personality of each player, [and] computes the value to him of war as fought out by every coalition set. Each such value is the expected . . . value of a transition of the whole system of sizes from the present values to hypothetical future sizes. The transition values are proportional to differences in *satisfaction* with the system of sizes. The transition values are also multiplied with fudge factors [for] intransigence at the bargaining table and distaste for risk.[17]

This satisfaction is an actor's preferred trade-off between their own growth in SIZE versus the degree of balance for the other members of the system. In other words, the actors have a preference scale that at one extreme (deviants), favors their own growth no matter what the war does to the relative distribution of the other actors' SIZEs, or at the other extreme (balancers) favors the balanced system to their own growth. The "fudge factors" determine the speed with which the actors bid for alliance partners.

---

16. Ibid., 5. The quotation Reinken used is from Deutsch and Singer, "Multipolar Power Systems and International Stability," *World Politics*, 16 (April 1964): 403.

17. Donald Reinken, (The University of Chicago, typewritten, n.d.).

Obvious Results. It does not take a rocket scientist or a computer to trace through the implications at the extremes of the preference scale. If the preference for balance is very high among all actors, then all actors are satisfied with the existing balance, and systemwide neutrality is the outcome. If the preference for balance is very low for all actors, then the system quickly becomes unstable (an actor is eliminated). However, getting the computer program to replicate this obvious tautology would indicate that the program was logically consistent at the extremes of the preference scale, and would increase the confidence that that program could be used in the middle range of the preference scale. This replication was accomplished, and the computer did realize the obvious patterns.

If all the actors had a low preference for balance, then in the first cycle of a run[18] four actors attacked the fifth. In subsequent cycles they continued to attack until the fifth was reduced to elimination. Although the reason for the designation will be stated in the following section of this chapter, this system state is herein characterized as one of disequilibrium.

If all the actors had a very high preference for balance, then no attacks occurred, and there was inaction. This system state is herein characterized as one of static equilibrium.

Although such results cannot be considered surprising, it was the realization of these obvious patterns that made it legitimate to explore some of the non-obvious implications of the computer model.

Non-obvious Results. The following questions lack obvious answers: What will happen if all the actors have only a moderate preference for balance—a mixture of balance-seeking and growth-seeking? What if one actor is a deviant, and the other four have a moderate preference for balance? What if there are two deviants? How do changes in the cost of war interact with varying preferences for balance?

The obvious point about these non-obvious problems is to recognize that because real international systems are open systems—in which all of these factors as well as many others are varying simultaneously—there is no way to systematically control these questions without a computer. Researchers need some means of creating a controlled experimental situation, and the computer provides such a laboratory.

Reinken describes the result for the situation in which the actors have a moderate preference for balance. This system state is one of dynamic equilibrium.

---

18. A run is one round of the realization model, beginning, for practical purposes, with a declaration of war by one actor and concluding after a battle is fought. The resultant change in the system of SIZEs then becomes part of the initial conditions for the next run. A family of runs is a group of runs categorized, in the present work, according to whether there are zero, one, or two deviant actors. Deviants have zero preference for balance.

Again, the first cycle is an attack of four against one. In the second cycle, however, the previous victim is not attacked again. Instead, three of the previous attackers join him in attacking the fourth previous attacker. During the third, fourth, and fifth cycles, a hitherto unattacked actor is attacked by all the other actors. At this point in the run, the SIZEs of the actors, initially all equal, have become all unequal. In all subsequent cycles of the run, the largest actor is attacked by all the others and made smaller than they. One such run was carried out on the computer for over 275 cycles.[19]

This result was unanticipated, because it contravened the traditional dogma—what Reinken called a "bland assumption"—that wars should be 3-2. It also demonstrated that Riker's theory of the minimum-winning coalition was less than general. A minimum-winning coalition will not form if the overall payoff is too small.[20]

There were two other experiments—families of runs—one with one deviant actor, and the other with two deviants. The deviants had zero preference for balance, whereas the other actors had moderate preferences, as they had in the first experiment. The implication from these experiments was clear: the system behaved exactly as it did in the first experiment, except for a shift in the thresholds separating disequilibrium, dynamic equilibrium, and static equilibrium.

It will be remembered that the parameter governing these thresholds was the preference for balance. As the number of deviants increase, the other actors must increase their commitment to balance. In somewhat different language, this is to say that the balancers must not dabble with the idea of joining the deviant to achieve short-run growth; thus, their tolerance for deviancy must decline, and they must quickly punish the deviant if the system is to remain stable.[21] If they do so dabble, because they seek their own growth, the system state quickly becomes disequilibrial and leads to actor elimination.

Of particular note in this system state, is that the deviant was the last actor eliminated, leaving a nondeviant as the last survivor. Reinken's interpretation of this result illuminates how the research scientist should judge deterministic computer results—namely, *not* as predictions of empirical events: "[O]ne sees that the deviant tactic is an incomplete recipe for hegemony. The deviant gets rid of others, but only as the jackal of a larger actor. If this is the best he can do, the jackal will be eaten last. On the other hand, deviance of this sort does begin to clear the competitors away *and stochastic luck added to the model could give a jackal a hegemonial chance.*"[22]

"Stochastic luck" is an umbrella term for chance factors arising from factors exogenous to the realization-model. Chance factors that might benefit such a

---

19. Reinken, "Computer Explorations," 471.

20. Reinken, "Computable Models," 34-35.

21. Those of a mathematical bent might compare this result with the tit-for-tat strategy proposed by Anatol Rapoport for the computer tournament organized by Robert Axelrod. See *The Evolution of Cooperation* (New York: Basic Books, 1984).

22. Reinken, "Computable Models," 32. Emphasis supplied.

jackal include terrain, weather, treachery and spies, the unexpected death of skillful general who slips on a bar of soap before battle, or the actions of a democratic legislature that restricts or expands the latitude of military decision. These factors *are not* and *should not* be included in a basic theory sketch. But a deviant actor in the real world, even if he had the results of his own computer project, might take a chance—or might have good information—that the goddess Fortuna would smile favorably on a hegemonic strategy.

Distinguishing Stability and Equilibrium. In the computer runs that led to the elimination of an actor, it was specified that the system state should be characterized as one of disequilibrium. The reason for this specification was not because an actor was eliminated, but because it was primarily the operational codes of the actors that led to the action pattern. That action pattern was not optimal with respect to the international system, thus the designation of disequilibrium. On the other hand, Reinken's language is different, and as stated above, somewhat obscures the relationships which this chapter is attempting to make explicit: "A system containing merely growth-seeking actors will obviously be *unstable*; there would be no provision for balancing or restraint."[23] This statement must be considered slightly elliptical. Instead of "be unstable" it would have been more accurate to state "become unstable," the difference being that the system cannot technically be called unstable until the actor is reduced to nonessential status. Clearly, it is the disequilibrium that leads to the instability.

As Reinken stated: "Kaplan and I customarily measure instability by the loss of an actor."[24] In the computer model, this would change the structure of the system from five to four actors.[25] But it was the particular disequilibrial actions and styles (regime characteristics) that led to the instability.

Instability could, of course, result from factors other than strategic action and style. The statement cited above, that a deviant might hope that stochastic factors would facilitate a drive for hegemony, makes this difference clear. The unstable system is one in which the structure of the system is too far out of balance for nondeviants to correct. Recall from the previous chapter the insufficient number of actors in the Chinese warlord system.

But there could be a weak, temporary instability that can be reversed in a stable system. That instability could be generated by exogenous parameters. Although a theory of international politics should only explain those instabilities generated in the international system, it should in principle explain the result of instability on the international system, regardless of how it is generated.

---

23. Reinken, "Computer Explorations," 469. Emphasis supplied.

24. Reinken, "Computable Models," 6n; idem, "Computer Explorations," 472.

25. What Reinken called a "minimal model" was included in his dissertation. The minimal model investigated the relationship between numbers of actors and preemptive strikes. Thus, it directly relates to the question of the numbers of actors and stability. On the theoretical argument for five actors as a minimum for stability in "balance of power" systems, see chap. 7.

Consider again the situation of static equilibrium, in which the high preference for balance leads to inaction. It will be remembered also that the structure of the system was such that all the actors were given equal capabilities. Reinken's interpretation of these runs is instructive:

About the occurrence of inaction . . . for high [preference] this much is useful to say: The initial equality of all the actors meant also the lowest possible imbalance. Every possible initial war . . . even a four-to-one war, does not offer them enough extra SIZE to outweigh, given their high [preference], the concomitant increased imbalance.

From that explanation alone, the reader could accept the assertion that if the high [preference] runs had begun with considerable initial inequality, there would have been war. One can now imagine external interference with the SIZEs of the actors between wars keeping the system constantly in motion, despite the high [preference].[26]

Reinken's characterization of these runs as indicating "dynamic stability" also seems unwarranted. The system is subjected to a temporary instability, arising from factors external to the international system of action (i.e, internal to national actor-systems), and coupled with a high preference for balance, dynamic equilibrium maintains the structure by preventing the preponderance of any actor.

Although each concept can only be understood in the context of the other, Kaplan's meaning of equilibrium and stability are more obvious if the propositions to which they refer are separated into action and structure, respectively. Given a particular structure, it is possible to derive plausible hypotheses about the range of action (rules) that are necessary to maintain that structure—which herein has been labeled equilibrium analysis. Given a particular range of actions, it is possible to derive plausible hypotheses about the effects on structure, which herein has been labeled stability analysis. Of particular note is that it is a stability that results from international action. If those actions are within a normal range, the system remains stable. Actions beyond such a range are hypothesized as leading to the rapid destruction of structure, especially the elimination of an essential actor.

INTERNATIONAL TRANSFORMATION

Kaplan originally placed transformation under the heading of rules, though later he explicitly abandoned that heading in favor of conditions.[27] In a formal

---

26. Reinken, "Computer Explorations," 474. There is also the following formulation: "Stochastic SIZE disturbances would make [high preference systems] fight. For high [preference for balance] and unequal initial SIZEs, actors would fight against the currently largest until approximate equality was attained. Under the circumstances the model would still have looked useful as a representation of balancing *action* which offsets stochastic increases in capabilities." Idem, "Computable Models," 34. Emphasis supplied.

27. Compare Kaplan, *System and Process*, 9, and "The Hard Facts of International Theory," 22, presented at The University of Chicago, PIPES Workshop, 8 March 1990.

sense, there are two kinds of transformation conditions if one maintains, other things being equal, an international politics focus: disequilibrial actions and structural instability.

It will be recalled from the analysis of equilibrium and stability that optimal international action patterns (essential rules) are a function of structure and styles, whereas structural changes are a function of action patterns and styles. In the previous chapter, questions of style—operational code—were subsumed under the initial condition of regime characteristics. In the remainder of this chapter I return to this usage. In principle, the operational code or style of an international actor should be a function of intra-actor structural characteristics. But regime characteristics are more relevant to the extension of a theory rather than its basic theoretical form. In the specification of a particular type of international system in basic form, it is necessary to specify the mutual compatibility of the two basic analytical regions—namely, action and structure.

Thus it follows that structures and actions that become incompatible are the key to transformation analysis. In other words, it is the elimination of one or more of the necessary conditions linking these analytical regions that marks the onset of transformative processes. But in this form of analysis it is disequilibrial actions or structural instability, or both, that lead to changes in either the actors' regimes[28] or in the subsequent action patterns of the actors.

Although transformation analysis is the most underdeveloped aspect of the theory sketches, Kaplan's objective is to specify the range beyond which changes in his three foci lead to long-term instability and thus, transformation. Consider his statement of the conditions that may make the "balance of power" system unstable.

[T]he existence of an essential national actor who does not play according to the rules of the game; the existence of a national actor whose essential national rules are oriented toward the establishment of some form of supranational political organization; failures in informational inputs into the decision-making systems of national actors or personality inputs which are deviant in terms of the essential rules; capability changes which are characterized by positive feedback; difficulties in applying the other rules when applying either the rule to increase capabilities or the rule to restore defeated actors or inconsistencies between the rules and pressing national needs; and difficulties arising from the logistics of "balancing," from the small number of essential actors, or from the lack of flexibility of the "balancing" apparatus.[29]

For individuals who consider sixteen-ounce steaks to be a large meal, Kaplan has in this excerpt offered an entire cow. Moreover, in keeping with the

---

On the meaning of "conditions," see Appendix B.

28. If deviant operational codes led to the disequilibrium in the first place, then what is disequilibrial or unstable from the perspective of the overall system may be equilibrial or stabilizing from the perspective of the deviant actor.

29. Kaplan, *System and Process*, 27.

navigational flags employed in this chapter, it is necessary to parse this excerpt according to equilibrium, stability, and transformation. Although it can be expected that each of these changes could in principle lead to transformation, some would necessarily work through others.

For instance, the statement "personality inputs which are deviant" is clearly tagged to rule violations. In the computer model, personality inputs are equivalent to an actor's style, and some styles clearly lead to more frequent rule violations. This relationship, however, has been classified above as the subject matter of equilibrium analysis, and if deviancy is sufficiently extensive within the system, the system state is characterized as one of disequilibrium. Two other statements also belong to the analysis of equilibrium: "a national actor whose essential national rules . . . " and "inconsistencies between the rules and pressing national needs." These changes would all seem to lead to rule violations, and it is the latter change—on international grounds—that would lead to transformation. Thus, in a strictly narrow sense, we should be able to analyze some aspects of transformation on the basis of changes in two foci alone. Regime characteristics would work through the doors of international action and international structure.

With those exceptions, all the other statements in the excerpt are instances of a change in either international structure (information of, capabilities of, and numbers of actors) or international action (rules) of the system. Thus, these kinds of changes are treated herein as the subject matter of transformation analysis.

Still, there are quite a large number of elements and it must be emphasized that the modifications in each element depends on the values of all the other elements when the change is introduced. Thus, in considering transformation Kaplan states that it may be necessary to relate "the essential rules of a system to its parameters *depending upon the previous state(s) of the system.*"[30] This is to say that the restoration of a parameter to an equilibrial value after disequilibrium has changed stability may not restore a stable equilibrium, just as quitting smoking may not restore health after the onset of emphysema or lung cancer. Or, in the case of Billy Dee (see chap. 6), the restoration of neutrality to Billy's block may not return Billy to neutrality.

The analysis of equilibrium, stability, and transformation are thus all interdependent, as are the broad influences arising from international action, international structure, and regime characteristics that stream into these forms of analysis. In order to clarify these relationships Kaplan's position must be considered in light of the implications of interdependent axiom sets, some preliminary concepts from set theory, and the chicken-and-egg (time) paradox.

The next three sections serve to illuminate the logical relations among action, structure and regime characteristics in terms of whether the focus of inquiry

---

30. Ibid., 26; idem, *Towards Professionalism*, 57-58, 67; idem, *System and Process*, 10. Emphasis in original.

covers equilibrium, stability, or transformation analysis. In order to make the illumination accessible to a wider audience, it does not utilize strictly formal logical notation.

Interdependence

In an analytical system, if axioms are independent of one another it is possible to draw a sharp distinction between the axioms (antecedents) and theorems (consequents). International politics is unlikely to be systematized in such a rigorous fashion; one cannot, for example, distinguish sharply between an actor's capabilities and its role in a system, because these variables partially imply each other. For example, in a "balance of power" system a small actor with highly mobile forces may be a better balancer than a very large actor with comparatively immobile forces. Kaplan's systems recognize this feature of social systems, and this strongly affects the coding of variables and parameters. In terms of regime characteristics, action, and structure, what is variable and what is parameter depends on whether one is analyzing equilibrium, stability, or transformation. But Kaplan does not always make these distinctions transparent.

In the international system models,[31] for example, Kaplan's term "equilibrium" basically means rules of international action, which Kaplan formulates against the backdrop of structure (number of actors, their role functions, their capabilities, and the informational transparency of the system). Regime characteristics are held constant in that the actors are assumed to be rational. Thus, international structure and regime characteristics are parameters (antecedents) from which equilibrial action is inferred. Kaplan, however, refers to all these elements as "variables."

On the other hand, in the models of the international actors,[32] international structure is held constant and regime characteristics are distinguished according to the intra-actor structural characteristics (e.g., democratic versus dictatorial national actors). Thus, the political systems of the actors produce styles—operational codes—when embedded in a particular type of international structure, and the parameter for regime characteristic may be varied to introduce elements of disequilibrium into a system.

Stability analysis focuses primarily on the structure of the international system. In the computer model, for example, some degree of disequilibrial action (rule-breaking) plus the operational codes of the nondeviant actors, lead to changes in capabilities (structure). If all the actors manifest a low preference for balance (deviancy), the system quickly becomes unstable as an actor is eliminated. If there are few deviants, the system's stability is dependent on the skill of the remaining actors. If they dabble, the system becomes unstable. Thus, some mix of disequilibrial action (declaring war on the weakest actor) and the style of the

---

31. Kaplan, *System and Process*, chap. 2.
32. Ibid., chap. 3.

nondeviant actors are parameters from which structural stability or instability is inferred. In this form of inquiry, (disequilibrial) action and regime characteristics are parameters from which modifications occur in structure.

As stated above, when Kaplan discusses transformation conditions, elements of rule violation or changes in structure, especially capabilities, are the triggers. The changed structure or the violations then become the backdrop for system change, which means change in the number or kind of actors. In this formulation, an instability in structure (for instance, inequality in capabilities) and some elements of disequilibrial action are parameters from which changes in regime characteristics or the other rules are inferred. Such changes are precursors for a transformation of the existing system. Kaplan, however, always calls his essential rules and capabilities, "variables."

Kaplan must of course make some such argument that transposes variables and parameters, for without these distinctions Kaplan cannot maintain that equilibrium and transformation are functions of parameters.[33] Although this position is substantively sturdy, it is ugly.

Although Kaplan's mentions each concept properly in its context, his sign system is somewhat inadequate; that is, he *uses* "variables" and "parameters" in an interchangeable fashion. Variables, including rules, are sometimes parameters—that is, initial conditions—and his initial conditions are sometimes variables. Thus, most of the transformation conditions outlined in each model entail rule-breaking, but transformations are supposed to result from parameter change, and in the models of the international system parameters are supposed to represent the internal systems of the international actors.[34] This problem is not substantive; but the reader is no doubt aware that there are no substantive problems in multiplying Roman numerals.[35] The problem is that it is difficult to manipulate these concepts analytically or to apply them empirically. It is also difficult to know which elements explain equilibrium and disequilibrium, which explain stability and instability, and which explain transformation. In short, Kaplan provides no protocol for the use of "variables" and "parameters."

Set Theory

What is fully consistent with Kaplan's approach but which he does not explicitly use is the basic language of set theory.[36] In what follows no attempt

---

33. Ibid., 8; on Kaplan's usage of variables and parameters in the "balance of power" system see ibid., 22-36; on the international actors see ibid., 54-85.

34. Ibid., 20.

35. The reader will note that each of the two expressions "CXLII x CLXII = ?" and "142 x 162 = ?" are logically equivalent.

36. On the distinction between "use" and "mention," see Willard Van Orman Quine, *Methods of Logic*, rev. ed., (New York: Holt, Rinehart and Winston, 1959), 37-38, 209; on set theory see ibid, 225ff. Kaplan does implicitly use set theoretic methods. See, for example, *Macropolitics*, 57.

will be made to discuss set theory in any but the most elementary fashion. The reader should not put unnecessary weight on the formulations below, for those formulations lack the specificity necessary to make them concrete. The protocols do not, for example, specify the particular type of international structure under investigation, and do not indicate how the individual actors are to be indexed. *Thus, the protocols are not propositions to be tested, but merely rules governing the formulation of propositions. The protocols are really propositional frames.*

This exercise is very abstract and serves a very limited function—namely, to establish formal protocols for the proper use of variables and parameters, with particular reference to the questions of equilibrium, stability, and transformation. A researcher chooses a protocol based on the problem under investigation, but it must be pointed out that there is no easy or direct means of applying these protocols, and that the basic standards must be used as well.[37] However, the theory of international politics can only benefit by adopting set theoretic methods, which are necessary building blocks for more sophisticated usage of logical methods.

A very simple symbolic language would minimally require variables, sets, and logical operators such as "and," "or," "if-then," and "not." Readers familiar with basic logic will note that the logical notion of quantification ("for all x" or "there exists an x such that") has been omitted, and this should serve as a warning. For those notions would provide important boundary conditions necessary to make the following schemata concrete. The analysis which follows has no explanatory value about the international system as such. It is designed only to illustrate how Kaplan's three foci can be made analytically distinct, and what kinds of statements are justifiably used to demonstrate other kinds of statements, given that a particular research question is kept in mind.

With this caveat, Kaplan's foci then become sets, each of which contains variables which range over different values. These variables are propositions, coded in some appropriate way. Next, three sets are defined for Kaplan's foci: International Action (A), ranging from equilibrium to disequilibrium; International Structure (I), ranging from stable to unstable; and Regime Characteristics (R), ranging from rational to deviant operational codes.[38] Subsets are designated by superscripting, (A'), for example. The symbols "⊃," "v," "+," and "~" stand, respectively, for "if-then," "or," "and," and "not."

A parameter is now defined as any set of variables used as initial condition and from which results in other sets are inferred, however loosely. Thus, given a three-set system with interdependent axioms two sets must be selected as parameters in order to investigate the implications on the remaining set, sets, or

---

37. The basic standards are stated in chap. 1.

38. The intuitive form of the actual ranges may be conceived as spheres, in which the center of each sphere may be characterized as equilibrial, stable, and rational, respectively. When all three centers converge, the system is in stable equilibrium. As the three centers depart from this ideal limit, the system change is amplified. One can think of departures as occurring along any vector.

subsets. The selection of sets as initial conditions and results can be grounded on specific protocols, labeled according to the object of analysis.

X. Equilibrium Protocol: $(I + R) \supset (A)$. For the analysis of equilibrial action patterns, international structure (I) and regime characteristics (R) are parameters governing (however loosely) international action patterns (rules). Equilibrial action is a consequence of the joint antecedents for structure and actors' operational codes. When (I) is a stable structure and the actors are rational (R) with respect to that structure, then essential rules can be hypothesized to describe the optimal action pattern for that system. On the other hand, atypical structures (~I) or elements of deviancy or stupidity (~R) will lead to rule violations, that is, disequilibrium (~A). The value of (A) feeds back into the system in the examination of stability.

Y. Stability Protocol: $(A + R) \supset (I)$. For the analysis of structural stability and change that could result from international—rather than stochastic—factors, international action (A) and regime characteristics (R) are parameters governing (however loosely) international structure (role function and, capabilities, numbers, and information of actors). If (A) is optimal behavior and the actors can maintain international rationality (R), then no runaway changes should occur in international structure. However, action that is disequilibrial (~A) is potentially destabilizing (~I).[39] If the remaining actors are highly rational (R), then they may be capable of countering the disequilibrial actions. But if the disequilibrial behavior is sufficiently strong, or it occurs in the presence of actors that include some mix of deviant and stupid actors, then instability is likely to be amplified. The values of (A) and (R) feeds back into the system in the examination of system transformation.

Z. Transformation Protocol: $(A \lor I) \supset (R \lor A') \lor (R + A')$.[40] For the analysis of system transformation international action patterns (A) and international structure are parameters governing international rationality (R), or international actions (A), or both. It follows that if a system analyzed under the first two protocols is in equilibrium and is stable, then propositions formed in the transformation protocol will tend to characterize the dynamic evolution of a system over time. However, on questions of transformation, if a particular international action is disequilibrial (~A) or international structure is unstable (~I), or both, then changes should result in the regime characteristics (~R) or in the other rules (~A'), or both.

Transformation conditions comprise all possible permutations of a system under an exhaustive substitution of parameters, a factor which is unlikely ever to be known fully for any particular international system, partly because of the complexity of parametric interaction effects. But the protocols may serve as a

---

39. This is not a fully precise statement because even some equilibrial actions, such as "act to increase capabilities," introduces some instability, but only if the other actors do not adopt an equilibrating action pattern. In that case, it is the subset of actions that introduces the disequilibrium, ~(A').

40. A' is a subset of A such that $\sim(\sim A) + A' = A$.

useful guides through the myriad chain of implication among action patterns, structural conditions, and the international rationality of the actors. If action is equilibrial in Protocol X, it reduces the potential for instability in Protocol Y; and if X and Y are equilibrial and stable, then the system is in stable equilibrium. There will exist an entire range of these possible transformations. However, if variables take negative values, positive feedback may multiply the negative values throughout the system and undermine its characteristic identity. This will comprise a range of unstable transformation conditions in Z.

These types of distinction are necessary to investigate regulatory—system maintenance—and transformative processes. The protocols clarify macrosystemic relationships among equilibrium, stability and transformation. The stable system is one that disequilibrates within limits short of changes in the structure necessary to maintain equilibrium during the system's future. If a means of fixing time exists, then parameters may be assessed and variables can be analyzed across time to see if they follow from and lead to expected results.

Chicken-and-Egg (Time) Paradox

Many students of international relations make statements that purport to be timeless. This predisposition probably follows from the erroneous view of causality as simple succession, which was discussed in chapter 6. Kaplan's theory sketches were about systems of action, and time factors must be part of the analysis. One of his reasons for including time is the fact that decision-making systems exhibit equilibria that are not linear and continuous, but result from the discrete actions of actors over time.[41]

This creates a problem that is a complex version of the chicken-and-egg paradox (which must ultimately favor the egg, though in light of evolutionary theory not necessarily a chicken's egg). Implicit in the protocols stated above and in *System and Process* is the notion of different time frames. But what are the logical grounds for selecting a time frame? One approach is to treat this problem as contextual. This may at times be adequate, as it seems to be in historical analyses of the "balance of power" system. But this has been a major problem in the analysis of the bipolar system.

The "balance of power" system, at least in the nineteenth century, has a natural clock. There is the war frame, and researchers may state all the initial conditions at the end of a war, taking into account the appropriate evidence and context. A researcher can then assess the system state according to the protocol relevant to the particular research question. Because the "balance of power" system is fairly simple, the decision procedure for choosing a protocol can, for the most part, rest on the basis of: "I'll know it when I see it." One may then analyze what variables are changing between war frames—such as capability increases, changes in the number of essential actors, or whether deviant actors are being

---

41. Kaplan, *System and Process*, 25.

constrained. A similar situation exists in domestic politics, where researchers have elections to fix their time frame. The variation of party seats in the House of Representatives, for example, may be calculated as a percentage change against the parameter of seats after the previous election. However, this approach cannot be maintained in the twentieth-century bipolar system. No comparable clock exists, for example, in the postwar loose bipolar system.

This paradox is, of course, solved if an alternative switching device can be designed to function theoretically like wars and elections. For now it is sufficient to mention the problem as one which hinders the application of Kaplan's bipolar model. In another work, a phase switching approach is used to deal with this difficulty, and it expands the dynamic capacity of the bipolar model.[42]

THE LANGUAGE OF INTERNATIONAL POLITICS

This chapter has now established a fairly strict usage of theoretical language for international politics, and a set of protocols governing the use of this language in the formulation of propositions. Such a language reduces the possibility of ambiguous statements.

The statements analyzed in this chapter are purely formal and categorical. The absence of a specific type of system, specific types of actors, and coding criteria means that the formal protocols are "propositional frames" rather than "propositions"—that is, truth candidates—about any particular macrosystem. These protocols, however, give more precise meaning to the concepts of equilibrium, stability, and transformation in terms of the logical relations among action, structure, and regime characteristics.

Such distinctions are preparatory to developed empirical analysis. Because of common misconceptions of science—that propositions are timeless, that science is about prediction, that conditions cause outcomes by a process of temporal succession—there has been little clarity about what constitutes successful theoretical application. The technical characteristics of this chapter have been designed to make the language of international politics more distinct, and to bring the interrelationships among the elements of analysis into sharper relief.

---

42. Dunne, *The Life and Death of Bipolar Systems* (manuscript).

Appendix A:

A Note on the Use of Lanchester Equations

Subsequent to the invention of the Reinken-Kaplan realization models,[1] Joshua Epstein criticized the use of Lanchester equations. Epstein states that the equations are designed to answer the right question, but that "the Lanchester equations offer a fundamentally implausible representation of combat under all but a very small set of circumstances. . . ."[2]

He does recognize some benefits to the equations, particularly their dynamic qualities: "Unlike static numerical comparisons, the Lanchester equations recognize some of warfare's operational dimensions and allow one to estimate such things as the winner and loser, the daily number of survivors on each side, and the duration of the war."[3]

Despite these benefits, Epstein states three essential objections to the equations: the models lack feedback mechanisms and thus cannot capture the effect of withdrawal on the rate of attrition, the models do not permit the trading of space for time, and the models do not reflect diminishing marginal returns for increases in capabilities. Epstein then cites statistical studies for which he states that the Lanchester "laws" do not hold and offers alternative equations that he claims better capture the workings of real battle.

Epstein's equations incorporate parameters that may very well realize more aspects of a theory of combat. However, it is unlikely that his position can be supported on the basis of statistical studies of battle. If either his equations or Lanchester's were very highly correlated with the battle process, there would be some ground for believing that those equations represented a law, but such

---

1. See chap. 8.

2. Joshua Epstein, "The Calculus of Conventional War: Dynamic Analysis without Lanchester Theory" (Washington: Brookings Institute, 1985).

3. Ibid., 3.

correlations are highly unlikely.[4] In the more likely event that the best equations will exhibit only moderate to weak correlations, it would be difficult to know if the theory—if in fact such a theory exists—represented by the equations was confirmed. That would require detailed qualitative analysis of the historical record to determine if decision-makers operated on the basis of the theory, or other factors (the "fog of war", intelligence failures, terrain). This is not to disparage any advance that Epstein has made with respect to the mathematical model of combat, but to make clear that mathematical models are problematic in open systems.

Because Epstein argues against Lanchester equations on the basis of how well they represent actual combat, his criticism does not alter the results of the Reinken-Kaplan realization model. The Reinken-Kaplan model was a closed system. As stated in chapter 8, it served the purpose of a controlled experiment. I would argue that Epstein's model serves the same function. However, the question can be raised as to whether Epstein's or Lanchester's equations would yield different results in the Reinken-Kaplan model. In the models analyzed in this book, that seems highly unlikely.

The computer project did employ a war game. As has been remarked, in a five-actor system, there are ninety-one possible alliance situations (including the case in which all actors are neutral). The main function that the war game serves is to provide all the actors, at each point in their decision process, a reasonable calculation as to the outcome (profit and loss) of each war. (Epstein recognizes that the equations are capable of doing this). They then assess these possibilities in terms of their preference for balance. If they have a very high preference for balance, then no outcome will lead to war. If they have a very low preference for balance, then even very small profits will be sufficient to lead to war.

Epstein's equations are about the war process, and are highly dependent on a parameters governing the pace of war; that is, the rates at which actors are willing to suffer losses. As each process would still have an outcome, it is not clear that the actor's calculations about which alliance to join would be changed in any fundamental way in a "balance of power" system in which the actors were calculating exclusively in system terms.

However, a more complex model might be sensitive to the Epstein equations. In particular, democratic actors might be more sensitive to pace of war considerations than authoritarian or dictatorial actors. Also, actors might bet on the rates at which a particular coalition will prosecute the war, a factor which could conceivably control booty/loss parameters, particularly if actors had internal constraints limiting their pace of war capacity. Although it is not clear that such experiments would yield macrotheoretically interesting results, this cannot be ruled out.

---

4. See also the discussion of covering laws in chap. 2.

Appendix B:

On the Meaning of "Conditions"

In chapter 8 a general discussion of the meaning of "conditions" would have detracted from the argument about transformation conditions. Kaplan originally placed transformation under the heading of rules, though later he explicitly abandoned that heading in favor of conditions.[1]

The term "conditions" is not used consistently among social scientists. It very often refers to something material. In Marx, for example, economic conditions are supposed to generate the ideological superstructure. In some behavioral approaches, an external condition—the presence of food for example—is supposed to lead to a response, such as salivation. In these conceptions the notion that an event, E, is always preceded by a cause, C, is implicit in the concept of conditions. These efforts constitute a search for laws of succession.

Statements of the form "the drop in temperature below 32 degrees fahrenheit caused the puddle of water to freeze" are statements of empirical generalization or law. Such statements specify a cause, and its successive effect. In this illustration, and assuming a variety of unspecified boundary conditions, the appropriate temperature is always sufficient to produce the desired effect.

All efforts to derive the stability of international systems merely from the presence of the number of actors, to determine the cultural and political superstructure from the material substructure, to locate the causes of war and peace in the system or in the economic constitution of the actors, betray this

---

1. Compare Kaplan, *System and Process in International Politics* (New York: John Wiley, 1957), 9, and "The Hard Facts of International Theory," 22, paper presented at The University of Chicago, PIPES Workshop, 8 March 1990.

empirical notion of conditions. This conception of causal conditions is particularly naive when the initial conditions of a system are underspecified.[2]

There is also a logical sense of condition that is not necessarily material, and not necessarily dependent on laws of succession. In this sense it is customary to distinguish necessary from sufficient conditions. A sufficient condition is a guarantor for the occurrence of some phenomenon. It is always effective in producing some event. A necessary condition is a requisite for the occurrence of some phenomenon, it is always present in the case of an event. If there are multiple causes that function in a system of relations, wherein each cause is necessary but are sufficient only together and in proper proportion, then all the necessary conditions must be known. For example, to get a mature lawn from viable grass seeds, it is necessary to have 1) water, 2) suitable temperature, 3) oxygen and nitrogen, 4) soil, and 5) light. Each alone is a necessary condition. Together in the proper proportions they are sufficient to produce a lawn.[3]

Thus the logically coherent system specifies the relations among a system's parts. It is not temporal but logical in form. It states that if you change the value of a part of a system, there will be a corresponding change in another part of the system. Newton's universal theory of gravitation specifies the relations among the masses of bodies, their distance from one another, and the force of their attraction. Newton did not, however, believe he had found the cause of gravity, and it troubled him. The popular version that characterized the cause of gravity as "action at a distance" was characterized by Leibniz as a return to occultism. Scientists are no longer troubled by the formal characteristics of theories. Given the confirmations of Einstein's formulations, it is generally held that theories in the exact sciences are functional and formal logical systems, the concepts of which have empirical referents. A theory earns its status by mapping out all the potential logical—and invariant—relations in a system, and if the system is isomorphic with respect to the empirical referents, then the theory explains how the empirical system functions. The reader will note that this conception of function does not require teleological components in the theory.

Kaplan's systems do not achieve this ideal of logical completeness, and he recognizes this situation. He has also explained why the social sciences are unlikely to achieve this ideal.[4] The computer model illustrates a research strategy for increasing the precision and rigor of international theory in the face of these difficulties.

---

2. Waltz never overcame this conception of causality. See, for instance, his "Realist Thought and Neorealist Theory" in Robert L. Rothstein, ed., *The Evolution of Theory in International Relations: Essays in Honor of William T. R. Fox* (Columbia: University of South Carolina Press, 1991), 32ff. Readers of this small edited volume will note the honorific nature of the title and subtitle.

3. This account of necessary and sufficient conditions steals liberally from Willard Hutcheon (correspondence).

4. Morton A. Kaplan, *Science, Language, and the Human Condition* (New York: Paragon House, 1984).

References

Ashby, W. Ross. *Design for a Brain*. New York: John Wiley, 1952.

Axelrod, Robert. *The Evolution of Cooperation*. New York: Basic Books, 1984.

Bismarck, Otto von. *Bismarck: The Man and the Statesman*. 2 vols. New York: Harper and Brothers, 1898.

Bull, Hedley. "International Theory: The Case for a Classical Approach." In *Contending Approaches to International Politics*. Edited by Klauss Knorr and James Rosenau. Princeton: Princeton University Press, 1969.

Burns, Arthur Lee. "From Balance to Deterrence." *World Politics* 9 (July 1957): 494-529.

_____ . *Of Powers and Their Politics: A Critique of Theoretical Approaches*. Englewood Cliffs, NJ: Prentice-Hall, Inc., 1968.

Carr, Edward Hallett. *The Twenty Years' Crisis, 1919-1939: An Introduction to the Study of International Relations*. 2nd ed. London: Macmillan and Co., Ltd., 1946.

Cassirer, Ernst. *An Essay on Man: An Introduction to a Philosophy of Human Culture*. New Haven: Yale University Press, 1944.

Ch'i, Hsi-sheng. "The Chinese Warlord System as an International System." In *New Approaches to International Relations*, pp. 405-425. Edited by Morton A. Kaplan. New York: St. Martin's Press, 1968.

_____ . "The Chinese Warlord System." Ph.D. dissertation, The University of Chicago, 1969.

_____ . *Warlord Politics in China, 1916-1928*. Stanford: Stanford University Press, 1976.

Cohen, Morris R. *Reason and Nature: An Essay on the Meaning of Scientific Method*. New York: Harcourt, Brace and Co., 1931.

_____ . *Studies in the Philosophy of Science*. New York: Henry Holt and Co., 1949.

Cohen, Morris R., and Nagel, Ernest. *An Introduction to Logic and Scientific Method.* New York: Harcourt, Brace and Co., 1934.

Cook, Thomas I., and Moos, Malcolm. "The American Idea of International Interest." *American Political Science Review* 47 (1953): 28-44.

Copi, Irving M. *Introduction to Logic.* New York: The Macmillan Co., 1961.

Craig, Gordon A., and George, Alexander L. *Force and Statecraft.* New York: Oxford University Press, 1988.

Desch, Michael C. *When the Third World Matters.* Baltimore: Johns Hopkins University Press, 1993.

Deutsch, Karl W. and Singer, J. David. "Multipolar Power Systems and International Stability." *World Politics* 16 (April 1964): 390-406.

Dunne, Andrew P. *The Life and Death of Bipolar Systems.* (Manuscript).

Eibl-Eibesfeldt, Irenaus. *The Biology of Peace and War: Men, Animals, and Aggression* (New York: Viking, 1979).

Einstein, Albert. *Relativity: The Special and the General Theory.* Translated by Robert W. Lawson. 15th ed. New York: Crown Publishers, 1952.

Epstein, Joshua. "The Calculus of Conventional War: Dynamic Analysis without Lanchester Theory." Washington, D.C.: Brookings Institute, 1985.

Franke, Winfried. "The Italian City-States Considered as a 'Balance-of-Power' System." M.A. thesis, The University of Chicago, March 1965.

_____. "The Italian City-State System as an International System." In *New Approaches to International Relations*, pp. 426-458. Edited by Morton A. Kaplan. New York: St. Martin's Press, 1968.

George, Alexander L., and George, Juliette L. *Woodrow Wilson and Colonel House: A Personality Study.* New York: Dover Publishing, [1956] 1964.

Gleick, James. *Chaos: Making a New Science.* New York: Viking Press, 1987.

Gordon, Scott. "Guarding the Guardians: An Essay on the History and Theory of Constitutionalism." Typewritten, Indiana University, 21 September 1986.

Gulick, Edward Vose. *Europe's Classic Balance of Power.* Ithaca: Cornell University Press, 1955.

Guttenplan, Samuel D., and Tamny, Martin. *Logic: A Comprehensive Introduction.* New York: Basic Books, Inc., 1971.

Haas, Ernst. "The Balance of Power: Description, Prescription, or Propaganda." *World Politics* 5 (1953):442-477.

Hempel, Carl G. *Aspects of Scientific Explanation and Other Essays in the Philosophy of Science.* New York: Free Press of Glencoe, 1965.

Hobbes, Thomas. *Leviathan: or the Matter, Form, and Power of a Commonwealth, Ecclesiastical and Civil.* Oxford: Blackwell, 1955.

Hoffmann, Stanley. *Contemporary Theory in International Relations.* Englewood Cliffs, NJ: Prentice-Hall, Inc., 1960.

_____. *The State of War: Essays on the Theory and Practice of International Politics.* New York: Frederick A. Praeger, 1965.

_____. *Janus and Minerva: Essays in the Theory and Practice of International Politics.* Boulder, CO: Westview Press, 1987.

Holt, Edgar. *The Tiger: The Life of George Clemenceau, 1841-1929*. London: Hamilton, 1976.

Hopf, Ted. "Polarity, the Offense-Defense Balance, War." *American Political Science Review* 85 (1991): 475-493.

Hudson, Valerie M., with Vore, Christopher S. "Foreign Policy Analysis, Yesterday, Today, and Tomorrow." *Mershon International Studies Review* 39 (1995): 209-238.

Hutcheon, Willard. "Reason in History and Its Rationale." In *Rationality in Thought and Action*. Edited by Martin Tamny and K.D. Irani. New York: Greenwood Press, 1986.

Jervis, Robert. "Systems Theories and Diplomatic History." In *Diplomacy*, pp. 183-211. Edited by Paul Gordon Lauren. New York: The Free Press, 1979.

____. "Security Regimes." In *International Regimes*, pp. 173-194. Edited by Stephen D. Krasner. Ithaca: Cornell University Press, 1983.

____. "From Balance to Concert." *World Politics* 38 (October 1985):58-79.

Kaplan, Morton A. *System and Process in International Politics*. New York: John Wiley, 1957.

____, ed. *New Approaches to International Relations*. New York: St. Martin's Press, 1968.

____. *Macropolitics: Essays on the Philosophy and Science of Politics*. New York: Free Press, 1969.

____. *Towards Professionalism in International Theory: Macrosystem Analysis*. New York: Free Press, 1979.

____. *Science, Language, and the Human Condition*. New York: Paragon House, 1984.

____. "The Hard Facts of International Theory." Paper presented at The University of Chicago, PIPES Workshop, 8 March 1990.

Keohane, Robert. *After Hegemony: Cooperation and Discord in the World Political Economy*. Princeton: Princeton University Press, 1984.

Keohane, Robert O., and Nye, Joseph S., Jr. eds. *Transnational Relations and World Politics*. Cambridge: Cambridge University Press, 1972.

____. *Power and Interdependence: World Politics in Transition*. Boston: Little, Brown and Co., 1977.

Koslowski, Rey, and Kratochwil, Friedrich. "Understanding Change in International Politics." *International Organization* 48 (spring 1994): 215-247.

Krasner, Stephen D., ed. *International Regimes*. Ithaca: Cornell University Press, 1983.

Lasswell, Harold D. *Propaganda Technique in the World War*. New York: Alfred A. Knopf, 1927.

____. *Psychopathology and Politics*. Chicago: The University of Chicago Press, 1930.

____. *World Politics and Personal Insecurity*. New York: Whittlesey House, 1935.

Lorenz, Konrad. *On Aggression*. Translated by Marjorie Kerr Wilson. New York: Harcourt, Brace and World, 1966.

Malinowski, Bronislaw. *Crime and Custom in Savage Society*. London: Routledge and Kegan Paul, 1926.

Mattingly, Garrett. *Renaissance Diplomacy*. London: Cape, 1955.

Mearsheimer, John J. *Conventional Deterrence*. Ithaca: Cornell University Press, 1983.

Midlarsky, Manus I. *The Onset of World War.* Boston: Unwin Hyman, 1988.

Midlarsky, Manus, and Hopf, Ted. "Polarity and International Stability." *American Political Science Review* 87 (1993): 173-180.

Morgenthau, Hans J. *Scientific Man vs. Power Politics.* Chicago: The University of Chicago Press, 1946.

____. *In Defense of the National Interest: A Critical Examination of American Foreign Policy.* New York: Alfred A. Knopf, 1951.

____. "Another Great 'Debate': The National Interest of the United States." *American Political Science Review* 46 (1952).

____. *Politics Among Nations: The Struggle for Power and Peace.* 3rd ed. New York: Alfred A. Knopf, 1963.

Nagel, Ernest. *The Structure of Science: Problems in the Logic of Scientific Explanation.* Indianapolis: Hackett Publishing Co., [1961], 1979.

Neumann, John von, and Morgenstern, Oskar. *Theory of Games and Economic Behavior.* 3rd ed. Princeton: Princeton University Press, 1953.

Newhall, David S. *Clemenceau.* Lewiston, NY: The Edwin Mellen Press, 1991.

Padgett, John F., and Ansell, Christopher K. "Robust Action and Party Formation in Renaissance Florence: The Rise of the Medici, 1400-1434." Typewritten, The University of Chicago, March 1992.

Peirce, Charles Sanders. *Philosophical Writings of Peirce.* Edited with an Introduction by Justus Buchler. New York: Dover Publications, 1955.

Prosch, Harry. *The Genesis of Twentieth Century Philosophy: the Evolution of Thought from Copernicus to the Present.* Garden City, NY: Doubleday, 1964.

Puchala, Donald J. "Woe to the Orphans of the Scientific Revolution." In *The Evolution of Theory in International Relations: Essays in Honor of William T. R. Fox*, pp. 39-60. Edited by Robert L. Rothstein. Columbia: University of South Carolina Press, 1991.

Quine, Willard van Orman. *From A Logical Point of View.* Cambridge: Harvard University Press, 1953.

____. *Methods of Logic.* Rev. ed. New York: Holt, Rinehart and Winston, 1959.

Randall, John Hermann. *The Career of Philosophy.* 3 vols. New York: Columbia University Press, 1962.

Rapoport, Anatol. "Various Meanings of Theory." *American Political Science Review* 52 (1958): 972-988.

Reinken, Donald L. "Computer Explorations of the 'Balance of Power': A Project Report." In *New Approaches to International Relations*, pp. 459-481. Edited by Morton A. Kaplan. New York: St. Martin's Press, 1968.

____. "Computable Models for Exploring the Idea of the 'Balance of Power'." Ph.D. Dissertation, The University of Chicago, 1969.

Rice, Eugene F., Jr. and Grafton, Anthony. *The Foundations of Early Modern Europe, 1460-1559.* 2nd ed. New York: W.W. Norton, 1994.

Rosecrance, Richard N. *Action and Reaction in World Politics: International Systems in Perspective.* Boston: Little, Brown and Co., 1963.

____. "Bipolarity, Multipolarity, and the Future." *Journal of Conflict Resolution* 10 (September 1966): 314-327.

Ruggie, John Gerard. "International Regimes, Transactions, and Change: Embedded Liberalism in the Postwar Economic Order." In *International Regimes*, pp. 195-231. Edited by Stephen D. Krasner. Ithaca: Cornell University Press, 1983.

Sabrosky, Alan Ned. *Polarity and War: The Changing Structure of International Conflict.* Boulder, CO: Westview Press, 1985.

Samuelson, Paul A. *Economics.* 11th ed. New York: McGraw-Hill, 1980.

Scherer, F.M., and Ross, David. *Industrial Market Structure and Economic Performance.* 3rd ed. Boston: Houghton Mifflin Co., 1990.

Schneider, William, Jr., et al. *U.S. Strategic Nuclear Policy and Ballistic Missile Defense: The 1980s and Beyond.* Philadelphia: Institute for Foreign Policy Analysis, April 1980.

Singer, J. David. "The Level-of-Analysis Problem in International Relations." In *The International System: Theoretical Essays.* Edited by Klauss Knorr and Sidney Verba. Princeton: Princeton University Press, 1961.

Singer, J. David, et al. *Explaining War: Selected Papers from the Correlates of War Project.* Foreword by Bruce M. Russett. Beverly Hills, CA: Sage Publications, 1979.

Singer, J. David, Bremer, Stuart A., and Stuckey, John. "Capability Distribution, Uncertainty, and Major Power War, 1820-1965." In *The Correlates of War.* 2 vols. New York: The Free Press, 1979.

Singer, J. David, and Small, Melvin. "Alliance Aggregation and the Onset of War, 1815-1945." In *The Correlates of War.* 2 vols. New York: The Free Press, 1979.

Tucker, Robert. "Professor Morgenthau's Theory of Political Realism." *American Political Science Review* 46 (1952): 214-224.

Waltz, Kenneth N. *Man, the State, and War: A Theoretical Analysis.* New York: Columbia University Press, 1959.

_____. "The Stability of a Bipolar World." *Daedalus* 93 (summer 1964):881-909.

_____. *Theory of International Politics.* Reading, MA: Addison-Wesley Publishing Co., Inc., 1979.

_____. "Realist Thought and Neorealist Theory." In *The Evolution of Theory in International Relations: Essays in Honor of William T. R. Fox.* Edited by Robert L. Rothstein. Columbia, SC: University of South Carolina Press, 1991.

Wendt, Alexander. "Anarchy is What States Make of It: The Social Construction of Power Politics." *International Organization* 46 (spring 1992):

Whitehead, Alfred North. *Science and the Modern World: Lowell Lectures, 1925.* New York: The Macmillan Co., 1925.

Wright, Quincy. *A Study of War.* 2 vols. Chicago: The University of Chicago Press, [1942], 1965.

_____. *The Study of International Relations.* New York: Appleton-Century-Crofts, 1955.

Index

action (patterns), 2, 8, 9, 10, 11, 16, 17-19, 24, 52, 60, 74, 87, 109-10, 114, 115, 118, 125, 135-37, 138-43, 145, 163, 168-77 passim
  collective, 13, 149
  as essential rules. *See* essential rules
  inadequate approaches to, 18, 33-34, 40-42, 49, 53-54, 57, 60, 75, 76-77, 84
  (macro)strategic, 3, 17, 101-3, 114, 117
  and motives, 21-23, 83-84, 102. *See also* motives and confirmation; values, as levels of motivation
  and rules, 19
  theoretical function of, 19, 101-2, 105-7, 141, 158-61.
  See also equilibrium; initial conditions; rationality; *particular systems, concrete*
actors, 2, 9, 16-19, 21-24, 41, 81
  and consciousness, 43-44, 66, 71, 84, 88, 111-14, 119
  directivity and dominance of, 117, 122, 127, 138, 139, 148, 149, 155
  effect of numbers of, 73-74, 86, 116, 137, 138, 163, 167, 168, 170. *See*

also stability, and number of actors
  essential, 17, 116, 119, 124, 126, 127, 132-33, 135, 136, 137-40, 142, 145, 147, 151, 152, 154
  individuated. *See* individuation
  nonessential, 17, 116, 124, 126, 133, 135, 136, 139, 140, 142, 152
  supranational, 17, 19, 142, 143, 153
  bloc, 12, 13, 17, 18-19, 23, 24-25, 148-50, 153
  universal, 17, 19, 119, 147, 150, 151-53, 155
  theoretical function of, 2-3, 11.
  See also decision-makers; motives and confirmation; regime characteristics
actor-systems. *See* actors
actual systems. *See* systems, concrete
aggregation, 7, 8, 31, 49, 63, 80-81, 100, 112. *See also* concatenation; continuous systems, outcomes
Alsace-Lorraine, 40, 115, 144-46
Ansell, Christopher K., 121
applied theory. *See* theory, applied
appraisal, 1, 10, 30, 35, 68, 73
Aristotle, 62
Aron, Raymond, 52

types of
  dynamic, 166, 169
  stable, 126, 159, 171, 174, 176
  static, 166.
  See also formal protocols; rationality,
    and deviancy; stability
essential rules, 110, 115, 159, 161,
  170-73, 175
  of "balance of power" system, 117-
    18
  of loose bipolar system, 150-51
  theoretical function of, 113-14, 115.
    See also action (patterns); *particular
    systems, concrete, action patterns*
Euclid, 14
Euclidean geometry. *See* logic and
  mathematics, Euclidean geometry
explanandum. *See* model(s), covering
  law
explanans. *See* model(s), covering law
explanatory models. *See* initial conditions
explanatory presupposition. *See* theory,
  explanatory
explanatory theory. *See* theory, explanatory
extended theory. *See* theory, extended

failures in basic standards. *See failures
  in, under particular basic standards*;
  international structure, inadequate
  approaches to; types, inadequate
  conceptions of
fallacies
  of affirming the consequent, 165
  of misplaced concreteness, 100
  of selectivity, 8, 24
  of simple succession, 100-101
fallibilism, 100
first principles. *See* principles, universal
focal presupposition. *See* international
  politics, focus of
formal protocols, 173-76
Fox, William T.R., 12, 68, 158
frameworks, 48-49, 52, 56, 58-60

as theories, 2, 10, 14-15, 25, 47, 104
Franke, Winfried, 118-38
free market. *See* economic systems, free
  market
Fukuyama, Francis, 3

generalities, 41, 54, 151
generalization(s). *See* model(s) cover-
  ing law; logic and mathematics;
  theory
George, Alexander L., 31, 144, 146
George, Juliet L., 31
Gleick, James, 83
Gordon, Scott, 112, 122, 127, 144
Grafton, Anthony, 85
Gulick, Edward Vose, 114
Guttenplan, Samuel D., 83

Haas, Ernst, 113
Hegel, G.W.F., 34
Hempel, Carl G., 9, 38, 41
hidden-hand metaphor, 15, 31, 44, 68,
  69, 70, 71, 72, 78, 111-12
hierarchy. *See* actors, supranational,
  bloc
historical sociology. *See* historiography,
  schools of thought, historical sociology
historiography, 3-5, 9, 25, 30, 32, 33,
  42-43, 47, 55-56, 65, 103-4, 106
  national interest focus, 5-9, 11, 30-
    31, 34, 37-38, 39-41, 43, 45, 48-
    49, 57
  schools of thought
    historical sociology, 10, 25, 47-60,
      79, 113
    practical politics, 10, 25, 29-46, 67
history, 105-6
Hobbes, Thomas, 4, 45, 104
Hoffmann, Stanley, 1, 47-54, 56, 58,
  60, 62, 64, 86, 158
  appraisal, 47, 48, 50, 60
  core questions, 48-49
  inductive approach of, 49-50
  and social studies, 52-54

About the Author

ANDREW P. DUNNE is Research Associate in the Program in International Politics, Economics, and Security (PIPES) at the University of Chicago. Previously, he was Lentz Postdoctoral Fellow in Global Issues, International Conflict, and Peace Research at the University of Missouri at St. Louis.

ISBN 0-313-30078-X

EAN

9 780313 300783

HARDCOVER BAR CODE